Dr. Flint has written a brave and prov(landscapes rarely considered by conventional p boundaries of the current maps of accepted reali a theoretical backdrop based on quantum physics and effective clinical interventions, which are described in an easy to follow step-by-step process for achieving rapid change. This book goes beyond our one "official" consciousness into broader spectrums of the psyche and probes the more profound therapeutic challenges.

Lee Pulos, Ph.D., A.B.P.P.
Author: *The Biology of Empowerments*
The Power of Visualization

Your therapeutic system is brilliant and powerful. By far the most sophisticated one available in the treatment of trauma. I've been thinking about your approach: It is the only one I know of where the therapy is derived from a physics theory. This, I feel, needs to be explicated much more clearly and completely since it is unique. There are many physicists and biophysicists now working on the issue of mental-physical, mind-body relationships, modifying the physics to include the mental. None of them take the approach of using the physics to create a psycho-physiological therapy.

Phillip Warren, Ph.D.
Professor Emeritus (Psychology and Music)

Healing Your Mind and Soul presents a radical approach for working with clients who claim that conventional counseling and psychotherapy have been ineffective. It combines insights from quantum physics with folk traditions, many of which I have observed firsthand in my work with traditional shamans around the world. Large numbers of individuals are suffering from trauma induced by combat, by war, and by emotional or sexual violence. Mental health professionals ignore innovative treatments at the risk of their clients. At the same time, the procedures described by Dr. Flint call for research studies that will explore their effectiveness and the clients for whom this "field" approach is especially suitable.

Stanley Krippner, Ph.D.
Co-author, *Personal Mythology*

"When a practicing down-to-earth psychologist, using the latest and most effective methods to treat the problems of his patients, comes up with concepts such as "hidden reality" and "intruding fields," we had better sit up and take notice. Almost against the grain of his own conceptions, he had to conclude that there is more, far more, to the world than we might think with our everyday reasoning. This "more" is not just a fact of our psychology - it's a fact of our cosmology. How we interpret it in the framework of the theories of the sciences is still a matter of debate - Flint interprets these realities as indicating a further dimension of the physical universe, and I interpret it as the single, unified, deep (and ordinarily "hidden") "Akashic" field - but this is not the crucial question for now. The relevant and truly stupendous insight is that such a hidden reality exists in the world "out there," and that it affects our world "in here."

Ervin Lazslo
Author of more than 400 papers and articles and over 80
books including *The Chaos Point* (2006), *Science and
the Akashic Field* (2007), and *Quantum Shift in the Global
Brain* (2008).

My first impression was, "Wow... that looks like it's going to be fantastic." On further reflection, Garry explains the unexplainable. From the physics point of view, everything seems feasible to me.

James C. Cranwell
Guitar Virtuoso, Thinker
Creator of Flux Theory 101

It is riveting information and I intend to now read it again if I may, as there is so much more to absorb.

One thing-apart from the actual content — that particularly struck me — is how friendly and conversational the tone is, which really made the information accessible even when complex...

The tone is so much a dialogue between author and reader that I felt really included and as though we were engaged in a dialogue or journey rather that a lecture. I love that in a book.

Amy-Jo Salter
Editor of books on holistic health care,
equine health care, and several children's books.

Healing

Your Mind

and Soul

Therapeutic interventions
in quantum reality

by
Garry A. Flint, Ph.D.

NeoSolTerric Enterprises
Vernon, British Columbia

Library and Archives Canada Cataloguing in Publication

Flint, Garry A., 1934-
    Healing your mind and soul : therapeutic interventions
in quantum reality / Garry A. Flint.

Includes bibliographical references and index.
Also issued in electronic format.
ISBN 978-0-9809289-0-7

    1. Self-actualization (Psychology). 2. String models--
Psychological aspects. 3. Quantum theory--Religious
aspects. I. Title.

BF637.S4F626 2012   158.1   C2012-900801-X

Copyright © Flint, Garry A.
                NeoSolTerric Enterprises
                5609 Allenby Place
                Vernon, BC Canada V1T8P6
                Phone 250 558-5077
                E-mail: gaflint@uniserve.com
                Web site: http://www.neosolterric.com
                Cover by Jo C. Willems

First Printing: July 2012

Disclaimer
Great care has been taken in preparation of this book, but the author makes no expressed or implied warranty of any kind, nor does the author assume any responsibility for errors or omissions presented here. The material in this book is experimental and is based on clinical results. There has been no peer-reviewed research proving the efficacy of the treatment methods described herein. The author recommends consulting with another mental health-care professional before self-administering this method and assumes no liability for incidental or consequential damages in connection with or arising out of the information contained in this book.
        This book provides accurate and authoritative information about the subject matter covered. The author offers this information with the clear understanding that the information presented here is not a substitute for professional mental health, spiritual, or medical advice, nor is the author giving professional mental health, spiritual, or medical advice. If the reader wants mental health advice or any other professional advice, he or she should seek the services of a competent professional.

        Printed in USA
        LightningSource.Inc.
        La Vergne, TN.

Contents

Acknowledgments

I wish to thank the following people who gave me feedback on my ideas. They also made other contributions either to draft versions of this book or to topics related to the book: Dean Kansky, Colleen Kaffashan, Kathy Izzo, Jo C. Willems, Donna Cameron, Dave Ambrose, and Marcel and Teri Wester.

I especially want to thank Dean Kansky, Colleen Kaffashan, and Marcel and Teri Wester, who collaborated in exploring the limits of non-locality and the use of this model in accessing esoteric aspects of the personality.

I want to thank all my patients who took part in my learning path, contributed to my understanding of the hidden reality and spiritual growth, and to the final version of this theory.

In particular, I want to thank AP,[1] who led me to the Flux Theory web page and engaged me in many discussions about the physics of our virtual reality and its connection with humans. This person definitely had a major impact on the theory presented in this book, the importance of writing the book, and my life.

I want to express special thanks to James Cranwell for his enthusiasm, for reading the manuscript in detail, and validating the feasibility of my adaptations of his model to explain the hidden reality.

A special thanks goes to Philip Warren, who gave a fine-grain, thoughtful editing of the first draft of the book and made many suggestions about the text and the figures. Thanks to Stephanie McCleod, who gave excellent suggestions for Chapter 1. She also suggested rewriting the book, which I did.

A big thanks goes to the following friends and colleagues who read and gave feedback on the first presentable draft of the book: Lee Pulos, Teri and Marcel Wester, Carol and Glen Kepler, Marie Green, Debbie Bensching, Derick Curtis and Eileen Scharader.

Again, my colleague, Jo Willems, who created a spectacular cover, did the first grueling edit of the book and made many excellent suggestions. She also provided information that I was able to reference in the text.

Michael LaRocca did a superb job of editing the first version of this book. He was generous with his time and made many positive suggestions and corrections that made the book easier to read.

Al Desetta performed a heroic task of content-editing and transforming the book to make it more readable. This involved rewriting several chapters and reorganizing some of the others. I thank Al for the time and effort he put into this task.

Thanks to Susann Robins, who edited for clarity, suggested many significant changes, and freely pointed out where my writing was not clear, and Kay Gale at Writersservices.com for doing yet another copyedit of this manuscript.

Thinking I was done revising and editing, I let Heather Cameron read the manuscript. She voluntarily returned a five page, single spaced critique of content, organization and formatting of the text. For this I am greatly appreciative.

Then, I had Dana Flint do a final edit before the layout. She did an excellent job. As soon as I got over the shock of her thoroughness, I appreciated the changes and comments she made and the results in the manuscript. She clearly understood what she was reading and made many clarifying suggestions.

Finally, I want to thank Barbara Feiner for the final copyedit of the completed manuscript and, especially, Blake J. Boulerice, EbookIt formatting expert, who brought many errors to my attention, which resulted is several final edits..

Though unusual, I am appreciative of the intruding voices heard by some people. I learned that listening to these voices either led me to treatment solutions, to significant insight in the issue at hand, or to information relevant to the theory.

In particular, I want to thank my wife, H. Jane Wakefield-Flint, and daughters, Dana Flint and Susan Flint-Rajkumar, who made useful comments and preserved my sanity and well-being while I was writing.

A few sections of this book were taken from *The Theory and Treatment of Your Personality: A manual for change* (Flint, 2006) and were modified to meet the requirements of their use in this book.

Tapas Acupressure Technique™ and TAT™ are registered trademarks of Tapas Fleming and are being used with permission.

Introduction

We are all creations in the universe, built with and governed by unseen rules — the same as those that apply to everything else in our world. Did you know that even the latest discoveries in the most advanced mathematical theories are also speaking about you? This book bridges the gap between those theories and your experience of life. *Healing Your Mind and Soul* does this while offering explanations for several seldom-discussed topics that affect our daily lives.

This book is based on my 15 years' experience as a psychologist treating causes of unusual behavior in both normal patients and survivors of severe trauma. I explored a physics theory that was based on quantum physics research, which helped me explain the source of these behaviors. There was no readily available explanation because the cause was an activity in a different reality that we can't see. In physics, they call it the virtual reality; I call it the hidden reality. I learned a theory about the structure of the hidden reality and adapted this theory to explain the source of these behaviors and, as it turned out, much more.

From a unique perspective, I describe our experience in 3D-Reality from the point of view of the hidden reality — the virtual, dimensional activity described by quantum theory. Using theoretical physics, I introduce a structure of many unique fields — dimensions — that underlies our 3D-Reality.[1] It is taken for granted that this multi-dimensional, hidden reality affects our lives in many ways. In fact, the virtual fields cause everything we do and experience. I explain how dimensional fields in the hidden reality create our 3D-Reality. This includes our Personal Field — our history from conception to now — and how our behavior is affected by activity in the hidden reality. Some activities in the hidden reality can distort our behavior in unpleasant ways and sometimes get in the way of successful treatment.

More specifically, I learned about intruding spirits and how they affect our behavior. Intruding spirits can block therapy and negatively influence our experience of life. Working from a scientific perspective and with my clinical experience, I adapted the physics theory to explain the mechanics and treatment of these spirits.

Most assumptions about life, the afterlife, and 3D-Reality involve explanations that are not scientific. Normally, many facts about life usually require taking explanations on faith. I am not going to comment on that here. However, I do want to point out that there is a difference between taking an explanation on faith and taking one based on a scientific theory. The advantage of having a scientific basis for an explanation is that it connects the explanation to properties of our reality that have been established through scientific research. The theories in this case are string theory and quantum theory. Another advantage of a scientific theory is that credible, scientific explanations for phenomena in the hidden reality can lead to some control over our hidden reality and therefore control over our 3D-Reality.

The theory presented here is not a true scientific theory. It is an adaptation of a string theory that explains the 11 dimensions of the hidden reality. I altered the theory to describe what I observed in my clinical practice. My adaptation of the theory moved it out of the realm of a scientific theory with authentic validity. It is really a metaphorical interpretation of the hidden reality. My patients readily accept this metaphorical interpretation. Many of the resulting concepts are constructs of my own creation that have worked well with my patients. My experience is that the theory is close enough to the hidden reality to be useful in creating interventions using the hidden reality to cause change in a person's behavior. This finding lends support to the efficacy of this metaphorical theory.

Most interesting is that this theory explains the existence of intruding spirits and how they can attach themselves to us. The mechanics and treatment of intruding spirits are conceptually consistent with the memory-based theory of the dynamics of the mind presented in my earlier book, *A Theory and Treatment of Your Personality: A manual for Change* (Flint, 2006). *Healing Your Mind and Soul* is written in a way that makes this physics theory easily understandable for both general readers and mental health professionals. It makes clear the connection between intruding spirits and our memories.

I have worked extensively with the subconscious and offer a new definition. The subconscious — independent of the conscious and unconscious minds — can identify, access, and treat mental issues, and even operates within the hidden reality. It is an invaluable, underappreciated resource that can be used in the treatment process. I believe that the subconscious, operating in the hidden reality, is a quality of our soul.

There are three other interesting deviations from the typical view of the universe presented in the book. The first is that time is only a construct used to describe the unfolding reality. The second is that the three dimensions we use as measures are only constructs created in 3D-Reality to explain our dimensions. They are not dimensions in the hidden reality. Finally, everything is determined; there is no randomness in the universe. What is unpredictable in the universe is the interaction of the living because of the uniqueness of our life histories. Our reality unfolds involving the recreation and preservation of information and activity in the dimensional fields. The evolution of knowledge and living species on the earth started from nothing — no wisdom, no species. Over time, the amassing of memory in the multidimensions aided the gradual and orderly evolution of both wisdom and the physical characteristics of all species.

Furthermore, this book helps the reader understand many of our experiences that cannot be explained by our usual understanding of reality. For example, I analyze prayer and surrogate treatment — treatment from a distance. Furthermore, I develop two treatment interventions in the hidden reality: one that uses a source of wisdom and the other uses the field pattern of the patient's issue.

This is a self-help book that describes interventions taking place in the hidden reality via dialogue between the therapist and the patient in our 3D-Reality. This hasn't been written about before, as far as I know. The book also covers an explanation of consciousness, the mechanics of propagation, ancestral influence, the nature of reality, evolution, and the afterlife.

Chapter 1 covers how I became interested in intruding spirits — called fields or souls — and my search for a means to explain them. I develop the notion of the hidden reality, a reality we cannot see, that creates our 3D-Reality. The activity of intruding fields is explained as taking place in the hidden reality. No wonder the "sciences" of psychology and psychiatry have not studied intruding fields — you cannot see or measure them. Together, we will explore the science of the hidden reality with evidence I offer for the reality of our Personal Field. Examples of the use of the Personal Field in therapy are given, as well. There is also an overview of intruding fields, their activity in the hidden reality, and their treatment.

Chapter 2 explains the reason some of our memories in 3D-Reality relate to the intruding fields or souls in the hidden reality. The Process Healing Method (Flint, 2006) assumes that memories cause good things in our lives, as well as problems, such as anxiety, fear, depression, emotional pain, and so forth. Painful trauma memories, which can cause these and other mental health problems, open the door for intruding fields. The more intense the trauma a person has suffered, the more likely that fields will attach to him or her. There are many kinds of complex memories to which these fields can attach, and this chapter describes them in detail.

Chapter 3 explains the origin and structure of our presence in the hidden reality. I adapted Cranwell's (1998) Flux Theory of the Universe[2] to build a model of the dimensional fields creating our 3D-Reality, a model the average reader can understand and accept. This physics theory is used only as a way to make it easier to think about our hidden reality and fields. Relax; it is not necessary to fully grasp Flux Theory to understand the hidden structures in the universe presented in this book. However, when you have finished Chapter 3, you will be able to conceptualize or think comfortably about hidden dimensions. You will also understand that each of us has a Personal Field that is the record of all our experiences from conception to the present time.

Chapter 4 describes the basic mechanics of a simple intruding field. The problematic fields that attach to us are usually the Personal Fields of deceased people with their past life histories intact. This involves bringing memory structures (Chapter 2) and the physics (Chapter 3) together to provide a plausible description of the mechanics of entrainment and the treatment of these intrusions. A number of examples of treatment reveal the psychology of intruding souls.

Chapter 5 describes complex intruding field structures — a field that has its own history of intruding fields or generational fields. Generational fields can attach in various arrangements and amass over many past generations, like a stack of poker chips with each chip from a different generation. I describe the analysis and treatment of fields with complex field structures by using transcripts from actual sessions with my patients.

Chapter 6 discusses how the nonlocal property of fields works in treating people at a distance. I describe the human qualities required for prayer and distant healing, and the active ingredients involved in surrogate treatment. I give several case histories of surrogate treatment using the Emotional Freedom Techniques[3] and include a description of the use of hidden reality in Hellinger's Family Constellation Therapy.[4] The role of nonlocality in voodoo and witchcraft is briefly discussed.

Chapter 7 includes a number of experimental treatment interventions that use the hidden reality. I use most of them frequently in my private practice, such as giving my treatment knowledge to others through the Personal Field. I also give other examples of treatment, such as using another person's good quality as a template for change in the patient and identifying and treating the source of allergies.

Chapter 8 describes using nonlocal support to aid in treating torture survivors. This is an interesting application of the properties of nonlocality. Although other therapists have used this experimental intervention successfully, it has to be carried out very carefully to ensure the safety of the therapist and patient. The safeguards are clearly presented.

Chapter 9 describes an experimental treatment intervention designed to obtain a more efficient, complete treatment with faster results. All changes in the universe, orchestrated by what I call the Manager, are based on fixed laws of the universe, which appear in reality to give more happiness and less pain to the living. A helper discovered in the 9th dimension, Wisdom, has access to all wisdom based on love from all Personal Fields from the beginning of life forms. Wisdom can help us quickly create well-formed interventions for treating people to obtain positive changes.

Chapter 10 is a collection of experimental treatment interventions using Wisdom. The first is the most exciting and is included here as an undeveloped, experimental treatment method that allows the subconscious to treat field patterns of target issues. I have also included many strategies for other interventions to give you ideas for treatment and avenues for additional exploration. I describe an inexplicable intervention that seems to originate from a higher realm.

Appendix I shows you how to communicate with your own subconscious and use it as an ally to treat intruding fields. If you are unable to access your subconscious easily, then consult my previous book, *A Theory and Treatment of Your Personality: A manual for change* (Flint, 2006). This text presents the information needed for many readers to establish such communication.

Writing this book made a difference in my life, and I hope reading it will make a difference in yours, as well.

Part I
Theoretical Basis for the Hidden Reality

Chapter 1

Introduction to Intruding Fields

To understand what another person is saying, you must assume
that it is true and try to imagine what it could be true of.
George A. Miller, Ph.D.,
Father of Communications Theory

How I Came to Work with Intruding Fields

I work with the subconscious. It is a complex part of our personality that has been present from conception. Until trained to do more, the subconscious is usually active in creative activity, in life-threatening situations, and in providing insight or intuition in novel situations. The subconscious is like an inner observer who usually does not get hurt by trauma. By communicating with the subconscious, I learned to problem-solve difficult issues by identifying the structure of traumatic memories causing the issue. By chance, I learned that the subconscious could be taught to treat issues. Treatment involved asking the subconscious to remove the emotional pain from the memory structure of the issue. When the pain is removed from the memory, the unwanted issue usually never happens again. As a therapist, I developed a description of the personality for this approach using memory structures as the basic component. I call this the Process Healing Method.

In this method, I assume that collages of mostly old memories are used simultaneously to create our next response and to create a unique memory of that response in our ongoing behavior. In other words, behavior and the memory of that behavior are created simultaneously. Most behavior is a collage of previously learned memories that cause everything we do, think, and feel. This includes all thoughts, images, pain, and emotions that pop into our consciousness. The collages can cause problematic issues in our lives, such as anxiety, depression, emotional intrusions, negative self-talk, obsessions, and so forth. They are simply memory structures that are associated with emotional pain from traumatic experiences in our past. Painful experiences create an assortment of memory structures, ranging from simple to complex, to which pain of varying intensity is associated. Usually, these painful memories can be easily treated.

The Process Healing Method worked well until 15 years ago, when I encountered a treatment barrier while working with a patient who had severe problems. He was a long-time schizophrenic who heard intruding voices and had other psychotic behaviors. These intruding voices and psychotic behaviors were caused by parts of the personality that were unique memories. I use the word **parts** for any memory structure that causes unwanted activity that intrudes into our experience. The barrier stopped me from treating these parts. To overcome the barrier, I learned a new therapeutic strategy that led to a breakthrough with this patient. That treatment strategy, further developed since then, forms the basis of the material presented in this book.

When the patient in question was four years old, he was helping his father in the garden and was pulling up flowers by mistake. His father became outraged, raised his hoe, and cried, "I'm going to kill you!" This "near-death" experience created in the child what I call a compartmentalized part and other complex memories. Later, with continued punishment, his brain adapted by creating an automatic process to create these compartmentalized memory structures when experiencing his own or others' anger. Later, I will explain compartmentalized parts and complex memories, how they are formed, and how they can influence our behavior.

This patient, because of the automatic creation process, had literally thousands of these compartmentalized parts or complex memories independent of his Main Personality. He was 42 and had been creating them automatically for years. When he became angry or when someone became angry with him, his emotional response in the present situation triggered the very intense emotions that he had experienced in the past, and this caused the creation of a new memory structure or part. For example, when he felt moderate fear or anger, a slight dissociation might occur, experienced as confusion, when a new memory structure was being created. It might be a fleeting emotion, but a small memory structure or part was created. The created structure would become a memory of what happened in the situation. This process helped him deal with the situation in some way. Later, these parts or memory structures then manifested in him as auditory intrusions, such as hearing radios playing, engines revving, dogs barking, hearing footsteps around his house, voices yelling at him, or an internal dialogue about how fat or sexually deprived he was.

I was treating him by using the Tapas Acupressure Technique (TAT), a technique that had him apply a gentle pressure to three acupressure points on his nose and forehead while putting his other hand behind his head.[1] While this is an effective technique to treat many mental health issues and allergies, I mainly use it to treat a person's obsessions.

Initially, treatment went well. I was able to systematically treat many of his traumatic memories in each session. When using the Process Healing Method with a patient, I employ finger responses to communicate with his or her subconscious (see Appendix I). This is a well-known hypnotic technique for communication of this type.[2] I encourage the patients not to go into a trance because I want them to learn what I say to the subconscious, so they can later treat themselves. Some patients voluntarily go into a light trance to ensure that their conscious mind does not influence the subconscious' response. When using finger responses with no formal hypnosis, I have been able to communicate with the subconscious with over 95 percent of my patients in the very first session. Hypnotizability is not a factor.

After months of making progress by treating this patient's memory structures in this way, I ran into a treatment barrier. For two months, I struggled to treat him without making any progress. Then I went to a training workshop that included removing demons and fallen angels in patients who had suffered torture or ritual abuse.[3] Ritual abuse is done in a quasi-religious setting and may include the simulated or real sacrifice of something as part of the ritual. This creates an enormous amount of trauma resulting in the creation of compartmentalized parts and other complex memories loaded with pain or fear. At first, I did not believe in fields, demons, or ritual abuse, yet my skepticism disappeared the next week after I used the new treatment intervention with my patient. I removed 19 demons or "fields" and continued treating him with no further barriers.

How was this possible? Interestingly, therapists treating torture survivors usually use hypnotic techniques. These therapists can run into fields. The pain memories in torture survivors are very intense, and the fields are attracted to these pain memories and make themselves known. The same is true when I use the hypnotic Process Healing Method. In both cases, we do not stimulate the person overtly with some physical intervention. These hypnotic interventions use metaphors to obtain change. A **metaphor** is a construct of words or a word that is used to refer to something that it does not literally describe in order to suggest a similarity — for example, *structures* causing problems, *walls* preventing communication, or *unknown* influences.

Intruding fields are in the hidden reality. The subconscious can be taught to stimulate the hidden reality to treat an intruding field. However, when I was treating other torture survivors using Eye Movement Desensitization and Reprocessing (bilateral stimulation) or Emotional Freedom Techniques (tapping on acupressure points) as interventions, I don't recall having any problem with intruding fields. I believe the reason for this is that the 3D stimulation of the patient with eye movements or tapping creates activity in the hidden reality that effectively treats any intruding fields that were attached to the traumatic issue.

Theoretical research in physics shows that there are unseen, dimensional structures that underlie our physical 3D-Reality. I assume that this is the basis for our spiritual reality.[4] This unseen, virtual or hidden reality affects our lives in many ways. Each of us suffers a number of traumas during our lifetime. Severe short-term trauma or constant and ongoing traumas create different kinds of memory structures. All that we experience and remember are, of course, our memories, but they are recorded in what I call the Personal Field — our unique structure in the virtual reality. Therefore, all our traumas create a pattern of trauma in our Personal Field. When a person dies, my clinical experience suggests that the person's Personal Field remains intact and present in the virtual or hidden reality.

The workshop started me thinking about the mechanics of intruding fields. Over time, it became clear that when the Personal Fields of a living person and a deceased person had similar trauma structures, the Personal Field or soul of a deceased person could entrain with or attach to the Personal Field of a patient.

For example, if you were involved in a near-fatal car accident and somebody in the car died, that person's Personal Field could entrain with yours because you have a common trauma experience. This could complicate healing your grief. Furthermore, given the right conditions, intruding fields from an acquaintance, a family member, or anyone who died in past generations can entrain to a person. Besides blocking the treatment of some memory structure, the presence of an entrained field can cause problems in the living person by increasing emotions to motivate problematic behavior or by introducing atypical behaviors. All behaviors are **motivated** by positive or negative emotions. The more intense the emotions, the more likely the behavior will occur.

The workshop provided me with new opportunities to treat patients with severe trauma and also taught me that severe trauma or torture led to acquiring entrained fields. I found that the more traumas a person had experienced, the more likely a field would entrain. Constant, ongoing pain — such as near-death experiences, multiple, severe beatings, rape, and perhaps intense grief — create memory structures that are vulnerable to being entrained by a field. The result is that some traumatic memories are much more difficult to treat in therapy, because intruding fields serve as barriers to treatment.

I still worked with the subconscious as I had before, but now I was aware that fields could block treatment. I used various Christian methods to successfully remove them. I came to the belief that fields were active in the virtual reality, the reality we can't see, resulting in various forms of intrusions into our 3D-Reality — the reality we know and with which we are familiar.

Soon I started calling demons **fields** to remove any religious connotations and barriers in thinking about them. Throughout this book, I will call the Personal Field of a living person a Personal Field and the Personal Field of a deceased person a **field** or **soul**. A Personal Field is like a television signal, carrying information. The Personal Field is one of the 11 fields or dimensions constructing our universe, which are governed by the laws of physics.

I soon discovered and treated these intruding fields in other patients, as the following clinical examples show.

This is my simplest example. A little girl, who was in treatment because she witnessed her mother's spousal abuse, had a severe spider phobia. After teaching her subconscious how to treat painful memories, I treated this simple phobia for practice. I treated her spider phobia to give her an example of subconscious treatment in action. With treatment, the intensity of her phobia went from 10 (high) to about a 5 (lower) but then got stalled. With problem-solving, I discovered that there were three memory structures or parts that had been created by her phobic responses to spiders. As I treated these parts, I found the second part had an intruding field blocking treatment. After treating the intruding field and the remaining parts, treatment was finished. Later that day, the girl carried a daddy longlegs spider from her bedroom to the back-yard without fear.

In another example, a patient fell into a deep depression nine months after his father died. He was unable to hold a job and had been in therapy for two and half years without progress, so he came to see me. Working with his subconscious, I removed his deceased father's entrained field and the patient's depression lifted. He was able to start gradually phasing into work within two months. This will be described in greater detail in Chapter 4.

The treatment of intruding fields does not take up the entire therapeutic session; instead, it is usually a brief intervention that I use in my treatment sessions when the need arises. I would estimate that the treatment of an intruding field seldom takes longer than five minutes.

Because of my background in experimental psychology, I looked for ways to describe how fields attach to us and how they affected our behavior. I wanted to be able to explain them to patients in an understandable way. I also wanted an explanation that would be understandable and acceptable to all mental health professionals, enabling them to accept a radical shift in thinking and practice — namely, that it is possible to identify and treat intruding fields in their patients.

Why would a clinical psychologist want to explain and treat something that exists in our unseen or hidden reality? Most mental health professionals deny the possibility that intruding fields affect our behavior or that they even exist. My experience in the ritual abuse workshop reminded me about a therapeutic intervention using the Tapas Acupressure Technique (TAT) that helped me form a concept of intruding fields.[5] This intervention, no longer used as a TAT procedure, involves the treatment of inherited allergies, which implies that some allergies are not necessarily learned in this lifetime. Rather, some allergies appear to be caused by conditions in previous generations and were passed down as ancestral fields.

The allergy treatment involved obtaining from the subconscious what I call triggers for the source of the allergy — namely, whether the allergy was acquired after birth, prebirth, or preconception, whether the ancestor was male or female, adult or child, in what century, and on what continent the allergy first occurred. These appear to serve as coordinates to activate the ancestral person and circumstances causing the allergy near us in the hidden reality. With the cause of the allergy present in our hidden reality, it can be treated. I used this approach to allergy treatment to help me conceptualize intruding fields — namely, that they were in the hidden reality and were survivors from a previous lifetime. In the meantime, I used the Christian treatment of intruding fields, learned in the workshop, until I developed my current explanation and treatment of these fields.

Religious and alternative healers routinely work with intruding fields and frequently find that removing them causes a positive change in their clients. The removal of demons or spirits is practiced in many Latin American countries. Many First Nation cultures (native Indians) have ceremonies in which they send away demons. Many churches, such as Roman Catholic, Anglican, and some Protestant churches, have clergy who specialize in removing intruding fields or demons from people or their homes. Some deliverance ministries specialize in casting out demons. Dickason (1987) bases the reality of demons on the Bible and offers many case studies to demonstrate their influence on people's lives.[6]

In my clinical work, the removal of intruding fields often results in positive behavior changes. Therefore, it is a disservice to those who have suffered severe trauma to ignore the possibility of intruding fields and their removal. My profession requires an objective theory to explain intruding fields and a protocol to treat them. It is important that we understand their existence, their relationship to the living, and their treatment so that we can help patients live better lives.

Virtual Reality: Looking for an Understandable Explanation

I am using a physics theory to explain intruding fields for two reasons. First, fields do not exist in our 3D, physical reality. They are active in our virtual reality: an active, unseen, complex, 11-dimensional structure that creates all objects and activity in our 3D-Reality. We therefore need a frame of reference and a theory to grasp the idea of multidimensions to make it easier to understand virtual reality and fields. Second, a physics theory led me to develop experimental interventions that use structures in virtual reality. Mental health professionals may want to use other features of my approach and use the theory to develop other treatment interventions. Therefore, describing the theory in some detail may spur new ideas for further research leading to effective treatments.

At first, it seemed daunting to explain how fields function in virtual reality. Then an acquaintance introduced me to a physics theory called the Flux Theory, which is described as "a theory of everything."[7]

The Flux Theory describes virtual or unseen reality as composed of nesting geometrical structures. Each of these 11 geometrical structures has a unique field that amasses and carries information related to our 3D-Reality. The Flux Theory provided the basis for a plausible explanation of the field activity that I see in my clinical practice. It also explains nonlocal communication, which is involved in surrogate treatment or treating patients at a distance. The most significant evidence of the theory's effectiveness is that it led to very powerful treatment interventions that I routinely use in my clinical practice. The interventions work because the model I developed based on the Flux Theory appears to approximate the basic structure of the universe. Understanding this basic structure of the hidden reality has enabled me to work with interventions in the unseen reality that obtain positive change in my patients.

To understand intruding fields, I want to lead you to an intuitive acceptance of fields in our physiology and other fields that appear to radiate from our bodies. I will use brief descriptions from my research and my clinical experience to describe these fields. I want to help you accept the fact that electromagnetic fields and other fields exist in our virtual or hidden reality. These fields account for unexplained experiences in many people.

Electromagnetic Fields in Everyday Life

The idea of unseen fields creating and affecting our behavior may seem strange, until you realize that there are many facts about our brain and body that are hidden from us. Because we can't see field activity in our brains or the universe, it doesn't mean that these unseen fields are not there. The concept of fields is not a strange idea, once you understand a little about the physical laws of the universe.

Walter Schempf, the mathematician who improved the Magnetic Resonance Imaging (MRI) machine, discovered that the quantum variations in an electromagnetic field carried information about objects, including their shapes.[8] The MRI machine takes this information and creates the image of the brain or body part from the patient's electromagnetic field. This is not unlike what a collaboration of scientists has concluded — that we don't see objects themselves but only their quantum, or unseen, information, and from that unseen information, we obtain our image of the 3D world.[9]

In other words, we don't compose or create 3D-Reality. Rather, 3D-Reality is composed and created in the hidden, virtual reality involving all relevant information in the universe. For example, our physical world is created in virtual reality. We see the outcome of this hidden reality because of the emanations or reflections of photons or sound waves, to which we respond with perception. We don't see other features of the hidden reality, unless we have a means to detect them.

Electromagnetic fields in people, probably generated by cellular activity, although unseen, play important roles in communication between cells, cellular structures, and other structures in our body. We can read about these fields in newspapers, magazines, or on the Internet. Electromagnetic fields are present and active in our physiology and affect our everyday lives.

For example, some people cannot wear digital watches because their electromagnetic field interferes with the watch's operation. In a less common example, some people can cause a computer to fail when they are close to it — their electromagnetic field distorts the electrical activity in the computer. This type of electromagnetic field extends only a short distance from the person because it does not affect other watches or computers in the same room.

Besides the effect on electronics, electromagnetic fields can also affect our behavior. One of the favorite ways to demonstrate this is to stand behind a person and change a muscle test response by manipulating his or her Personal Field. A muscle test has to do with using muscle strength to determine whether or not a belief or condition is true or false, as you will see. Here is a demonstration that you can try.

While standing behind a person, ask them to hold their arm straight out from their body (see Figure 1-1, next page). Now press down on a spot just below the elbow with firm pressure. The person can usually hold their arm up even with some downward pressure. This is a "true" response. Now sweep your hand from the head down to the lower back, holding it three inches away from the spine without touching the person. After you do this, retest the muscle strength. The person is no longer able to hold their arm up. This is a "false" response. On the other hand, when you sweep your hand up from the lower back to the neck, the muscle test becomes "true" again. Try it and you will find that it works. This is your local field affecting only the person being tested. This demonstration doesn't affect the muscle strength of everybody in the room.

Figure 1-1 Muscle Testing Correctly

In discussing fields, I want to distinguish between the fields present in the dimensional structures of the universe in the hidden reality and other measurable fields. The intruding fields I am talking about are not fields that can be measured, like strong and weak nuclear forces, light, other known electromagnetic fields, and so forth. Each dimension has unique longitudinal waves, similar to sound waves, which create the structures and activity in 3D-Reality. An intruding field, then, is a field that exists in the dimensional structure of our hidden reality.

The Eleven Dimensions and the Personal Field

The Flux Theory is the version of the string theory that I use as the basis for my model. There is a basic element in the theory that serves to create the 11 dimensions in our universe — the 10 dimensional structures and particles in the 0th dimension. Each of the 1st through 9th dimensions, and maybe the 0th dimension, is capable of storing and communicating information within its structure. The 10th dimension serves a different purpose. I have redefined the function of the dimensions in the hidden reality based on my clinical experience (see Appendix IV).

I hypothesize that the behavior and physical structure of a person is defined by the 5th through 9th dimensions. The fields of the 0th through 4th dimensions are involved in creating molecular structures to fill in the virtual structures. The 6th and 7th dimensions store templates that are used to construct and maintain our physical body. The 8th dimension is a transition dimension involved in our accessing wisdom in the 9th dimension. I hypothesize that the 0th through 9th dimensions are all embedded in the 10th dimension, which operates following the basic laws of the universe to maintain coherency or logical order between the living and inanimate objects.

These 11 dimensions can be thought of as geometrical structures with the sides of the structures vibrating to store and communicate information. I call the vibrations carried in these dimensions "fields." The geometrical structure of each dimension is created by a particular longitudinal wave of information in its structure, like the station 102.7 on your FM radio, but more complex. The wave of a dimension I call a "dimensional field."

Our soul includes the 5th through 9th dimensions. When I refer to the Personal Field, I am referring to the 5th dimension. The 5th dimension carries all of our experience from conception to the present and is most important for our purposes here. Your Personal Field has the information or memory to direct all your experience, your sensory perceptions, and everything you think and do. You might wonder where the soul comes from.

At conception, your parents' souls, including ancestral fields from each parent, are joined to form your **conception soul**. With life experience, this initial soul is modified to become unique to you. This means that everything you learned, as well as all the pain and joy that you experienced, remains forever present in the universe in your soul after death. With death, it is my understanding that the soul — the 5th through 9th dimensions — continues forever in the universe. The soul of every dead person, including his or her Personal Field, is in the virtual reality and, as I mentioned before, can anchor to the Personal Fields of the living.

In my experience as a therapist, treating such normal issues as negative beliefs, intrusions, trauma memories, and so forth, all involve working with memory structures that are motivated by mild to intense negative emotions. These structures and emotions are in the hidden reality. In other words, all the experiences we have in our 3D-Reality are really reflections of what is happening in the hidden reality. In that reality, it is possible to acquire an intruding soul. I want to make it clear that not all people, fewer than half of my patients, have had intruding souls.

What is surprising is that the pattern of pain structures found in the Personal Fields of intruding souls appears to be similar to the pattern of pain structures found in the Personal Fields of my patients. By removing the pain in the memory structures in an intruding soul, the intruding soul is able to leave the living person's Personal Field. Once you learn the theory, you will see that it is understandable, logical, and effective as a therapeutic intervention. Kraft (1992) describes his experience and approach to treating these intruding fields.[10]

Another important fact you should know about Personal Fields is that they are not everywhere in the universe but can be accessed anywhere in the universe. Let me explain this. I believe that the stimulus-response process we see in human behavior is reflective of a similar stimulus-response process of Personal Fields in the universe. Just as a stimulus is needed to trigger a response in our behavior, a stimulus in some location is needed to trigger the presence of a soul in that location. Like the allergy example, this means that when you think of somebody or have a lock of their hair, their Personal Field is in your presence. This is strongly suggested by examples of successful treatment of patients who are in a different location than the person performing the treatment. The treatment of an issue in the presence of a nonlocal soul causes the treatment of an issue in the soul itself. This surrogate treatment is possible because of the non-local property of the universe.

The electromagnetic fields discussed previously appear to be local fields involved with running the body. Cells react to the changing properties of local fields; that is, the effects of change seem to be local in the cells or organs. Field effects appear to be able to operate reliably at a short distance from the body. However, here's what's interesting. Some fields are able to communicate or have influence over long distances. The following examples suggest that our memories can be outside our physical body and can be triggered in places that are some distance from our current location.

Communication in the Personal Field

In the 1920s, a great American scientist, Dr. Wilder Penfield, showed that by stimulating different parts of the brain, a patient could remember some scenes from the past.[11] Later, Karl Lashley tried to find the location of the cellular structures in the brain in which memory was stored. He trained rats to jump from a stand, across a pool of water, and through doors to get food. When the jump was not successful, the rat fell into the water. Penfield experimented by damaging various areas of the rats' brains to locate the cellular structure that provided the memory of the task. Following repeated failures to destroy the locus of memory, he finally concluded that memory was equally potent everywhere in the brain. This implies that memories are not in the cells themselves — cellular or neural memory — but outside the body in the hidden reality.

Other research suggests that the Personal Field is capable of both storing information for local use and manifesting information in distant places. This non-local quality of the Personal Field means that something done locally can be experienced or cause effects in some person in another place on Earth. A property of the Personal Field and the virtual reality makes this possible. The idea that a person can communicate over distance with people is of profound importance. This means that therapists can treat and remove visiting fields and use the nonlocal field in treatment interventions, such as in distant and surrogate treatment.

The U.S. Army Intelligence and Security Command demonstrated an interesting example of nonlocality in an experiment described by Pearsall (1998).[12] In this 1993 experiment, white blood cells were scraped from the gums of a volunteer, centrifuged to emulsify them, and placed in a test tube. A probe from equipment like a lie detector was inserted into the emulsified cells.

The volunteer who donated the cells was in another room and was shown a prepared video sequence that included both violent and nonviolent scenes. The response of cellular activity of the emulsified cells, as measured by the lie detector, perfectly matched the emotional swings observed in the volunteer as he viewed the violent and peaceful scenes, even though he was in the next room. This remote effect was successfully repeated at a distance of 50 miles and still worked two days later. This demonstrated that the cells were responsive to the volunteer's emotions at a distance. Evidently, the nonlocal property of the Personal Field enabled the individual's emotional information to affect his cells, even when those cells are moved some distance away.

In this example, I assume the Personal Field of the cells' donor manifested remotely in the presence of emulsified cells, because it was triggered with an identical cellular DNA signature. With the person's field active nonlocally in the presence of the emulsified cells, information was received by the cells causing responses matching the person's experience.

In addition, Pearsall (1998) describes many unusual changes that heart transplant recipients undergo when living with a donated heart.[13] In one case, a woman who detested television became a couch potato and TV sports addict after her heart transplant. Pearsall cited many other changes revealed in eating habits, speech patterns, social activities, and hobbies after heart transplant surgery.

In one especially striking example, a child received the heart of a young girl who had been murdered.[14] For two weeks after the transplant, the recipient told her doctor about dreams and memories revealing intimate details of the murder. These details involved the location and circumstances of the murder, the clothes worn by victim and murderer, and conversations that occurred during the murder. When the heart recipient's doctor called the police, the detailed information revealed by the girl resulted in the conviction of the murderer, who received a life sentence.

The girl's new heart brought or triggered details of the crime from memories that would only be found in the experience or Personal Field of the deceased donor. I believe that the common, cellular DNA signature from the heart and the pain from the operation enabled her Personal Field to attract the Personal Field of the donor. This joining of Personal Fields gave the girl access to information about the crime that could only come from the donor's Personal Field. I don't believe that it was cellular memory, because when the cells in the brains of the rats in Penfield's experiment were destroyed, the rats' behavior continued.

I have observed similar phenomena in one of my patients, where a perpetrator's field entrained with the victim. My patient experienced an attempted rape. The assailant attacked the patient and, although no rape or physical harm occurred, the terror she experienced enabled the field of the perpetrator to attach to her. Apparently, the perpetrator had a pain pattern similar to the patient's, which allowed his field to attach. When treating the trauma, the presence of the perpetrator's Personal Field triggered emotions that became a barrier to treating the trauma. The trauma could not be treated until the field of the perpetrator was removed. The subconscious was able to treat the perpetrator's field using a different intervention. Once the perpetrator's field was removed, the treatment of the patient's trauma proceeded routinely.

Still another example of remote communication is extrasensory perception (ESP). J. B. Rhine was a researcher whose interest in ESP led to studies that allegedly revealed the nonlocal properties of Personal

Field. In the past, psychologists and others ridiculed him because of their disbelief in ESP and the methods he used.[15]

That was soon to change by the experiments of astronaut Edgar Mitchell, who went to the moon on Apollo 14 in February 1971. He had a strong interest in the scientific basis of spirituality, had studied Rhine's work on ESP, and had several friends involved with research in telepathy. Before his trip to the moon, Mitchell and his friends designed some experiments. At a prearranged time, Mitchell would "send" symbols to the earth, while his six friends or receivers would try to receive the symbols. Mitchell sent four sets of data. Later analysis revealed that the data received was close to the data that Mitchell sent, an outcome that would have occurred by chance only once in 3,000 tries. Mitchell's experiment and later research on the mechanics of transmission interested other scientists in doing research on consciousness.[16]

This experiment showed that the great distance between sender and receiver didn't reduce the sender's ability to send information by thought. Mitchell's research suggests there is a field that is available or accessible throughout space and over long distances. Based on my clinical work with nonlocal communication and these research vignettes, I assume the Personal Field of Mitchell and his receivers activated near each other to obtain the results in this distant communication experiment.

Animals also show similar ESP capabilities. Rupert Sheldrake (1999) collected examples of animal behavior from many species suggesting that animals are using some form of ESP. Sheldrake explored these extrasensory capacities and hypothesized what he calls the morphic field to explain these phenomena.[17]

Perhaps the best example of communication in another dimension is the following: A couple owned a dog. The husband was the captain of a U.S. Coast Guard buoy tender and would arrive home 30 minutes after docking at unpredictable times. Whenever his ship came into port, at some point, the dog would "ask" to go outside, stand at the front of the walk, look in the direction of his owner's return, and wait 20 minutes for his arrival. This behavior was so consistent that his wife used it as a signal to freshen up and start preparing dinner to be ready when her husband arrived. Because of the randomness of her husband's return, there was no obvious means for the dog to know when his master was coming home. This suggests the dog had an extrasensory way of sensing when the husband was within 20 minutes from home. In this case, I believe that it was the connection to the man's Personal Field that allowed the dog to be alerted.

A final example of how Personal Fields affect others is supported by McTaggart's (2001) review of Elizabeth Targ and Fred Sicher's study of the effects of prayer on illness.[18] In this well-designed study with controls for all possible explanations, Targ and Sicher spent months identifying qualified religious and spiritual healers around the country. The study involved the healers praying for HIV patients one hour a day, six days a week, for 10 weeks, with every other week off. A team of scientists studied the patients with documented HIV symptoms before and after the experiment. There was an experimental and control group. The control group was a group of patients who did not receive prayers.

The results showed that the experimental group with prayer support was healthier and experienced fewer deaths than the control group without prayer support. Targ and Sicher repeated the study, making it even less subject to criticism, and again found that prayer for the experimental group had positive effects on every measure of health in the study.

These examples show how a person's Personal Field can influence or communicate with others, send information, receive information, and even affect a person's health and well-being.

The Use of the Personal Field in Therapy

As a practicing psychologist, my interest in the Personal Field stems from seeing how the subconscious works in the hidden reality and in the cells and neurology of my patients. The subconsciouses of most of the patients in my clinical practice demonstrate activity in the hidden reality.

For example, I have occasionally noticed a patient's subconscious using one of my interventions before I taught it. On one occasion, a patient's subconscious used the Tapas Acupressure Treatment (TAT) intervention. In this case, the patient reported the distinct experience of thoughts streaming through her conscious experience, similar to patients who have this experience when I use the TAT method to treat obsessive thoughts. By questioning the subconscious, I concluded that the subconscious of my client had obtained this knowledge of TAT from my Personal Field.

In other cases, patients often shake or rub their head before I teach the subconscious how to use the Process Healing Method. They are experiencing a sensation in their brain or on their scalp. This reaction is often caused by an internal experience patients have when the subconscious is treating some issue. By asking leading questions, I have found that the subconscious had read my Personal Field and was busy treating issues that I routinely treat. Treating these issues allows the subconscious to treat issues independently without the involvement of the Main Personality.

A colleague who is a First Nations Elder (a Native American older than 50)[19] told me that, prior to 1800, the Elders would have meetings without anyone speaking. This didn't surprise me, because I had heard of the Rife tribe in South America, a tribe that didn't have a spoken language. His comment prompted me to wonder if nonverbal communication would be possible with a patient.

With my next First Nations patient, I started the session by asking if I could talk to his subconscious. With a surprised look, he said that he heard a "Yes." I asked if it was all right for the subconscious to read my Personal Field and learn all my treatment knowledge and the wisdom of my teachers. The patient again heard a "Yes." I then told his subconscious I was offering my treatment knowledge to him and that he could take it.

After a few minutes, I wanted to put this to a test. I asked him to rank on a scale from 0 (low) to 10 (high) how anxious he would be if he had to give a prepared speech to 100 people. He said 13. I asked his subconscious if it would be safe to treat this issue. He heard a "Yes." I then asked his subconscious to treat the basis for this public speaking anxiety. Within minutes, the anxiety moved from 13 to a scale of 2. The patient stated that he now believed that he would have no problem giving a prepared speech before 100 people.

I have come to trust that communication in the 5th dimension is possible and have since explored what I can do with it. Although this method doesn't work with all patients, I have often communicated my treatment knowledge in my Personal Field to patients in my office, as well as to participants in a workshop. I have shared my treatment knowledge over the telephone with patients who were thousands of miles away. I tell them that it is possible for their subconscious to access my subconscious when they are having a problem with a barrier, and that perhaps their subconscious can find a solution from my subconscious. I have patients who report receiving help from my subconscious when working with their own barriers or when working with barriers in their children.

For example, I have a collaborator in another city who has been using Process Healing on himself for years. Whenever he runs into a problem, he asks his subconscious to contact my subconscious and get help for removing the barrier. He reports that in most cases the barrier is resolved. It only fails to work when the complexity of the problem requires a novel intervention. In another example, a therapist and her 10-year-old son both learned the Process Healing method, and she had been effectively using it at home with her child. The therapist told me that whenever her child had a treatment barrier, she would ask the child's subconscious to contact my subconscious and get help resolving the barrier. The therapist said that this usually worked.

In most cases, when I am successful in transferring my knowledge to my patients' Personal Field and communicating with their subconscious, the patient can hear a "Yes" or "No" in their thoughts in response to my questions. Similarly, some readers who quiet their mind and ask themselves if they can talk to their subconscious will hear a response in their thoughts. However, it is quite normal if you do not hear a response after your request. There are many reasons for this. The primary reason is that some aspect of you is blocking the response for some protective reason. During therapy, these barriers to communication with the subconscious can be resolved by using finger responses to communicate with the barrier or subconscious and by problem-solving.

Recently, the subconscious of some patients, to whom I had just given the treatment knowledge via the field, spontaneously responded to me with finger responses — raising the index finger as "Yes" and the thumb as "No." This happened before I had taught the patients or their subconscious the finger responses. These examples confirm to me the efficacy of passing knowledge from my Personal Field to a patient. It appears that the patient's subconscious can access my Personal Field and then successfully use the information accessed to both interact with the therapist with finger responses as well as to begin therapeutic interventions on his or her own.

This is also true with surrogate treatment of a patient in another location. Because of the nonlocal property of Personal Fields, it appears possible to treat patients with or without their awareness when they are located some distance from the therapist. When I do surrogate treatment, I assume the patient's Personal Field manifests near mine. Then,

I can treat the issue in my Personal Field by using EFT or ask their sub-conscious to treat the issue to change their Personal Field. Both approaches result in change in their behavior. This will be explored in detail in Chapters 7 and 8.

With this overview of fields and their treatment, let's look at how virtual or hidden reality is related to trauma, memory, and behavior — a connection that goes to the heart of the phenomena of intruding fields.

Chapter 2

Memory, Trauma, and Behavior

Introduction

Behaviors are memories — everything we think and do, our dreams, intrusive thoughts, images, emotions, and sometimes pain. A basic assumption for the Process Healing Method is that memories are collages of mostly old memories that are assembled to simultaneously create new memories and responses. Memories are created in an unfolding process caused by the changing environment that determines our behavior in everyday life. This is very close to a model of verbal behavior and remembering that was previously offered by Bartlett in 1932.[1]

Problematic issues in our lives are simply memory structures associated with emotional pain from punishing experiences that occurred in the past. With continued clinical experience, I discovered that complex trauma memory structures in the fields of deceased persons could entrain with or attach to similar trauma memory structures in my living patients. As I came to understand the mechanics of how an intruding field joins with the Personal Field of a living person, I discovered a way to treat these fields. The mechanics involved in the treatment of fields is consistent with the theory underlying the Process Healing Method.

Therefore, given the importance of memory in the entrainment of Personal Fields, this chapter will provide a detailed look at the development of memory. I will discuss simple and complex memory structures to show you how active conscious and unconscious experience — active memories and active emotions — work together to produce behavior. I will then describe the trauma-based memory structures that are the basis for problematic behavior. These memory structures caused by a motor vehicle accident, a medical crisis, sexual or physical abuse, or torture can have intense negative emotions associated with them. (To become more aware of the complexities of memories, and the use of the subconscious, I suggest reading Flint, [2006]). These same trauma-based memory structures attract or enable the intrusion of fields. Here is what happens when fields are associated with the memory of a problematic issue.

Based upon my clinical experience, I learned to treat most problematic issues as memories. By communicating and problem-solving with the subconscious, I am able to identify the memory structure of the problematic issue. Treatment of the issue then involves removing the emotional pain from the memory structure. When the motivating pain is removed from the memory, the issue created by the memory no longer occurs and the problem is gone.

However, when an intruding field is entrained to a trauma memory, one cannot treat the trauma memory, because the intruding field or soul, independent of the patient's memories, can activate emotions or behaviors in the victim that serve as barriers to treatment. The treatment of fields and trauma memories have different interventions that are carried out by the subconscious. The field barrier has to be treated before the trauma can be treated.

To fully understand this phenomenon, let's look at how memory is formed.

The Structure of Internal Dynamics of Memory

When I started working systematically with the subconscious in 1992 to help improve my skills as a therapist, I had no model for the inner dynamics of memory and the creation of behavior.[2] Over the last 20 years, based on problem-solving and my clinical experience, I developed a model for the memory structures underlying the inner dynamics of behavior.[3] This is another way of saying that I made up metaphors or constructs based on my experience that fit together logically and were plausible to my patients — it made sense to them. I have used the model effectively in constructing treatments for many patients.

The model is called the Behavior System (see Figure 2-1). The Behavior System consists of the Basic Neurostructure, the Active Experience, and Memories I, II and III. There are other structures and processes that are not shown, such as the Emotion System, Heart System, Kinesthetic System and the association and dissociative processes. This model of the dynamics of the memory system is useful when problem-solving treatment barriers in patients.

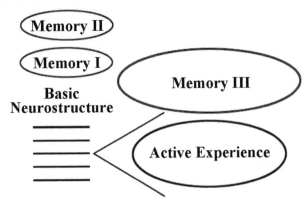

Figure 2-1 The Behavior System

The Creation of Behavior and the Basic Neurostructure

The Process Healing treatment model assumes that active memories are assembled in a collage to cause behavior. Each memory has a unique structure created at the time it formed. A memory can be as simple as the word "and," or as complex as a compartmentalized part who can "run the body" and have a linear association to all memories—an autobiographical memory—of behavior occurring during a severe trauma.

Freeman in his article "The Physiology of Perception" points out that all functions in the brain interconnect.[4] I accept as a basic truth that massive interconnections exist between all memories and brain functions. Bartlett suggested that all verbal behavior is assembled from previously learned verbal behavior.[5] I extend this to assume that memories of behavior we have previously learned are the basis for most of our ongoing behavior. Therefore, I define a person's response in the present as a **collage** of previously learned memories — a collection of memories that contain the physiology to cause the desired response. How is the desired response created?

The Basic Neurostructure is a neurological process that creates a response and a memory of the response simultaneously. It takes many responses to see what we call behavior. The **Basic Neurostructure** is an assumed neurological process that organizes internal and external stimulation, some of the active memories, and last response into a collage needed to create the next response. The governing rule for creating the next response is to get more happiness and less pain. Each response has a unique memory structure.

All memories have a unique memory structure. I assume that a **memory structure** is composed from the complexion of some aspects of brain activity at the moment it is created. It is this unique structure that is the basic building block for all memories. For example, words like "and" and "there" have a unique memory structure. The word "there" is available to be plugged into any sentence that I use. When someone says "Hi, Garry" and I reply "Hi there," the expression "Hi there" becomes a memory in itself. It's a memory that includes a collage of the neurology to create the thought and expression of "Hi" and "there." Therefore, a unique collage of memories causing neural activity creates the response, "Hi there." Thereafter, "Hi there" is triggered by anybody who says "Hi, Garry."

Memory structures are therefore created as we progress through life with varied experiences and behavior. Memories that are not active are called **dormant memories**. Most of our memories are dormant. Old, inactive, dormant memories are triggered into activity by a change in the situation. The last response/memory is adjusted to a new response/ memory with a new unique memory structure and collage. Many of the memories included in a collage immediately go dormant after the response, because the situation has changed. Other memories activate with a new situation. A new structure is associated with a collage of suitable memories to cause the next response. In other words, the last response is the basis for the next response, which has a new, unique, memory structure.

Because neural activity is always changing, all memory structures created in a changing environment are unique. The last response and some old memory structures are organized and assembled into a collage for the next response and associated *with* a new memory structure. The collage is selected to activate neural activity to cause the desired response. When the collage is activated, the neural activity of the collage causes the desired brain or body activity causing the response. Each memory has a unique collage and its own memory structure based on the complexion of neural activity in the brain when the structure was created. However, when trying to treat painful memories, there can be a problem.

Association Problem: *with* and *to*

The problem has to do with memories associating *to* the memory structure. Normally, old memories associate *with* a base memory structure as a collage to create the neural connections for the memory and response. Now, during a trauma, because of the circumstances and the emotional intensity, one or more memory structures can associate *to* the base memory structure. There is a difference between associating *with* and *to* the base memory structure (See Figure 2-2). When a memory structure associates *to* a base memory structure, the association prevents the col-

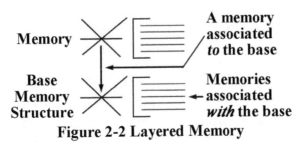

Figure 2-2 Layered Memory

lage of memories associated *with* the memory structure from being treated. The painful emotions associated with the memory structure cannot be replaced. This is the reason so many beliefs are hard to change. Here is an example. If I have a trauma memory of a car accident, part of another memory might associate *to* the memory of the trauma. Therefore, treating the trauma first involves treating the memory associated *to* the trauma memory. After I treat the memory associated *to* the trauma memory, I can treat the trauma. Memory structures with memories associated *to* them are called layered memories.

Easily-Created Memory Structures
Another problem caused by severe trauma early in life is that the victim learns to **easily-create** memory structures, such as compartmentalized parts or layered memories. This means that with each experience of moderate emotional pain or fear, a new, problematic structure can be created. This leads to the creation of many problematic structures. Without first treating the complex structures causing the easy-creation of memory structures, treatment of the patient becomes difficult because problematic structures can be created faster than you can treat them. The structure causing this easy-creation has to be addressed and treated early.

Memory Structures and Treatment
Memories are assumed to run all biological structures in the brain and body, namely, cells, organs, brain centers, muscle groups, and so forth. Each brain and body structure has its own memory that is interrelated with all other relevant structures. This means that it is possible, in

theory, to discover — or, in other words, to problem-solve — a means to treat the memory of any maladaptive structure or process in the brain and body.

A patient's symptoms are memory structures. Therefore, treating a symptom involves identifying the memory structure of the particular symptom and then treating the memory structure that causes the symptom. Usually negative emotions motivate the symptom and cause it to be problematic. Symptoms are typically a behavior, belief, memory, emotion, pain, an intrusion into consciousness, a kinesthetic response, depression, or some other problematic symptom. **Treatment** involves removing the emotions from the memory structure causing the symptom so that it is no longer problematic. Treating symptoms as memory structures allows all symptoms to be treated in the same way — by problem-solving to identify the memory structure of the target symptom and then treating the emotions. In this method, the subconscious is taught to remove the emotion or pain associated with the memory structure of the symptom and replace it with neutral to positive emotions.

When treatment of some symptom doesn't work, you simply problem-solve to find the barrier to treatment, treat the barrier, and then treat the symptom again. Not all symptoms can be treated in one session. Some symptoms have multiple, unique memory structures and require more problem-solving. In addition, when memory structures remain inactive or dormant during a therapy session, the symptom may occur weeks or months later in therapy. Once they occur and are recognized, they can then be treated. This is the reason I believe the subconscious does not see dormant memories and has to work with active memories to treat them.

The treatment of a problematic memory structure in one patient does not work as a cookie cutter treatment with all patients. An intervention for problematic symptoms requires problem-solving to identify the specific memory structure of each patient's symptom. While symptoms can be similar across all patients, they can be more or less complex and be represented differently within a patient. The Process Healing Method helps the therapist identify the uniqueness of the symptom in the individual, namely the memory structure. What is a cookie cutter is that the treatment method has worked with most patients and similar memory structures in different patients are treated in the same way. As a result, it is my belief that the success rate is higher and therapy progresses faster. There has been no research validating my belief.

The Active Processes in Our Personality

Active Experience is a metaphor that serves as a container that helps us think about the brain activity involved in creating behavior. The **Active Experience** contains all active memories, emotions and neural activity of the brain and body, namely internal and external stimulation. The Active Experience is a construct that simplifies our thinking about the brain's and body's activity and allows us to talk about dormant memories and unconscious and conscious active memories in a meaningful way.

When discussing memory structures and behavior, it is important that you know the difference between the subconscious, conscious, unconscious, and active and dormant memories, as I use them in this book.

The subconscious is not the unconscious and does not usually run the body. For the sake of simplicity in this chapter, I assume the **subconscious** is a body-wide language system that starts shortly after conception and becomes more or less functional at birth. The subconscious is like a part who has been with us from the beginning. It is independent of the content and emotion memories that run the body — that is, it is not distorted by emotions and usually has a clear "vision" of the particulars about active memories and the associated emotions. It can learn a treatment method and complex procedures using the treatment method. It serves as an ally in problem-solving by helping to identify the memory structures of all issues, as well as barriers to treatment.

It is easy to see that most therapists would have difficulty embracing this definition and use of the subconscious. I, of course, have a different point of view. By using finger responses to communicate without deliberately inducing a hypnotic trance, I have been able to communicate with the subconscious of over 95 percent of my patients in the first session. With some patients, you can ask to talk to the subconscious and the patient will hear a "Yes" in his or her thoughts. With other patients, it is more difficult to communicate with the subconscious. Sometimes, the person watching someone's therapy finds his or her fingers responding as I ask the patient questions.

Conscious refers to our awareness and experience of active memories in the Active Experience; these are conscious active memories. **Unconscious** refers to the absence of awareness of active memories in the Active Experience. These are unconscious active memories. Only the conscious and unconscious active memories participate in the creation of our behavior and experience.

I also make a distinction between dormant memories and active memories. **Dormant memories** are memories that are not active in the Active Experience. Most of our memories remain dormant until they are triggered into the Active Experience, like seeds that don't germinate and grow until the right stimulation occurs. Since all brain functions and memories interconnect, anything said or happening in the environment can provide stimuli to trigger the dormant memories in the persons present. When I say or write, "I don't drink any more," I trigger all the positive and negative drinking-related memories in my patient, as well as the reader.

Dormant memories have to be triggered active before the patient or subconscious can experience them. For example, the memories needed to answer a question are dormant before the question is asked. The answer to the question, "What is the color of your shoes?" is not conscious until I ask the question. The answer is triggered into conscious experience. Furthermore, I have found that dormant memories can't be treated. Memories have to be active in the conscious or unconscious to be treated. How do I know this? For a year, I asked the subconscious of a patient if the all of her parts were treated. Every week the subconscious said, "Yes." There were always parts to treat the next week. I concluded that the subconscious could not see dormant memories.

Active memories are memories that are active in either the conscious or unconscious experience. A response in our ongoing behavior is caused by a collage of memories assembled from active memories in the conscious and unconscious experience. The creation of behavior does not use memories that are dormant. The unconscious influences in our life are unconscious active memories — not dormant memories. Memories are either active or dormant.

Hypnotic techniques cause most active memories to become dormant — the active memories are coaxed into dormancy by verbal suggestions. Lankton and Lankton use the hypnotic state to retrieve or trigger active resources in the patient, the behaviors related to the issue, and then trigger and link the resources to the problem behaviors with self-empowering interventions that will use the resources to resolve the issue in a healthy way.[6]

It is incorrect to refer to unconscious memories as the problematic memories in our behavior. It is more accurate to refer to old memories as the cause for our problems. **Unconscious memories** are active memories that are either problematic or not problematic contributors to the collage forming our immediate behavior. Problematic memories can be triggered active in our unconscious, because we learned them in the past. Self-empowering memories can also be active in our unconscious.

The Active Experience

Active memories are memories that have been triggered from a dormant state into the Active Experience. They can be either unconscious or conscious active memories, and may be included in the creation of a collage of memories to run some brain or body activity.

For example, when I say, "Let's think about going swimming," all memories associated with swimming become active. The next response is a collage that includes some of these memories. The Basic Neurostructure, taking into account all active memories and internal and external stimulation, manages the Active Experience to form responses and memories that lead to getting more happiness and less pain.

Initially, there was no organization in the Active Experience, so the behaviors were simply random activity. With further development, the number and complexity of memories increased and some processes formed that help simplify the Active Experience (see Figure 2-3). I believe that normal developmental activity led to the formation of the associative and dissociative processes. The **associative process**

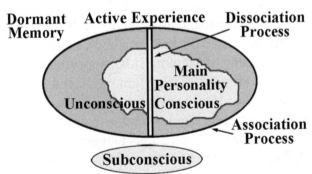

**Figure 2-3 Components of the
Active Experience**

permits only useful dormant memories to activate in the Active Experience. This lessens the number of slightly related but irrelevant active memories and improves the efficiency of the Basic Neurostructure. This screening and elimination of irrelevant memories will also allow for more efficient use of the conscious experience. Later, the dissociative process forms. The dissociative process is formed when conscious experience becomes useful in directing behavior. The **dissociative process** associated with a memory causes the memory to remain active, but active in the unconscious experience. The dissociative process is cause of the unconscious — the unconscious mind.

To understand more about memory, let's look at three categories of memory — Memory I, II, and III — and how memory structures amass in different stages of development. This is important, because complex memories can involve all three memories. The development of these memories also reflects the complexity of the process in the hidden reality.

Memory I, Memory II — Predispositions

This is a technical section that can be skipped if you find it too challenging.

I first conceptualized Memory I when I working with the subconscious to treat the problem of the easy-creation of parts. I hypothesized the construct of Memory I as one of the structures that caused this problem. I was able to treat and disable the easy-creation of parts. I define Memory I as consisting of primitive memories formed from conception to birth.

Memory II starts sometime before birth and lasts until ages four or five. This structure was originally based on the work of Stone and Stone's idea of sub-personality.[7] Interestingly, there are two parts in Memory II that are called the Protector and Controller. More important is that the amassing of Memory II is happening at the same time Memory III is developing. Both Memory II and Memory III are involved in responses to reoccurring situations. The response in Memory II becomes associated to and a trigger for a response in Memory III. This happens in situations that are reoccurring and calls for a safe, defensive response of some kind, like when a child has to constantly deal with pain or conflict caused by angry parents. These responses appear something like habits. I call these habit-like responses predispositions.

A **predisposition** is simply a learned tendency to respond to a situation in a predefined way — a response triggered in Memory II that triggers an associated response in Memory III. As a Roman Catholic Bishop once said: "Give me a child to age five and I have him for a lifetime." Predispositions can color a person's behavior for the rest of his or her life. Often, they can be negative or self-destructive. Because the response in Memory II has to be treated before the associated response in Memory III can be treated, I think of the Memory II response as the predisposition.

Here is an example of a predisposition. When pain becomes active in the Active Experience — that is, when a person experiences pain — the pain triggers a predisposition. The predisposition causes a response that rapidly dissociates the pain to the unconscious so the person doesn't feel it. This predisposition could be the result of living in a home that did not tolerate talking about painful experiences. Another example of a predisposition would be denial. If someone is confronted for doing something wrong, the experience of blame or criticism triggers a strong emotional response. This, in tern, triggers a predisposition leading to a behavior pattern, a memory structure in Memory III, that causes the person to automatically deny the criticism.

Predispositions are usually associated *with* or *to* memories in Memory III. They can be complex and are the basis for many personality issues. Many complex memory structures in severely traumatized patients involve predispositions associated *with* or *to* memory structures in Memory III. Symptoms involving predispositions or habits complicate treatment. Most therapies do not address the idea of predispositions. However, I have found that treating predispositions both simplifies and speeds up therapy.

Memory III

Memory III starts around birth and continues until we die. In this memory system, the Main Personality develops and amasses most of our experiences. These amassed memories are later used to create responses to current demands of our internal and external environment. What I call "ego-states" occur in specific environments in which systems of memories and collections of behaviors are triggered to give specific response patterns. For example, when I walk into a police station I may become immediately guarded and a little bit on edge because of my beliefs about the police. However, when I enter a church, I may feel a sense of reverence and safety. Both of these responses are caused by collages based upon memories in Memory III that were composed earlier when behaving in those situations. People can usually recognize their different ego states.

Main Personality

The Main Personality starts just before birth during the development of Memories I and II. Remember, the Basic Neurostructure operates on the Active Experience, which consists of internal and external stimulation, active memories, and emotions. The complex activity of the Basic Neurostructure creates collages for our ongoing behavior to get more happiness and less pain. As we age, Memory III becomes increasingly dominant in providing active memories for the creation of behavior. Memory III has memories amassed during life that operate as the Main Personality (see Figure 2-1). The Main Personality has a unique memory structure, like a part, associated with the amassing of memory structures, giving us a more or less conscious and unconscious autobiographical history of experiences as our life unfolds from prebirth to the present.

Recall that when a new memory structure is created, a collage of memories is formed consisting of part of the collage of memories from the previous response and other active memories to create the new response now demanded by the environment. This process creates both the immediate response and the memory of the response at the same time. Our behavior, therefore, is a sequence of memory structures causing ongoing behavior.

The memory structures also have emotions associated with them to motivate the response. By "motivate," I mean the positive or negative emotions associated with a memory that drive the memory to action. The more intense the emotion, the more motivated the memory — that is, the more likely it will become active. Intrusive thoughts, for example, are memories having emotions associated with them. When the emotions are replaced by neutral emotions in a treatment process, the intrusive thoughts or memories are no longer motivated to intrude. In most cases, after treatment, the intrusions are gone.

While the Main Personality is in Memory III and is mostly the basis for behavior, unconscious active memories not in the Main Personality can also influence behavior. These active memories can add emotions to the behavior, provide emotional intrusions, or be the cause of distorted behavior, such as a change in mood, hearing voices, blurting out words, making a sudden arm movement, or causing a tic.

For example, whenever someone became angry with the schizophrenic patient mentioned in Chapter I, it triggered very intense emotions that he had experienced in the past when his father threatened to kill him. These intense emotions triggered a predisposition involving many aspects of the Behavior System, leading to the easy-creation of a part or memory structure. This freshly created memory of an experience could later intrude as a verbal reprimand or other auditory intrusions, such as cars revving or dogs barking.

Memories, the Active Experience, and Behavior

Let's look in more detail at how memories amass in Memory I, II, and III. At some point in development, the creation of behavior and memories starts. Shortly after conception, spontaneous neural activity in the brain and body starts occurring. This neural activity creates unorganized responses of the fetus (see Figure 2-4). The empty circles in the open space represent this activity of unorganized responses, which

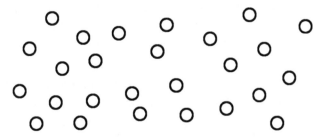

**Figure 2-4 Spontaneous Activity
Starting in the Brain**

continues until further neural development takes place. For a period of time, no memories are created and the neural activity causes more or less random behavior. This spontaneous random neural activity and responses are soon organized.

Before long, the neural structure on the left, the Basic Neurostructure, develops and starts organizing random activity into memories and responses (see Figure 2-5, next page). I use the idea or construct of the Basic Neurostructure to explain the creation of behavior in this model. The Basic Neurostructure initially selects random neural activity to assemble collages that are chosen, because they lead to more satisfaction or happiness and less pain. Note that

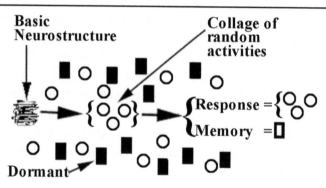

**Figure 2-5 The Formation of
Behavior and Memory**

more happiness and less pain is the primary leverage used in treatment. The open circles in the closed brackets in the center of the figure represent the chosen collage of random neural activity for the next response. The collage, created with a unique memory structure, becomes a response and memory from the chosen neural activity. The instant the memory collage forms, the memories in the collage create the response and the new memory — the empty white box. The memory soon becomes dormant — the black boxes. At this point in the development, the dormant memories are simply amassing and not contributing to the creation of behavior.

As the numbers of dormant memories amass, a greater number of dormant memories are triggered into activity by existing conditions involving external and internal stimulation (see Figure 2-6). More memories are included in the creation of behavior. The open squares represent the active memories. When the memory isn't active, it is dormant. The black squares represent the dormant memories. The Basic Neurostructure gradually uses additional active and previously

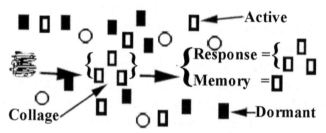

**Figure 2-6 The Creation of Behavior
from Active Memories**

learned memories to create the next response. When the response becomes irrelevant in the Active Experience, the memory structure becomes dormant. In this way, the unique dormant memories amass and expand the memory.

To simplify talking to the subconscious about the memory structures in the brain that cause behavior problems, I created constructs to make it easy to describe the structures in the Behavior System (see Figure 2-7). In this case, Memory I is a construct containing all dormant Memory I memories represented by black squares.

Memory constructs to simplify discussion

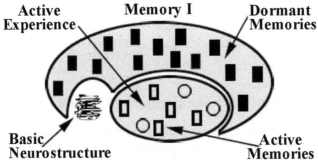

Figure 2-7 Constructs of of the Active Experience

The Active Experience is a construct containing all active memories, which are represented by open squares, and spontaneous activity represented by open circles.

The memories in Memory I are all state-dependent with simple neural activity as the state-defining property. State-dependent means that some pattern of simple neural activity and specific content can trigger a dormant memory in Memory I into the Active Experience. The content is a feature of the memory itself. Over time, many memories created *in utero* amass in Memory I.

While all memories in Memory I are dormant (the black squares), the Active Experience includes active memories from Memory I with content related in some way to the current situation. As you can see, the Active Experience construct is useful to distinguish dormant memories from active memories. The collage created for the next response includes a new memory structure and the association of some of the spontaneous neural activity and structures of active memories in the Active Experience. In this behavioral model, I assume that a Basic Neurostructure, an Active Experience, and a unique memory are used in most systems in the brain, such as the Emotion System, and other systems such as the Heart System, the Kinesthetic System, and other brain functions.

Initially, the Basic Neurostructure operates on primitive neural activity in the Active Experience to create collages of behavior amassed in Memory I (see Figure 2-8). Simple neural activity is the common property of the memories that define Memory I, which is

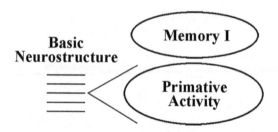

Figure 2-8 The Creation of Memory I

described as being state dependent on neural activity. At some point, learned memories triggered from Memory I are gradually included in the creation of behavior. As time passes, the creation of behavior in the Active Experience shifts from using only primitive spontaneous activity to using the activity of memories triggered from Memory I. Eventually, the collages of most responses created are assembled from active memories from Memory I.

I created the Memory II construct after I learned about David and Deidre Stone's ideas about sub-personalities.[8] I borrowed their ideas and, by working with the subconscious, discovered there were positive and negative predispositions learned early in life found in what I called Memory II. Memory II is also a state-dependent memory that is based on both neural activity and sensory stimulation before sensory experience occurs, as the defining properties for memories in Memory II (see Figure 2-9). Memory II begins when sensory stimulation starts. In this case, neural activity, sensory stimulation, and memory content must be present to trigger a response from Memory II. Memory II starts amassing memories from some time before birth to about age four.

Sometime before birth and surely by birth, sensory experience starts. Memory III amasses memories formed with the state-defining

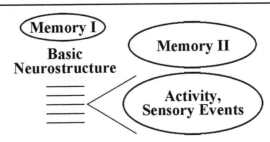

Figure 2-9 The Creation of Memory II

properties of activity, sensory stimulation, sensory experience, needs, and emotions (see Figure 2-10). Memory structures in Memory III require all of the state-defining properties to trigger them into activity. These memories continue to amass throughout the rest of our lives.

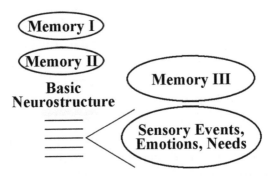

Figure 2-10 The Creation of Memory III

As time passes, activity in the Active Experience includes continuing behavior, emotion memories and related content, internal and external stimulation, and active processes, such as composing speech, editing speech, and organ and brain functions. Some of these activities in the Active Experience relevant to the situation are in the collage causing the next response. The memory structure for a response and the memory of the response are created simultaneously.

Thus, memories from Memories I, II, and III are all available to be triggered into the Active Experience and be selected for inclusion in a collage for a response.

The Virtual Active Experience

When I speak of active memories, I am referring to memories, emotions, and processes that are active in the Active Experience that lead to the next response. But think about it: in our 3D-Reality we have dormant and active memories that also must be dormant or active in our Personal Field. Therefore, we have dormant field memories, active field memories, and a virtual Active Experience.

What are changing as we behave are the stimulation, memories, and emotions active in the virtual Active Experience. For example, when you are bouncing a basketball, you are bouncing the ball in your virtual Active Experience. Everything we do takes place in the virtual reality. The virtual Active Experience consists of activated field memories of behavior and emotions entrained and synchronized with virtual internal or external stimulation; in other words, stimulation entrains memories and emotions to activate in the virtual Active Experience to create a response.

These active virtual memories are available for the creation of the next response according to the laws of the universe. Other field memories not entrained and synchronized are dormant in the Personal Field, because they are not relevant to virtual situation at the time — our situation in 3D-Reality — and are not available for the next response. Only the memories and emotions entrained and synchronized as active in the virtual Active Experience are available for creating the next response. For example, when a stoplight turns red in the 3D-Reality, it also turns "red" in the virtual reality, so all relevant virtual memories triggered by the red light are triggered into the virtual Active Experience from which our virtual response is created. The virtual response is then carried out and experienced in 3D-Reality, namely, to step on the brake.

In addition to the Active Experience, the incremental creation of a person's life consists of changes in hundreds of thousands of interdependent structures in our body. These structures appear to be self-organized, responding to stimulations and consequences in the environment in a massive, multiprocessing activity. Each of these apparent self-organized structures represented in our virtual reality has a unique virtual Active Experience. I believe that the 10th dimension organizes the active fields in the Active Experience for each structure and manages the environment, locally and nonlocally, to create the next response. The 10th dimension then is responsible for all the self-organization we see in our 3D-Reality. The 10th dimension manages your entire environment, from your cellular level to your interaction with others — an interaction involving someone in front of you or someone 2,000 miles away talking to you on a telephone.

Dissociated Parts and Compartmentalized Parts

It is crucial to understand the underlying causes of amnesia and how they relate to the problem of barriers that block therapeutic treatment. The underlying causes are dissociation and compartmentalization — both cause amnesia.

Dissociation is a process that moves memories from conscious experience into unconscious experience. Dissociation is what we use voluntarily or automatically to hide memories that are irrelevant or that we don't want to remember. Dissociation can also hide skills that run automatically. For example, driving can be a dissociated skill that runs our behavior. Your dissociated memory knows enough to drive the car and handle most situations without your being completely aware of driving. In any dangerous situation or if your cell phone rings, you come back into consciousness.

Compartmentalized parts are created with executive function and amass an autobiographical memory of the trauma. They can self-generate problematic behavior based on their unique trauma memories, such as emotion or verbal intrusions or other atypical behavior. They can take over and run the body. Compartmentalized parts are memory structures that can be difficult to change and can cause personality problems and barriers in the treatment process.

The following describes these two processes in greater detail.

Dissociation

Many behaviors in our everyday life use the dissociative process. The dissociative process starts early as we begin to give attention to conscious memory activity. The dissociative process was gradually learned to effectively move irrelevant memories and stimulation from the conscious experience to the unconscious experience. This simplified our conscious experience so our conscious attention deals with only relevant active memories and stimulation.

The partition in the Active Experience construct represents dissociation (see Figure 2-11, next page). This creates the conscious and unconscious Active Experience. Both the conscious and unconscious Active Experience have active memories. This division of memories is useful, because it further simplifies the conscious Active Experience and causes intention to become more efficient in creating responses. Conceptually, it makes a clear distinction between dormant memories, conscious and unconscious active memories, and the subconscious.

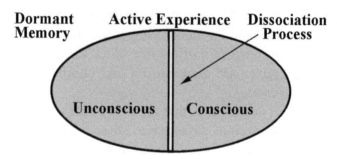

Figure 2-11 The Dissociation Process

When you remember the details of a trauma that are very upsetting, and, later, you cannot remember the details, then the details have been dissociated. We call these memories dissociated memories. A dissociative process can work to dissociate some or all of a memory. These dissociated memories can be active in the unconscious and can still participate in the creation of behavior.

We learn many skills consciously and then dissociate them to the unconscious to clear them out of the conscious mind. Dissociating skills, such as composing and editing language, reading, or driving a car, serve a positive function. When these dissociated skills are triggered and appear to run the body, I refer to them as dissociative parts. An example would be a man who can't stop acting like his punishing father. In certain situations, the dissociated learning from his father is triggered and, without wanting to, the man behaves as a bully like his father.

Repression and suppression of memories, whether voluntary or involuntary, also use the dissociative and associative processes. Repression occurs when intensely painful experiences are rapidly dissociated, before conscious awareness, to the unconscious by an internal predisposition. The predisposition automatically dissociates the experience and, in the process, creates an associative barrier for the triggers. These repressed memories are hard to recover, because the memories and the triggers for the memories are strongly dissociated and have associative barriers.

Suppression of experience can happen by choice or gradually over time. Basically, the experience is dissociated. Many people can suppress or deliberately end thinking about some painful memory or thoughts just by intent. This practice can become an automatic response to dissociate unpleasant memories into the unconscious. These memories are easier to retrieve than repressed memories, because they have less intense emotions and the triggers are more available than they are in repressed memories, which have associative barriers.

When a person concentrates, he or she is using both the dissociative and associative processes to remove distractions from the conscious experience to focus attention. The associative process governs what is triggered into the Active Experience. The dissociative process moves unwanted information or memories out of the conscious Active Experience. Both the dissociative and associative processes can come under voluntary control.

When these processes operate independently, irrelevant information caused by memory intrusions disturbs the person's concentration. When I become aware of this condition in a patient, I can contact the dissociative and associative processes by working with the subconscious, and join the processes so the patient has better concentration. The processes then work together and fewer intrusions occur to distract the person when he or she tries to focus on something.

Compartmentalized Parts and Trauma

Painful experiences cause an assortment of memory structures ranging from simple to complex, to which pain of varying intensity associates. Memory structures all have content, which would be sensory experience and behavior associated *with* the memory structure. Moreover, an emotional component associated *with* the memory structure motivates the content. As stated before, most trauma memory structures are associated *with* intense emotional content, namely, the emotions caused by the trauma.

For example, when a teenager has strong, positive feelings for a member of the opposite sex, the teenager can't keep that person out of his or her mind. That's a highly motivated memory structure with intense positive emotions involving an image or thought of the special person. In the same way after a severe trauma, such as a sexual abuse experience, a memory structure with intense painful emotions may result in flashbacks to that trauma when in the presence of related triggers. The more intense the emotion, positive or negative, the more motivated or likely the memory or behavior will become conscious or manifest as behavior.

A trauma usually has a start and an end (see Figure 2-12, next page). With moderate trauma, a person can remember the details of the entire trauma. When I run down a path, slip on some gravel, and break my arm, my experience includes a memory of the entire experience, the pain of the accident, as well as the pain at the hospital when they set my broken arm. In addition, when I get home, I can tell my wife all the details of that experience.

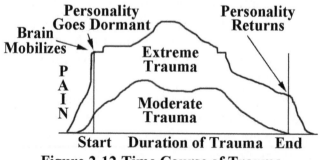

Figure 2-12 Time Course of Trauma

Extreme trauma in a novel situation causes a completely differ-ent response by the brain. When the pain is very intense, in a novel situation, the brain mobilizes, and the Main Personality goes dormant. Compartmentalized parts form as the result of intense trauma (see Figure 2-13). During severe trauma in a situation where there is *no pre-vious memory to handle the situation*, the intense emotions and the triggers in the situation rapidly activate memories related to the crisis situation (1). This rush or flood of memories (behavior) and emotions independent of the Main Personality causes the Main Personality to become dormant (2). A new memory structure forms at the start of the trauma (1). All the experience during the trauma associates *with* the new structure in an autobiological memory (1 to 3). This trauma

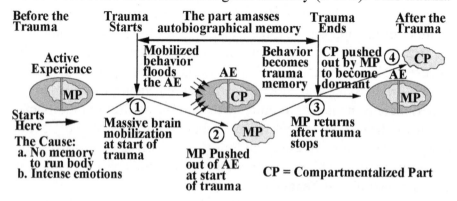

Figure 2-13 The Creation of a Compartmentalized Part

process creates a compartmentalized part, a "personality" part, who is more or less independent of the Main Personality and remains dormant until triggered.

When the emotions decline to a comfortable level (3), the Main Personality rushes back into the Active Experience and the compartmentalized part is displaced out of the Active Experience into a dormant state (4). Amnesia occurs because the Main Personality moves out of the Active Experience (2) and then, as the pain subsides, into the Active Experience (3) so quickly that there are few or no neural associations between the compartmentalized part and the Main Personality. The absence of neural associations between the compartmentalized part and the Main Personality causes amnesia between them. Therefore, the compartmentalized part is a trauma memory of which the active personality is unaware.

It is important to be aware of this difference between compartmentalized and dissociative parts, because they both show the symptom of amnesia. Recall that dissociative parts are like skills that are hidden from consciousness by the process of dissociation until they become active. When triggered, they can appear to operate like compartmentalized parts. The difference between them is that the amnesia of compartmentalized parts is a structural amnesia with a unique memory structure and an absence of neural connection with the Main Personality, as opposed to process amnesia, which involves a dissociative process that allows some connection with the Main Personality. Only the compartmentalized part has the executive function — the capacity to organize life in a meaningful way and amass memories.

In clinical practice, the awareness of one compartmentalized part for another part can range from complete amnesia to co-consciousness. On the other hand, one part may have complete amnesia of the other, while the other has complete awareness of the activity of the first part. This structural amnesia has profound implications for therapeutic treatment. A compartmentalized part or memory involves the formation of a new memory structure created by intense emotional trauma and the absence of memories available to manage the trauma. These two conditions result in the creation of a unique memory structure that is usually not easily accessed by the Main Personality. A compartmentalized memory, therefore, cannot be treated in usual therapeutic ways. What happens during the trauma when the compartmentalized part is created?

During the trauma, the new part preserves the experience by creating an autobiographical memory over the time course of the trauma. In addition, since this part is running the body, it appears self-organized and has executive function and involves all aspects of the self-generation of behavior. This includes selecting information, planning, self-monitoring, self-correcting, problem-solving, decision-making, and controlling behavior. The Main Personality or society will see many of the appropriate behaviors created during a trauma as dysfunctional at a later time.

Compartmentalized parts usually have more pain than dissociated parts and are harder to find and treat. They have the capacity to run the body — executive function — either independently, when the Main Personality is dormant, or co-consciously with or without the awareness of the Main Personality. In contrast, I don't believe that dissociative memories or parts can take over and run the body creatively, because dissociative memory structures do not have the executive function. It is for these reasons that complex dissociative memories are easier to treat, in my experience, than compartmentalized parts.

Treatment Using This Model

This explanation of dissociation and amnesia is different from what is usually taught in psychology. Because the basis for the Process Healing Method involves paradigm shifts in its description of brain processes, it is difficult for most therapists to grasp the ease of getting rapport with all parts of the personality before beginning treatment. This treatment method is respectful to all parts of the personality from the onset of treatment, an approach not found in other popular treatments for dissociative disorders. This simplifies treatment, since all parts can be convinced to want treatment and to integrate or join with the Main Personality.

There is a treatment leverage that is important to all parts of the personality. They want more happiness and less pain. Treatment involves removing pain from the trauma memories of the part, strengthening the positive qualities of the part (and similar qualities in the Main Personality) with positive emotions, and joining or integrating the memory or part with the Main Personality. Integration, in this case, means that two unique memory structures associate their memories to each other, resulting in both memory structures having the same memories. The Main Personality and integrated part remain unique and can then run the body at the same time with no conflict, to achieve more happiness and lessen pain. Why? They have identical memories and a more complete autobiography. With this intervention, young parts grow up very fast.

Memory or Trauma Structures to Which Fields Entrain

With this understanding of the mechanics of creating behavior and memory, let's review the memories or trauma structures that are believed to be the basis for the entrainment of external fields with someone's Personal Field. There are six structures that can have varying amounts of emotional pain associated with them. These are basic pain, layered memories, dissociative parts and memories, compartmentalized parts and memories, stacked parts, and predispositions associated *to* or *with* complex parts. Let's look at each in more detail.

Basic Pain

Figure 2-14 shows a unique memory structure. The memory structure is the basis for all simple or complex memory structures. Some

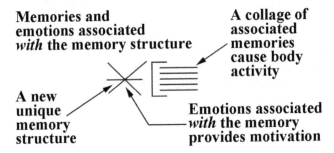

Figure 2-14 A Memory Structure

pattern of neurological activity at the creation of the memory structure allows it to be unique and have associations *with* content and emotions. Recall that the collages of both content and emotion memories associate *with* a memory structure to create the memory and response. Memories learned in a punishing environment result in negative emotions associating *with* the trauma memory structures. The more intense the emotions, the more likely it is that the memory will become active. Positive and negative emotions motivate all our behavior, parts, and memories.

Basic pain is defined as the sum of pain associated with simple memory structures that have emotional or physical pain associated with them. Everyone has basic pain. If our life becomes more complex and traumatic, the amassing of basic pain, as well as other more complex painful memories, increases and can become significant. Additional complex memory structures often have intense emotional pain. Intruding fields entrain to patterns of basic pain and other simple and complex memory structures associated with intense, painful emotions.

Layered Memory

Layered memory structures are created when one or more additional memory structures associate *to* the base memory structure (see Figure 2-15). When a memory structure is associated *to* a memory, the usual treatment method does not work to treat memories associated *with*

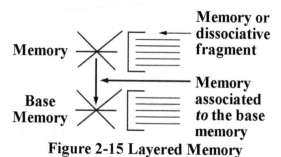

Figure 2-15 Layered Memory

the structure. Layered memories can have intense emotional pain associated *with* them and create problematic beliefs or traumatic memories in us that are difficult to change. Persons with extensive trauma history can have many layered memories that have a significant amount of emotional pain. This pain can be the basis for soul intrusions.

Dissociative Parts and Memories

Recall that dissociative parts are like skills that can automatically carry out behavior, such as editing and composing speech, or driving a car without awareness. These repetitive skills are learned consciously but, because of overtraining, eventually dissociate to the unconscious. Sometimes the novelty of a situation with emotional pain is intense but not intense enough to trigger the creation of a compartmentalized part. Trauma survivors can learn to automatically dissociate these painful experiences. The memory of dysfunctional behavior that involved relating to a punishing parent can be dissociated. This dysfunctional behavior can later be triggered to distort behavior.

Hypnosis can also be used to create dissociated memories or parts. People with a traumatic history often have dissociative parts and memories created by hypnosis. Therapists hide the traumatic memories and behavior by associating the dissociative process to the behavior by hypnotic suggestion. This moves the behavior to the unconscious. Depending on the extent of traumatic history, a person can have many dissociative parts and memories with intense negative emotions. Nevertheless, be clear that dissociative parts are usually more like skills and very different from compartmentalized parts. It is these dissociative parts and memories, as well as other memory structures with intense emotions, to which intruding fields can entrain.

Compartmentalized Parts and Memories

Remember that compartmentalized parts or memories are created during a trauma with intense emotions and *with no memory to handle the trauma situation.* Because the Main Personality was "pushed" into dormancy at the start of the trauma, and, later, the trauma structure was "pushed" into dormancy by the quick reentry of the Main Personality into the Active Experience, there were few or no neural connections between the trauma structure of the compartmentalized part and the Main Personality. For example, a survivor of a severe motor vehicle accident, a near-death experience, physical or sexual abuse, or extreme torture can have many compartmentalized parts crowding the timeline of life. This causes an amnesic condition with the compartmentalized parts represented in Figure 2-16 as blips on the timeline of the Main Personality. Intense and negative emotional pain motivates these parts in the Personal Field. Intruding fields often entrain to a pattern of pain that includes compartmentalized parts carrying extreme pain.

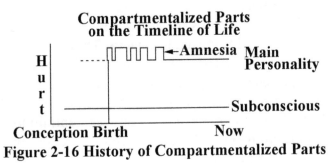

Figure 2-16 History of Compartmentalized Parts

Stacked Parts

Stacked parts form when traumatic pain is constantly increasing and therefore becomes repeatedly novel. Each novel plateau of pain causes the brain to mobilize and create a compartmentalized part. When this happens within the context of ongoing pain, the new part associates *to* the previous part. This results in each part associated *to* the previous part, starting with the base part (see Figure 2-17). Situations with extreme shock or increasing traumatic intensity can lead to the

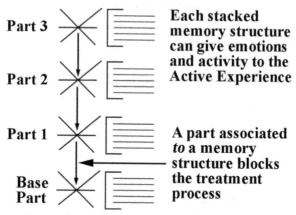

Figure 2-17 Stacked Amnesic Parts

creation of a stack of two or more parts. Stacked parts, often found in torture survivors, can be easily treated. However, stacked parts can have an enormous amount of emotion associated with them that is attractive to similar structures in intruding fields. It turns out that stacked parts serve as links for reentrainment that make treating some intruding souls more difficult.

Predispositions

Early in life, memories in Memory II are created that trigger memories in Memory III that work like habits. These memory structures are called predispositions. These are like habits triggered by activity in the Active Experience that give a routine response to the activity. Predispositions often have strong negative emotions. With a large number of predispositions, intruding souls can entrain to either the emotions associated with the structures or the complexion of the predispositions structures.

Complex Parts

Under certain circumstances, a predisposition can associate either *to* or *with* a complex memory structure in Memory III. A complex example is a predisposition structure. Figure 2-18 shows a predisposition structure associated *to* the base part in Memory III. The

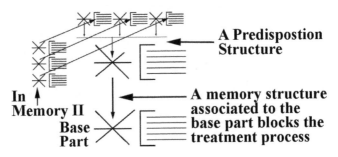

Figure 2-18 A Complex Predisposition

predisposition structure includes a complex layered memory structure in Memory III with three predispositions in Memory II associated *to* the layered structure. Each of these three memories, layered *to* the structure in Memory III, has a memory in Memory II associated *with* them. Intense trauma created this structure. Though I now don't find much problem treating these kinds of complex structures, initially I had a problem treating them when the complex structure was unknown and hadn't been identified. Intruding fields can entrain to pain associated with complex memory structures similar to this complex structure with or without predispositions.

In the next chapter, I look closely at the underlying structure of the hidden dimensions in virtual reality, so you can understand more fully the physics of the Personal Field and field intrusions.

Chapter 3

The Physics of the Hidden Reality: Personal Field

Understanding the Personal Field

In the first chapter, we established that dimensional structures, called fields, underlie reality. Then, we discussed the development of memory and described several memory structures that are important for understanding the mechanics of intruding souls. In this chapter, I will describe the structure of the universe in some detail to demonstrate how virtual reality creates our Personal Field as well as our 3D-Reality and makes possible the phenomena of intruding fields. (I am using the Personal Field here as the soul. Later I will define the Personal Field as the 5th dimension.)

Since the Personal Field is a mysterious feature of our reality, a scientific explanation of how it works is useful, but not necessary, to understand and treat field issues. These fields are hidden from 3D-Reality and exist in the virtual or unseen reality. Understanding multidimensions in virtual reality involves becoming comfortable with constructs related to physics that underlie our perceived 3D-Reality. These constructs — the zero points, flunots, and strings that define the dimensions — are discussed in this chapter.

I write as though my theory is real and that it has some connection to theoretical physics and research. It is really a physics theory modified to fit findings from my clinical interventions and dialogue with patients. At best, the theory presented here, just like physics theories, is a metaphor describing reality. Some work better that others. This one works for understanding change in human behavior

The Origin of Our Personal Field

The Personal Field of the fetus is the joining of the Personal Fields of the mother and father. However, the development of our Personal Field actually starts before birth with the creation of the egg and sperm. Bruce Lipton cites research that shows that emotional events in the lives of parents, both positive and negative, modify the genetic information in the egg and the sperm before conception.[1] He stresses that the parenting of children starts before conception and affects the development of the fetus just as smoking and drinking can affect it after conception. Since the genetic information (DNA) of the egg and sperm can be changed by the verbal and emotional experience of the parents before conception, it is interesting to speculate the possibility of changing the DNA or cellular memory in children and adults with some kind of treatment intervention.

In this model, the Personal Fields of people do not reincarnate. However, Personal Field experiences from previous generations of ancestors can be carried into our present generation because of their presence in our parents' Personal Fields. These ancestral fields can affect the development of our emotional experience, beliefs, and behavior. I believe that spiritually sensitive people who can experience these ancestral fields mistakenly interpret ancestral experiences as their own from a previous lifetime. This misunderstanding of ancestral experiences leads to the belief in Karma.

When the egg and sperm join at conception, a number of zero points unite to participate in the unfolding of reality to create the development of the embryo. Zero points are sources of energy in the vacuum of the universe that create photons and dimensional structures many thousands of times per second. Curiously, the photons and dimensional structures are believed, in this theory, to be destroyed immediately after their creation, only to be immediately recreated. I will describe the creation process in detail later in this chapter.

The parents' dimensional fields that create the sperm and the egg merge to form the dimensional fields creating the fertilized egg. With the splitting of new cells, additional zero points respond and cause the continual creation of the fetus as a living being in the 11-dimensional virtual reality. Ho points out that the DNA of the mother and father carry the building blocks of the whole person (see Figure 3-1).

DNA are structures in 3D-Reality that are created in the hidden reality. Primarily, DNA provides the templates for growth[2]. The 5th dimension records the physiology and activity of the fetus. The 6th and 7th dimensions maintain the most recent templates for the structures of the fetus. As the incremental creation of molecules, cells, organs, and systems progresses, the features of the particular growing human emerges in 3D-Reality. Here's what's interesting.

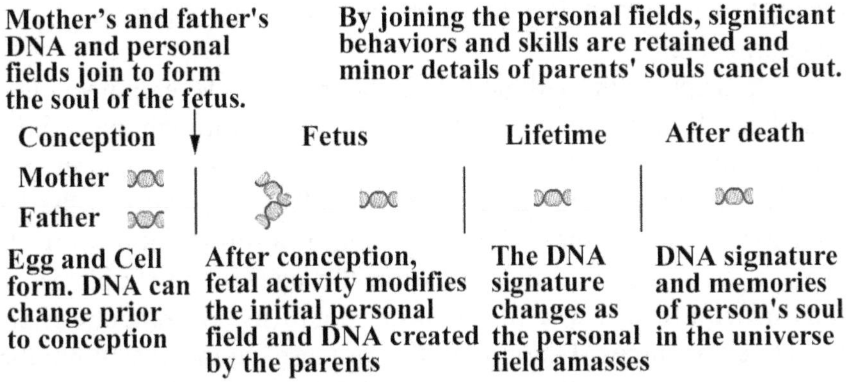

Mother's and father's DNA and personal fields join to form the soul of the fetus.		By joining the personal fields, significant behaviors and skills are retained and minor details of parents' souls cancel out.	
Conception ↓	Fetus	Lifetime	After death
Mother ✕			
Father ✕			
Egg and Cell form. DNA can change prior to conception	After conception, fetal activity modifies the initial personal field and DNA created by the parents	The DNA signature changes as the personal field amasses	DNA signature and memories of person's soul in the universe

Figure 3-1 The Role of the DNA from Preconception to Death

At conception, the mother and father's Personal Fields join to form the embryo's Personal Field. The Personal Field of the fetus consists not only of the entrained Personal Fields of the parents, but also of the souls of ancestors and other ancestral influences that happened to be carried by the parents' Personal Fields. Therefore, the Personal Field of each neonate includes the field representations of all the parents' good and bad habits, as well as good and bad field influences from the past generations of ancestors, called ancestral fields. Ancestral fields can be predispositions for skills, allergies, addictions, or a particular belief or behavior. A more detailed look at inherited ancestral fields and other subtle influences will be presented in Chapter 10.

The joining of the parents' Personal Fields results in the representation of similar traits adding to increase their impact on the person and the canceling out of other traits that are present in one parent and opposed in the other parent. The blending of these fields forms the initial Personal Field of the fetus. The laws of the 10th dimension orchestrate the physical growth and development of the fetus based on information from the DNA in the parents' Personal Fields and internal and external environmental influences in the virtual reality.

The mother's and father's subconsciouses also entrain to provide the knowledge and wisdom of both subconsciouses. Although I have treated damage to the subconscious caused by ancestral fields, the fetus' subconscious resulting from the parents' subconsciouses is usually undamaged, healthy, and becomes supportive to the Main Personality. In some cases, the subconscious operates to provide extranormal skills passed from generation to generation from the subconscious of ancestors who acquired these skills. These extranormal skills provide stronger connections to the 9th dimension and sensitivity to other field information.

Let's apply our 11-dimensional theory to the development of the human body from inception. As the fetus evolves through the creation of cells, the number of zero points increases to meet the demands of the developing person. The growth of the fetus, managed by the 10th dimension, is merely the orderly creation of a representation in the 0th through 9th dimensions based on the use of the templates and other information in the dimensions defining all aspects of the developmental stages. Throughout this process, an increasing number of zero points serve the fetus and, later, the adult by creating a lifetime of behavior and a unique Personal Field. As noted before, some zero points continue creating the soul after death, namely, the Personal Field or 5th dimension, and the 6th through 9th dimensions. This process is probably true of all living creatures: mammals, birds, fish, insects, and so forth.

Understanding Virtual Reality: The Flux Theory

The theory of fields I offer in this book is a creatively generated string theory metaphor based on Cranwell's Flux Theory.[3] My theory may not be accurate, but, according to Cranwell, it is feasible.[4] The theory leaves out and probably distorts many important details of string and quantum theory to explain the phenomenon I see in my patients. Most physics theories about behavior are mathematical models that warp or ignore behavior to fit the model. This theory adjusts the physics model into a collection of metaphors to describe behavioral data I have observed in my clinical practice. The redeeming feature is that the theory explains the subtle field influences in my patients, provides the rationale for treating these influences, and is the basis for experimental interventions using constructs in the hidden reality that work very well. What more can you expect from a theory?

While it is not necessary to fully grasp Cranwell's Flux Theory to understand the hidden structures in the universe, there are three reasons that it is important that I describe the physics theory in some detail to explain intruding souls.

First, fields are not observable in our reality and need a frame of reference to make them real. They are active in our virtual reality and consist of multidimensions. A physics theory will explain the idea of multidimensions, so it will be easier to think about virtual reality and intruding souls. Second, Flux Theory led me to develop experimental interventions that use structures in virtual reality. Knowledge of the theory is needed to understand the basis for these interventions. Finally, there may be other mental health professionals who will want to use facets of the theory to develop new treatment interventions. Therefore, explaining the theory in detail may contribute to this development.

Interventions based on the modified Flux Theory have proved successful in creating changes in my patients' behavior. During an intervention, they often report feeling an energy movement in their bodies, often from head to toe, or memories flashing through their consciousness. After the intervention, they usually perceive personal changes in their memories and behavior. Therefore, the use of the Flux Theory to explain and treat behaviors and intruding fields is justified by its application and outcome in my clinical practice.

I will first present the basic ideas of the theory according to Cranwell's Model. Then I will introduce my own insights and observations from clinical experience and construct a model using my understanding of Flux Theory.

Most of my patients, possibly because of naiveté, various personality dynamics, or hypnotic reasons, understand the theory as plausible and accept it as an explanation for the interventions. The theory provides answers about philosophical or theological questions they have about our reality and life. It accounts for unusual experiences. In some patients, unknown voices are heard — voices that reflect wisdom. Although I don't truly know their source, these voices have validated the theory and have led me in fruitful directions both in treatment of the patient and in this theory's development.[5]

Overview of Virtual Reality

The structures that underlie our 3D-Reality are dimensional structures that we cannot see. I am going to show them as graphic representations in Figure 3-2 (next page). This figure shows the 0th through 7th dimensions as the dimensional structures actively involved in 3D-Reality. The 3rd, 6th and 7th dimensional structures create the general physical presence of what we see as 3D-Reality. Our Personal Field amasses memories in the 5th dimension. These dimensions are involved in the creation of behavior and other aspects of our experience. The 0th through 4th dimensions complete the physical structures or are involved in communication within and between the structures. The three dimensions we

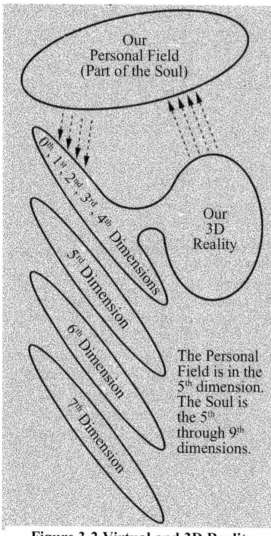

Our
Personal Field
(Part of the Soul)

0th, 1st, 2nd, 3rd, 4th Dimensions

5th Dimensions

5th Dimension

6th Dimension

7th Dimension

Our
3D
Reality

The Personal
Field is in the
5th dimension.
The Soul is
the 5th
through 9th
dimensions.

Figure 3-2 Virtual and 3D Reality

see in our 3D-Reality are our perception of the structures created by the hidden reality. Of course, to us, our 3D-Reality is real, measurable, and concrete. The measurements, time and the 3 dimensions, are simply constructs invented to describe our 3D-Reality.

We cannot see the activity of the dimensional structures; they are in the virtual or hidden reality. However, they are all operating as directed by the laws of the universe. What we do see are the photons emanating from or bouncing off the virtual structures. We perceive the photons as light and colors to see our 3D-Reality. We also bump into, hold, and touch virtual objects that apparently seem solid because of the electromagnetic properties of the structures. In other words, the cause for all the chemical activity in the universe takes place in virtual reality.

Zero points, shown as the speckled background in Figure 3-2, are in the void and are the pervasive source of creation. Zero points create the dimensional structures that underlie all living and inanimate objects we observe in 3D-Reality. A unique set of zero points creates each object — a grain of sand, a plant, a rabbit, or a human. Millions of independent objects in the biology and physiology of all living plants and animals have their own unique set of zero points.

The creation of the 11 dimensions unfolds according to fixed laws of the universe. Recall that the photons and dimensions are created and immediately destroyed. Therefore, our 3D-Reality is created incrementally, like a movie, only with many thousands of frames a second. Each frame and any changes in that frame are recreated by the zero points in the next frame. This creation process includes not only the changes, but also the amassing of memories in various dimensions. In this movie-like environment, our reality is an unfolding, evolving process.

Here is an example of the unfolding reality. Some readers will remember the old flip books that created the movement of figures by fanning a book to create the action. As you fanned the book, each successive page or image frame had a new position of the characters and objects in the picture. The story of the flip book unfolded as the pages were flipped. This is the precursor of the modern-day movie. Our reality unfolds like a flip book, frame by frame.

Assume the frames of our unfolding reality are happening in seconds rather than nanoseconds. During the creation of the flip book, the cartoonist looks at the current frame, the printed copy, imagines the history of the characters involved, and sketches in desired changes in the content of the printed copy. The sketches are adjusted to maintain the coherency with the history of all characters and objects that were present in the printed copy or that were introduced. These changes are printed in the next frame. The flip from the current frame with changes to the next frame is the action of the zero points. With each change, the history of all related objects is preserved in all dimensions by the zero points. A change in any frame results in the change appearing in the next frame.

Everything we do in 3D-Reality is governed by our history. We bring our unique history to a situation that governs our behavior. The cartoonist, who is analogous to the 10th dimension, creates the next action in each frame and maintains coherency in the content. He or she imagines the history of the characters and carries that forward. In the flip book, we can only see the coherent results on each page of the sequence of flipping frames. However, the sequence of change created by the cartoonist is directed by the history of the characters, which involves beliefs, experiences, motivation, and the state of inert objects, to operate coherently as the flip book unfolds frame by frame. Expanding this notion, we find that all the living and inert objects in 3D-Reality have their own frames. When you consider all the processes in our physiology and interrelationships that are operating as we behave, you can see the complexity of our unfolding reality.

Let's take the case of an eagle watching a cat, a cat watching a mouse, and the mouse watching the cat. Each of these animals has memories of unique experiences that are independent of each other but participate in the unfolding reality. The 10th dimension, the "cartoonist," that operates robotically according to the laws of the universe, manages the evolving behavior governed by the memories of each animal. The 10th dimension causes changes in the 0th through 9th dimensions in the current frame, which takes into account all memories and templates in the Personal Field of all related living and inert objects in the frame, namely the eagle, the cat and the mouse. These changes are the cause for the next frame. The zero points then create the next frame, the flip of the page, which includes the changes made by the 10th dimension. This causes change and movement in 3D Reality. The 10th dimension creating change in the current frame leads to change in 3D-Reality. When the zero points recreate the frame, the change in 3D-Reality occurs. I call the 10th dimension the Manager.

The Manager causes what we experience and call self-organized behavior. We only think we are self-organized, because we know our history, can explain our behavior based on our history and the situation, and identify with the outcome as caused by us. It is coherent with our history and all others around us. With experience, we formed beliefs that we are self-organized and cause our behavior. The real cause for our self-organization and behavior is in the hidden reality, namely, amassed memories of all the related living and inert objects and the Manager.

Therefore, our observed 3D-Reality is a complex turmoil of interacting biochemical, living processes, and inanimate objects unfolding in virtual reality. The movements of living and inanimate objects affect each other and result in changes in the current frame of the unfolding virtual reality and, therefore, the unfolding of 3D-Reality. The Manager maintains the coherency among all objects that are related in some way. The occurrence and activity of intruding souls are consistent with the function of the zero points and the Manager, as we will soon see.

Let's review how all these dimensions operate to create a living person or animal. The soul, 5th through 9th dimensions, is present from the moment of conception. Within the soul is all the information necessary to construct an adult. Let's start with the physical being from the outside in. The 7th dimension organizes all the structures in the body into our 3D-image, what we see — the complete human. The 7th dimension has a template from the parents that is passed down to our soul by means of fields we call the DNA, which directs each of us to become a unique, tangible person. The organized structures include our bones, muscles, hair, the brain structures, the skin, all internal organs, and all neural cells. The templates for these structures, organized by the 7th dimension, are present in the 6th dimension. I also believe that the 6th dimension carries a running memory of the growth and development of these structures, which in turn is orchestrated by the DNA. Templates in the 3rd dimension manage chemical elements and molecules that make up the organs. The 4th dimension is involved in communication. The 0th to 2nd dimensions provide the building blocks for the elements and molecules. Photons are means of communication between cells and structures in the body. Vibrating structures causing local fields provide another means of communication. The 5th dimension records all of the movements and behaviors, physical and mental, and amasses our personal history of experience from conception to our current age. Much of the information inherited by our soul, given to us by our parents, gradually changes with our experience to become unique to us.

As stated before, our reality is unfolding like a sequence of movie frames. Changes in our 3D-Reality are reflected in the current frame of all dimensions and are incorporated into creating the next frame. The changes in the 5th dimension amass with each frame and become the primary memory of all the activity of a living organism, from conception through death. Our memory in the 5th dimension and the other dimensions of our soul remains available in the universe after death. The souls of living or dead persons include the 5th through 9th dimensions.

Because I believe that I encounter and work with the 5th dimension in treatment, I usually call this dimension the Personal Field. It also provides the structures to which intruding fields attach. In any case, it appears that focusing on the 5th dimension simplifies the theory and the treatment process.

String Theory and Dimensional Structures

One way to understand multidimensions is to understand string theory. It uses the concept of strings as one of the important building blocks in our universe. Strings build the dimensional structures and are the carriers of information. As a brief introduction to the structure of the universe, suppose a metal screen with half-inch squares represents a simple dimension. The points where the wires cross is a universal element found in all dimensions of the universe. You will learn that this element, called a **flunot**, adjusts and operates to create all dimensions of the universe, as well as subatomic particles. The strings in all dimensions vibrate in a way that allows them to amass information and participate in the creation of 3D-Reality. Each of the 1st through 10th dimensions is similar to the screen wire with cross points but become much more complex in the higher dimensions.

To understand the creation process, we have to understand the void. A **void** is obtained in an enclosed space when all known physical matter, like air, particles, and electromagnetic fields, are removed. Even when a space is void, the space is packed with zero points. Physicist Tom Bearden describes the void as "filled with virtual particles (zero points) and their activities!" from which "anything physical . . . is continually being CREATED AND SUSTAINED (Bearden's caps) as an underlying tremendous set of direct vacuum interactions," later adding "be it living or dead."[6] These zero points are unknown point sources that are also creating photons, which are immediately destroyed for a reason beyond the scope of this book. It is like many blinking Christmas tree lights all packed together, completely filling the void in space. I assume that the zero points are also creating the structures in our universe, which, just like photons, are being created and, then, immediately destroyed.

A zero point creates a photon and what is called a longitudinal wave (scalar wave). The photon is an electromagnetic wave with electric and magnetic components of the wave. The longitudinal wave is similar to a sound wave but much more complex. This wave is a complex field associated with dimensional structures in virtual reality. The wave consists of a flunot and strings that can be one of the 11 dimensions but adapts to serve as only one dimension in a structure in virtual reality. **Longitudinal waves**, created by many zero points, create the structure of flunots and strings in dimensional structures. This can be confusing, but the physics equation for the longitudinal wave includes many different field structures within the equation. The longitudinal wave can cause any one of the 11-dimensional fields that correspond to the dimensions in our virtual reality.[7] Since most dimensions created by zero points cannot be independently measured, physicists lump them together in what they call the longitudinal wave.

Since photons are created and destroyed, I assume that the longitudinal waves are also created and destroyed. Therefore, we have an unfolding universe, much like the frames in a movie. As the size of the dimension increases, the length of the strings between corners or flunots gets shorter. The 10th dimension has very, very short strings. Because the strings are very thin and the flunots very small, our 3D-Reality is 99.9999+ percent space.

Every object in the universe — every cell, sand particle, mountain, tree, animal, and human — has its own collection of zero points creating that object seen in 3D-Reality. Let's consider a puppy as an example. Every 3D structure in the puppy, such as electrons, molecules, cells, organs, and hair, involves constantly changing dimensions in our virtual reality. All dimensions involved in creating the puppy have a particular quality — namely, they are related to the creation of all interacting aspects of the puppy. That is the reason coherency is important. Some dimensions carry an electromagnetic field that is capable of amassing information and being used in a way to contribute to creating the puppy that we see in our 3D-Reality. As the puppy behaves, information changes. The change is preserved in the dimensions as it is recreated in the next frame of creation. Its history amasses in some of the dimensions creating the puppy. This amassing of history is what allows us to observe orderly changes in the activity of the puppy.

When we look at the objects on our desk — the pens, pencils, a stapler, and papers — all have a unique collection of zero points that are actively creating the objects. When we move the objects around, the frames change and the objects are recreated in a new location. The Manager — really the 10th dimension — maintains **coherency** — the way things affect each other in a logical and orderly relationship. When objects are moved, the relationship of all objects to each other is orchestrated by the Manager to maintain coherency. The 0th through 9th dimensions are assumed to be embedded in the 10th dimension. The process will not be discussed here, but the 10th dimension maintains coherency between all objects in the universe according to the laws of the universe, which includes most of the physics and the chemical laws that we have in our 3D-Reality.

Structures and Communication in Virtual Reality

The communication in our virtual reality can take place only as waveforms vibrating or traveling along the strings connecting the points of dimensional structures, called matrices. See Figure 3-3 for examples of 2- and 3-dimensional matrix structures.

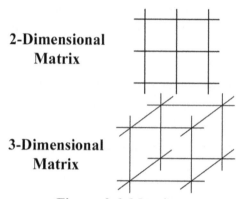

2-Dimensional Matrix

3-Dimensional Matrix

Figure 3-3 Matrices

All virtual dimensions are matrix structures. These structures look like wire frames with strings connecting the corner points in the structures. Except for the corners and strings, everything else is space. Communication and memory in the structures can only take place in the form of longitudinal waveforms, similar to sound waves. The strings in the structures carry the waveforms. Communication in a matrix does not pass through the space surrounding the strings. Looking at the 2-dimensional and the 3-dimensional matrices shown, one can imagine communication as waveforms traveling through the corners and along the strings connecting the corners. Unique memories are amassed in different dimensions as a complex waveform of life experiences or templates for structures. The zero points recreate the structures including the waveforms with or without changes, thereby preserving and amassing memories. Therefore, what we experience as living and inert objects in our 3D-Reality are really complex virtual structures created by the 0th through 10th dimensions. Understanding this concept goes a long way toward explaining how fields from the dead can intrude into the living.

As an illustration, imagine a box made with wires with just corners and edges. Now imagine one end of a room filled with these boxes piled edge to edge (see Figure 3-4). If all you can see were the corners and edges, then you would have a 3-dimensional structure. Between the

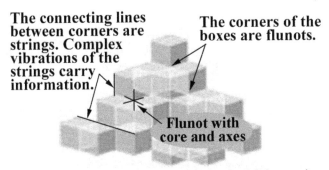

The connecting lines between corners are strings. Complex vibrations of the strings carry information.

The corners of the boxes are flunots.

Flunot with core and axes

Figure 3-4 Stacked Boxes in the 3rd Dimension

corners and edges is empty space. All dimensions in the universe have structures with corners and edges with empty space between them. Those corners are the flunots; the edges are the strings. Communication is carried along the wires or strings through the corners of the 3-dimensional boxes. As the dimensions increase, say from a 2-dimensional structure to a 3-dimensional structure (see Figure 3-3), the number of axes or strings in a stacked structure increases and the corners have more axes passing through them. The corners or intersections in a matrix of any dimension are the flunots. The presence of waveforms on the strings in structures is where the amassing of memory, and perhaps communication, takes place in the virtual dimensions.

The flunots or corners in 3-dimensional structures would have three axes passing through the center of the flunot, making six radii that extend toward adjacent radii of other flunots. When they join, an edge or string forms, connecting the flunots. All dimensions form in the same way, but the structures can be more or less complex. For a flunot to work in all dimensions, each flunot or corner has enough axes to form a 10-dimensional structure. When all the axes are not used, as in a 3-dimensional structure, the unused axes curl up to the core of the flunot.

Thinking about Multidimensions

Let's see if we can conceptualize or picture multidimensions. Imagine that our reality is a 0-dimensional matrix called a point, and that we are a wave communicating in that point. Locate the point on the right side of Figure 3-5 (next page). Look at the point and make believe that you are living as a waveform there. Not much is happening. We move around, but there is no string to vibrate to form a wave. Our perception, if it is even possible when living in the point, does not reveal the

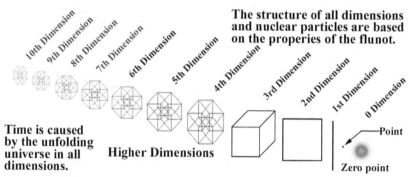

Figure 3-5 The Structures of All Dimensions

complexity and existence of other dimensional realities. Although we accept our reality as a point, we know hidden dimensions are there, but we cannot see them. Frankly, if you were living in the point, you would not see or perhaps even think about the other dimensions of our reality. Without a string, there may be no memory preserved in the structure.

When we expand the point, so we live in the matrix of the 1st dimension, a line, our experience is a waveform on a straight piece of string, a fine string at that. Find the 1st dimension — the 1-dimensional space — in Figure 3-5. Our perception of the line would still not include all of our reality. We can vibrate or communicate along the string, but the dimension would restrict our communication to only two directions. A 1-dimensional structure would be strings connected end to end. Our communication could only travel along those strings. Although we know there are more dimensions in the universe, we cannot see any more than what exists in our 1-dimensional reality. The other dimensions are virtual dimensions that we know are there, but can't see. In other words, they are in the hidden reality.

If we expanded our reality to a matrix with two dimensions, we would be living in a matrix of wire squares with no depth. It's like living on the lines crisscrossing a chessboard. Identify the 2-dimensional matrix in Figure 3-5. Our waveforms could communicate to the right and left and in front and behind, but not up and down or across because that is not in our reality. We still don't experience the full perception of other dimensions. While living in the second dimension, the third dimension is virtual or hidden, and beyond our perception.

Now, let us expand our reality to three dimensions. In Figure 3-5, the strings connect corners to form a box-like wire frame structure, representing a 3-dimensional matrix. The 3rd dimension in the universe is not a physical object in our 3D-Reality. Rather, it is a dimension that participates in creating structures in virtual reality that contributes to what we perceive as our 3D-Reality. In the 3rd dimension, complex waveforms can communicate or travel right and left, in front and behind, and up and down, but not across the box matrix. In the 3rd dimension, we have communication that is more flexible, and we are not as limited as we were in the 1st and 2nd dimensions, but it is still like a wire box with plenty of space between the wires in the structure. How complex is this creation process?

Here is an example of the complexity of the creation process. Zero points emit photons and longitudinal waves. Longitudinal waves are said to be capable of representing any of the 11 dimensions in the hidden reality. In other words, the longitudinal (scalar) waves (including both electric and magnetic waves) from many zero points form a composite of the 11 dimensions to create who we are. This is similar to the ripples observed when 11 pebbles are dropped into a still pond, which becomes a complex collage of ripples after they merge. While all of the dimensions represented by longitudinal fields participate in forming structures, some dimensions preserve our experiences and the templates of physical structures as the basis for future growth and behavior. In other words, the waves in several dimensions amass history in complex waveforms that carry and preserve features of our physical makeup and life history.

Yet, having said all this, we still haven't fully experienced the virtual reality of multidimensions.

Just as there were unseen virtual dimensions when we lived or communicated as a point or a line, there are additional virtual dimensions when we live or communicate in the 3D-Reality. Let's change our perspective to be aware of the virtual reality. Since all dimensions of the universe are virtual dimensions to us, our thinking and perception in our 3D-Reality hide the complexity of the virtual dimensional structures in the universe. This change in perspective will help you to imagine the virtual structures, while seeing them as creating our 3D-Reality. We know they are there and we can't see them. We can see and measure the 0th, $1^{st,}$ and 2nd dimensions and the composite of the virtual dimensions in what we observe as the three dimensions in 3D-Reality, but not the dimensions that create our 3D-Reality. Our 3D-Reality is really a composite of the activity of nine dimensions and is not explicitly represented as a 3D structure in the virtual reality. Our 3D-Reality could be called an illusion created by our virtual reality, albeit real.

The dimensions embedded in the virtual structures underlying our 3D-Reality include structures defined by the 5th through 7th dimensions, as described in Chapter 1. These structures work in concert with particles, molecules, and communication provided by the 0th through 4th dimensions to complete the virtual object.

How, then, can we look in all directions, if communication can only happen along the strings of the structures?

Recall that structures formed by the 0th through 9th dimensions in our virtual reality are pulled together by gravity and electromagnetic phenomena. The 3rd, 6th and 7th dimensions form the structural basis for our observed 3D-Reality. The structures of 0th through 9th dimensions that are creating an object are embedded in the 10th dimension. Here's how we see objects. When zero points create objects, they emit photons. The photon light waves bounce off or emanate from the structures in the virtual reality and travel along the strings of the 10th dimension in a fine zigzag path. The light travels in the form of a wavy pattern, following the strings connecting the corners in the 10-dimensional matrix, until we receive the wave. Our biochemistry converts the wave into a photon. Our 3D-Reality is embedded in the 10th dimension constructed by the 0th through 9th dimensions. We can see everything in 3D-Reality, because light traveling in the 10th dimension is revealed to us as photons. This photon activity is how we perceive our 3D-Reality.[8]

The 9 dimensions are embedded in the 10th dimension and the communication between the 9 dimensions appears limited. How do the dimensions communicate with each other? Because photons travel in the 10th dimension as waveforms, some communication between dimensions is done with photons. This form of communication has been found in our physiology. In addition, the 2nd and 4th dimensions are found to be electromagnetic fields involved in communication within the body. There is some wave structure that provides a process in the waveforms that is responsive to communication via the 2nd and 4th dimensions and photons. If we find this form of communication in ourselves, why not find it in the hidden reality?

We can't see these dimensional structures as virtual objects, but we perceive them in 3D-Reality because of photons emanating from or bouncing off of them. At any moment, what we see is created by the virtual structures, which we then experience as sensory stimulation. Let's take, for example, a ball flying through the air and approaching our mitt. It is the photons emanating from or bouncing off the moving virtual structure — the ball — that our visual receptors decode as a spherical shape in our 3D-Reality.

How do we explain touch? When we catch the ball, the gravity and electromagnetic bonding that determine the structure of a ball in the virtual reality bump into the gravity and electromagnetic bonding that determine the structure of the mitt in the virtual reality. Of course, we define these objects as a ball and a mitt in 3D-Reality as solid, because we can touch and feel them. They even look solid. I am asking you to imagine all the objects around you as constructs of dimensional matrices that are more than 99.9999 percent space but, nevertheless, have the electromagnetic bonding of millions of necessary structures that gives these objects the feeling and appearance of being solid in our 3D-Reality. It is the electromagnetic bonding of each object, say the hand and the ball, that gives us the experience of touching solid objects. Interestingly, the photons emanating from these structures traveling in the 10th dimension take the shortest zigzag line between points in the universe to allow us to see our mitt and the ball.

At this point, don't worry about understanding every aspect of the virtual dimensions. Some theory is necessary for you to understand the construction of our virtual, dimensional reality. This information prepares you to accept that virtual dimensions are possible, do exist, and have the power to influence our behavior, particularly when they take the form of intruding fields.

A Closer Look at the Void, Zero Points, and Flunots

Now let's look a little closer at zero points and flunots. Recall that zero points are point sources pervasive in the universe that are destroying and recreating the structures of all physical objects in the universe. This creates a reality that unfolds frame by frame similar to the unfolding of a movie film. Each physical object, from the smallest to the largest, has its own set of zero points creating its virtual reality — the virtual dimensions of the object. The physical objects are constructed from virtual dimensions composed of flunots and strings. The flunots have 10 axes passing through them that are available to form 11 dimensions. When the axes are not used to form a dimension, they curl up to the base of the core. As the dimensions get higher in number, more axes are used and the distance between flunots gets shorter.

According to Cranwell's Flux Theory, the flunot is the basic structure of all objects in the universe. His theory eliminates the need for a preexisting field having a specific shape and form to organize our reality or for a big bang to start the universe.[9] He hypothesizes the universe started with strings, or simple, infinitesimal structures. The strings eventually joined to form the axes of a flunot. Over time, the flunot evolved into a structure that has 10 axes passing through its center (see Figure 3-6). These flunot structures adapt to construct the zero- to 10-dimensional structures that serve different functions in our universe.

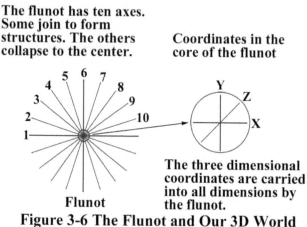

The flunot has ten axes. Some join to form structures. The others collapse to the center.

Coordinates in the core of the flunot

Flunot

The three dimensional coordinates are carried into all dimensions by the flunot.

Figure 3-6 The Flunot and Our 3D World

The figure at the left side of Figure 3-6 shows the 10 axes or strings passing through the core of the flunot. A dimensional structure forms when a fixed number of strings or axes of a group of flunots join to form a structure of some dimension. The unused strings curl up to the core of the flunot and are not involved in the structure. For example, a 3-dimensional structure has many flunots, with three axes (or six radii) of each flunot joining the radii of other flunots to form a structure consisting of box matrices. A stack of empty frame-like square boxes with a flunot located at each corner of the stacked boxes would be an example of such a structure. The connected axes form the strings, which carry information contained in complex waveforms unique to the 3rd dimension. The zero points preserve this information in the creation process.

Moving from the 3rd dimension to the 4th or 5th dimension, the number of axes used in the dimensional structure increases. In addition, as we move higher in the dimensions, the distance between the flunots creating the structure becomes shorter. So, as the dimension of the structures increases in number, the structures become more compact or dense. The 10th dimension, which manages the evolving virtual reality, has the shortest axes. The 0th through 9th dimensions are embedded in the 10th dimension.

The flunots are the corners of all structures in the universe that make up the virtual reality that underlies living and inanimate 3D-Reality. The radii or strings connecting the flunots take up very little space, because the flunots and axes are so small. A structure in any dimension is really a matrix — namely, a wire-frame-like structure made up of flunots and axes with open space in between. Gravity, namely the flunots attracting each other, holds the matrix of dimensional structures together.[10]

The 10 axes provide up to 20 radii that can extend from the core of the flunot. Each dimension uses a different number of radii. These radii adjust to connect to the axes of other flunots to create matrices for the 1st through 10th dimensions. Many flunots of the same dimension are necessary to form a structure.[11]

Flunots of the zero and first dimensions form subnuclear particles.[12] With the 0th dimension, all the axes curl up in various arrangements to form subnuclear particles. Physics research with linear accelerators and cyclotrons has shown that when a beam of electrons hits various elements, it causes axes to break off from protons in varying numbers and the remainder ball up to form many subnuclear particles. These subnuclear particles form when the unused axes of a 0-dimensional structure or particle curl up to the core of the flunot in different ways.[13] Since the flunot with one axis is an electron, one can see that the size of the curled-up axes and flunot are infinitesimal. This allows numerous structures of many dimensions to imbed or occupy the same space with no contact.

Dimensional Structures, Information, and Memory:
A Crucial Link

What's the point of all of this talk about zero points, flunots, and dimensional structures we are unable to see?

The single most important point to remember is that each dimension can carry unique information in waveforms. Complex waveforms on the strings of the dimensional structures carry information in the form of memories.

For example, the simplest waveform is like a jump rope that can have one end moving up and down to produce a transverse waveform traveling the length of the rope. This is simple information. If the vibrations of the rope displayed the music of a symphony, the vibrations or waveforms would be very complex representing the sound of each instrument in the orchestra. If the zero points preserved the waveform of the symphony on the jump rope, then it would be available to all persons who played with the jump rope. This is what I mean by information and memory. Complex vibrations of the axes (strings) of a structure, regardless of dimension, carry the information unique to that dimension. Recall that the axes and flunots are infinitesimal and many dimensions can exist in the same space. As the size of a dimension increases, say from 5 to 8, the length of the edges of the structure decreases, which allows a higher frequency of vibration. Structures with higher frequencies of vibration can carry more information. Each structure in the universe, from the smallest to the largest, has unique information amassed on the dimensions creating that structure.

All dimensions work following the same basic laws of physics and chemistry. The xyz's that Cranwell identifies in the core of the flunots (see Figure 3-6) enables all dimensions to participate in creating the virtual reality. I suggest that the 10th dimension connects to the core of the flunots, the xyz's, and is responsible for managing the coherency or how everything interrelates to each other in all dimensions. The management of coherency leads to changes in virtual reality. This virtual reality is what we see in our 3D-Reality.

Since virtual reality is created and destroyed in discrete frames, something like motion pictures, but instantaneously, what causes change in the new frame? With a new frame, the Manager or 10th dimension adjusts the content in the frame based on the unique memories of the living content, including motivation, and the inert objects. It is as if the Manager responds to the question, "What's next?" and causes change to honor the history of all related living and inert objects. The Manager responds robotically to create the changes and manage the effects of the change on other objects in the frame by causing changes in the 0th through 9th dimensions of each object. The zero points respond to these new changes and manifest the changes in the following frame. This is a repetitive and recurrent process — namely, the last frame is the basis for the next frame.

Here's an example. Imagine yourself standing in front of the refrigerator. The Manager creates all the different choices that cross your mind. The choices are based on what you see and the subtle motivation attributed to each choice contained in your memories. Your memory is used by the Manager to direct your behavior. When maintaining coherency, in general, the Manager takes into account the memories in all related living and inert structures and any change in the universe that affects these structures or that these structures affect. The Manager orchestrates the 9 dimensions. This takes place with each new frame. If something falls out of the refrigerator, the Manager immediately orchestrates your response to the change in the frame.

Let's return to the analogy that reality is unfolding like a movie. Movies use about 30 frames per second to create the action-packed drama we see on the screen. Zero points, on the other hand, are like multidimensional projectors that create all 11 dimensions of the dimensional structures and their information underlying our 3D-Reality. Some physicists estimate that the zero points create and annihilate photons, and all dimensions according to my assumption, many hundreds of thousands of times per second. Therefore, the movie in the universe has many hundred of thousands of frames per second, creating the 9-dimensional virtual movie we see as the unfolding 3D-Reality. The duration of the frame we see in our 3D-Reality is brief but thousands of times longer than a frame in the creation process. It is this incremental creation process that causes us to experience the seamless unfolding of experience in our 3D-Reality.

The Manager is believed to orchestrate the change of all related objects in our biochemistry and in our community to maintain coherency. When responding to a new frame, the activity of the 10th dimension takes into account all the motivating factors in our life history and in the life history of all other, related living organisms, not to mention the interplay of physical objects in our reality. All objects in the universe are created codependently with all other related structures. The Manager causes physical and biochemical interactions of objects in virtual reality to cause the next frame of the movie.

This understanding leads to other interesting speculations, such as about the nature of time. We don't see time and it doesn't exist. Time is simply an observed property caused by zero point activity and the 10th dimension changing and creating objects to appear like an unfolding movie. Time is an artifact of the creation process, an arbitrary measure defined by the movement of the moon around the earth. It is a useful and necessary construct in mathematics and physics to describe acceleration, motion, other properties in our reality, and other dimensions. Time is a construct made up to account for our unfolding experience — nothing more and nothing less.

Another interesting question proposed by this concept of the universe is the following: how is it that we remember and have a history?

The Creation of Autobiographical Memory

We have memory structures in our biochemistry, which record memories that are retrievable in a linear fashion — our autobiographical memory. These biochemical memories are the 3D representation of structures active in the hidden reality. The 5th through 9th dimensions remember all activity in the brain and body (see Figure 3-7). The memory in the 5th dimension is the closest in content to what we experience in our 3D-Reality. This dimension serves as the memory that amasses all aspects of our behavior and experience in the form of complex waveforms.

What causes memory in the waveforms of the 5th dimension when we behave in our 3D-Reality? Basically, the zero points recreate and preserve the memory of the current physical state of objects and of all we think and do by amassing them as memories in the 5th dimension. All activity in our physiology has a unique 5th dimensional representation that amasses with previous history. This memory includes all behavior related to our basic needs, sensory experience, reinforcement and punishment, and the entire movie of our life created by the 0th through 9th dimensions. The history of a rock is simple, but the history of a human or a skunk can be very complex. History starts at conception and continues to amass until death. How is memory related to the creation of the next frame?

Everything we do internally and externally to respond to changes in our internal and external environment is a result of activity in the representations of our biochemistry in the virtual reality. These responses are assumed to be orchestrated and created by the Manager. When the Manager causes a small change in any dimension in your Personal Field, the zero points preserve the memory of the change and create the change in the next frame. This change is reflected in both our virtual and 3D-Reality. The Manager then operates again, according to laws of the universe, to modify the current frame of our virtual reality to cause the

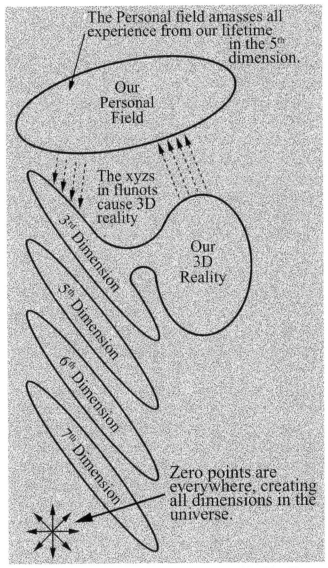

The Personal field amasses all experience from our lifetime in the 5th dimension.

Our Personal Field

The xyzs in flunots cause 3D reality

3rd Dimension

5th Dimension

6th Dimension

7th Dimension

Our 3D Reality

Zero points are everywhere, creating all dimensions in the universe.

Figure 3-7 The Creation of the 3D Reality

next response. Coherency is maintained with all related structures in other Personal Fields or physical objects that we affect and that affect us. The Manager does this by making changes in the virtual representations in the current frame, and the zero points then create these changes in the following frame of all structures affected while amassing and preserving memories in each of them. This interplay between the zero points and the 10th dimension changes the information in all dimensions. The changes amassed in the 5th through 9th dimensions serve as the templates and memories for both structures and activity in our current virtual and 3D-Realities.

The interaction between unique living organisms and inanimate objects in virtual reality is like a loose gun in the universe, because the outcome cannot be predicted. This is not caused by free will but by the interactions involving the varied and unique histories in the 5th dimension of all living objects. This is where creativity comes into play in a universe that, otherwise, is completely determined by fixed laws. We are completely determined as we move from frame to frame, but the changes caused by interactions of the living and objects, each with different memories, are novel or very novel in the outcome.

Some massive 3D structures appear self-organized (living plants and animals) and others appear chaotic (weather, objects in the physical environment). In both of these cases, all of their interactions are fairly unpredictable, yet determined by the laws of the universe. This is caused by the fact that the activity of one living organism based on its history is unknown to the activity of another organism with its history. The interaction of these two organisms with different histories leads to novel interactions, thus the creation of a new and original history in both. This unpredictable relationship between virtual structures causes surprising changes in all aspects of the universe. In particular, it leads to the growth of knowledge and wisdom in the universe. This will be discussed in detail in Chapter 9.

We know that information and memory exist in waveforms in virtual reality, but where does our behavior come from? How do we "do what we do," which is to be creative or respond adaptively to our environment? It involves a property called self-organization.

Self-Organization and the Common Theme of Creation

A **self-organized system** has an internal structure that increases in complexity over time without any external influence. We see self-organization when we move our arm to scratch our ear and, when suddenly our nose itches, our movement changes to scratch our nose. The change in direction from our ear to our nose is an example of self-organized behavior in our body. Extending this to our behavior allows us to see that our entire behavior is self-organized, using accumulated information in the form of memories to respond to internal and external stimulation to create the next response.

If you think about it, self-organization is governing our lives and the world. We see it in and between each other and in other living matter, plants and animals, using accumulated information or memories to respond to internal and external stimulation. The laws of the universe directing the 10th dimension cause self-organization in the virtual reality of all living things. We see the accumulation of history and self-generated behavior evolving in 3D-Reality. This self-organization, then, is a property of our virtual reality, and we see the results of it in our 3D-Reality. We think we are self-organized, but, actually, we only experience the self-organization managed by the 10th dimension that is maintaining coherency between our environment and ourselves in the virtual reality.

Some physicists believe the zero points cause the self-organization observed in our 3D-Reality. Contrary to this belief, I believe the zero points recreate the frames of our unfolding reality, including any changes, but are not responsible for the changes or self-organization. A frame is like a pixel in a television screen refreshed by the basic circuitry, which is analogous to the zero points. The storage of information for the pixel is displayed. When the storage of the pixel information is changed by the TV signal, the circuitry refreshes the TV screen with the changed pixel. The pixel now shows the change of color to match the storage area. A simple recreation by the circuitry manages any changes in the storage area. This refreshing of the pixel, like the zero points, is a rule-bound reflection of the change caused by the input from the TV signal.

Zero points have a rule-bound way of handling change from frame to frame in virtual reality. A change in one frame is recreated by the zero points in the next frame. Zero points do not show the property of self-organization or of increasing complexity caused by changes in 3D-Reality. I assume that zero points don't have history. They simply recreate the frame with the change and preserve the history of changes in various dimensions in virtual reality. This is the amassing of history. This occurs from frame to frame. Self-organization involves the 10th dimension's activity or management in virtual reality respecting the history of the living and changing the content of frames to maintain coherency. The zero points recreate the frames, including the changes created by the 10th dimension, that lead to increased complexity in memories of the 5th through 9th dimensions of objects in virtual reality, which are observed in 3D-Reality.

With self-organization, over time, living matter in virtual reality learns and is responsive to the changes in information and, in this way, forms a richer history. Living matter created a history from its beginning to the present. The human experience, which appears self-organized in 3D-Reality, is a result of the properties of the virtual reality. The zero points are assumed to simply respond to changes in one frame of our unfolding reality, to create the change in the next frame. In this way, the activity of the zero points supports the self-organization and coherency of objects that are handled by the 10th dimension.

A Model for Strange Phenomena

How is the entire history of the 5th through 9th dimensions from other generations involved in our 3D-Reality? Think about all the strange phenomena in the universe, such as ghosts and their apparently beneficial, playful or destructive behavior, as documented by Belanger (2006), Hensley (2005), Bearden (2002), Kraft (1992, 1993), and Dickason (1987). Poltergeist phenomena and other unexpected activities of souls are described by Roll (2003). Bearden (2002) describes other paranormal phenomena and sightings.

I want to touch on these strange self-organized phenomena here. These phenomena involve activities of the 5th through 9th dimensions in a way that manifests as transitory images, sensory stimulation, physical effects, communication, and even physical presence in our 3D-Reality. These effects may involve activities of the 0th through 4th dimensions combined with the 5th, 6th, and 7th dimensions of the intruding soul or object. Some speculations will be made in Chapter 4 about the mechanics of the conscious awareness of various activities of intruding souls. However, most scientists discount these reports, denying the reality of anything that cannot be measured and observed on a consistent basis. They believe that if something cannot be perceived and measured, then it cannot be real. What they don't get is that the constructs of 3D-Reality, time and the three dimensions, don't work to adequately explain and describe the hidden reality.

The 10th Dimension Is the Cause of Our Reality

The 10th dimension manages the creation process and makes changes in each dimension in virtual reality to obtain the most optimal response at all levels of biochemistry and behavior. These optimal responses are made by taking into account the history of all dimensions of an individual and the history of all other interacting living and inert objects. Any activity and changes we experience in 3D-Reality are reflected in all dimensions and are remembered in some form in the 5th through 9th dimensions. The 5th through 9th dimensions each have their own interdependent histories related to an individual.

All behavior is caused by the activity of the 10th dimension to maintain coherency in us and with the environment. This is a recurrent process, in which the state of the current frame is the basis for the next condition or frame. The activity of the 10th dimension to maintain coherency and the recurrent process of the zero points is the cause of our unfolding reality at all levels of our being. This happens in fine increments in our virtual reality to give us the experience of ongoing, progressive self-organized behavior in our 3D-Reality. The complexion of living and inert objects that we affect and that affect us always influences the outcome of the self-organization of our behavior.

The Illusion of Free Will

The theory presented assumes that basic laws of the universe are completely controlling our lives by giving apparent self-organization to our behavior. What does this mean for us? On the surface, it means that there is no free will. What we perceive as free will in this model is simply the operation of the 10th dimension directing our behavior based on our history, leading us to make what we believe is a free-will choice. The occurrence of a "free will" experience requires all the determinants of the free-will experience to be in the 5th dimension or the environment. Without that, the free-will experience would not occur.

This does not mean that we are unable to control our destiny. To control our destiny, we have to have the idea or strategies in our history to enable controlling our reality and therefore our destiny. You might expect our subconscious to have free will. However, my patients' subconsciouses initially cannot heal trauma or engage in automatic treatment between sessions until they are taught how to do it. This is what relationships, listening, reading, and therapies are about: to introduce ideas and concepts that lead the patient to have the insight and inclination to change his or her life course. This is the basis for what we call free will. It is not free because it is based on our autobiographical history.

The extent to which we are risk-taking is based on the net sum of our life experiences. We can either make choices that seem right or make choices that go against our better judgment. In either case, it is the outcome of the Manager maintaining coherency. The way we can control our destiny is by attending to the forces in our relationships and environment that control us. We can stop spending time with people who will take us in a direction we don't want to go. Choosing to change, modify, or avoid these forces is another way of controlling our destiny. Therefore, we can control our destiny, but it is in the context of our history of conditioning and the environment in which we live. Our will is definitely not free of our history or of the environment.

The Loving Nature of the Manager

The other interesting feature of the self-generation of our reality is that reality appears to be based on love. From clinical experience, I believe the basic laws of the universe, as reflected by the work of the Manager, lead to getting more satisfaction or happiness and less pain. Getting rewards and avoiding pain or punishment are outcomes that bring more happiness and less pain to our lives. When a person is confronted with constant, ongoing pain, the Manager manifests in the person the choice to experience such pain in order to experience a lower intensity of pain. This is a loving response. Even choosing suicide or avoidance behaviors hurtful to self or others, based on a history of severe, ongoing pain, is consistent with the goal of experiencing less pain. Can all behavior, then, be viewed as based on love?

All people, even those considered most despicable by cultural norms, operate under the same principles to obtain the optimum response determined by their history — to achieve more happiness and experience less pain. This is the concept referred to at the end of Chapter 2 — all parts of the personality want this. Successful therapeutic treatment of compartmentalized parts using the Process Healing Method involves replacing the pain of the trauma memories with neutral to positive emotions, strengthening the positive qualities of personality parts, and integrating the parts and the Main Personality — namely exchanging memories until all parts and the Main Personality have the same memories. When all parts are integrated with identical memories, the Manager can then orchestrate the Main Personality and integrated parts to run the body and mind with no conflict to achieve more happiness and less pain.

However, the intrusion of fields into aspects of the Personal Field can prevent treatment by distorting our experience. The history of the intruding field affects our history and is included in the creation of our behavior. When our experience is distorted by fields, our behavior can manifest in unexpected and unexplainable ways. Let's turn, then, to the particulars of how such intruding fields can be identified and removed.

Part II
The Treatment in the Hidden Reality

Chapter 4

Treating Intruding Souls

About Treating Intruding Souls

I have worked with many personality parts and unusual memory structures in people using the Process Healing Method. During the course of therapy, no matter what I try, I encounter a barrier that prevents the treatment of the targeted issue. Once I exhaust all other possible causes for this barrier, I usually find an intruding soul — the Personal Field of a deceased person — who has entrained with the Personal Field of the patient. The behavioral history of the intruding soul, such as emotional pain, beliefs or problematic behaviors, can be activated and distort the patient's Personal Field and, therefore, his or her behavior. These distortions are usually subtle in our conscious awareness and overlooked because we become used to their presence. Who would think intruding souls could cause problems in our behavior? Yet, they do, and they can cause large problems.

My work with intruding souls and other field phenomena in my clinical practice has convinced me that the souls of all dead organisms from the beginning of living matter are available as fields in the 5th through 9th dimensions. Under the right circumstances, these fields can intrude. When a soul's emotional pain entrains with similar pain in a living person's Personal Field, the resulting emotions and behavior caused by the intruding soul will, in some cases, block therapeutic treatment, or cause distortions of emotions, treatment, and behavior.

Treating intruding souls with this method requires that you have contact with the subconscious; otherwise, there is no way to communicate productively with the souls. (If you want to treat intruding souls in yourself or others, read Appendix II, where you will learn how to contact and communicate with your subconscious.) In addition, it helps to have rapport with all parts of the personality to gain the cooperation of the various parts to support treating soul intrusions or barriers.

As you read this, you and your subconscious are probably going to learn most of the skills to find and treat intruding souls. Treating intruding souls is generally a routine intervention after you learn the treatment techniques for the various structural barriers that can arise in the souls. With practice, the treatment of souls will become easier and it may even become automatic for the subconscious to treat them.

In this chapter, I will show you how souls entrain and synchronize with a living person by describing the mechanics of their entrainment to emotional trauma in Personal Fields. I will then explain the treatment of both simple and complex intruding souls, using actual case histories from my practice. When you read "field," know that I am talking about intruding souls.

The Mechanics of Intruding Fields

You may wonder exactly how intruding souls entrain when they join with the Personal Field of a living person. The answer to that lies in a person's memory.

There is a difference between the movie of our memories — the content of sensory experiences — and our physiological responses. Figure 4-1 shows the content of a memory — the movie with the sensory experiences — and the physiological responses, such as perception,

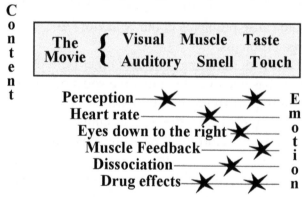

Figure 4-1 Content and Emotion Memory

heart rate, and so forth. Although emotions are assembled as collages in the Emotion System, I believe that both positive and negative emotion collages usually associate with the physiological activity of a memory. The reason for this is that treatment changes the physiology and the association of emotions without changing the movie. After treatment, the content of the movie can be remembered without a physiological or emotional experience.

The stars in Figure 4-1, which are attached to the remembered physiological activity, serve to indicate where the emotions in a memory are believed to associate. Because memories of experience remain intact after treatment, I assume that the movie or sensory aspect of the memory is usually structurally separate from the emotions that associate with the memory structure. A memory structure, then, consists of all three parts: the movie, the physiological responses, and the associated emotions.

When a person dies, it appears that the person's Personal Field remains available in the universe. This field changes from a living soul, with a Personal Field, to a dead soul, with a Personal Field, and, obviously, no physical body. All the information in the Personal Field is preserved. My experience with intruding souls suggests that these souls appear self-organized and function like our living Personal Fields. I developed this opinion by talking to intruding souls entrained to my patients and from reviewing the ghost and haunting literature. The only emotions and behaviors available for fields to cause disturbances in a living body arise from the emotions and behaviors in the memories of the entrained soul. Because there is no body, the only condition in the soul that appears to lead to entrainment and synchronization is the shared positive or negative emotions and common behavior in the soul's field and in the field of the living person (see Figure 4-2). Synchronization occurs when similar information in the person's Personal Field and the intruding soul operates at the same time.

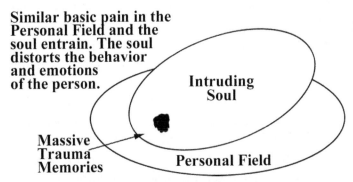

Similar basic pain in the Personal Field and the soul entrain. The soul distorts the behavior and emotions of the person.

Intruding Soul

Massive Trauma Memories

Personal Field

**Figure 4-2 An Intruding Soul
in the Personal Field**

As described in Chapter 2, emotions associated with a memory structure serve to motivate the response defined by the collage of memories associated with the structure. The more intense the emotions associated with a memory structure, the more likely the response will occur. When a soul entrains to a person, it is entraining to the painful emotions of trauma memory structures that are present in the person's 5th dimension. In stressful situations, when trauma-based emotions are active in the living person, the emotions of the intruding soul, related to that trauma, activate or trigger additional emotions in the person. These emotions intensify the trauma-based emotions. Therefore, any response in the person with which the soul's emotions are associated causes an increase in the intensity of motivation for the response, and the response is more likely to happen and with more intensity.

In the simplest case, when an intruding soul associates to a living Personal Field, the basic pain of trauma in the soul entrains and synchronizes with matching basic pain in the Personal Field. Again, only the emotions and behaviors of the soul, which are entrained to and synchronized with the emotions in the person, influence the person's Personal Field to cause problems. The emotions brought by the soul add to and further motivate behaviors, both protective and problematic, related to the trauma. In addition, some souls, once entrained, can give verbal, visual, emotional, or somatic intrusions in the person's experience; others can cause behavior or take over the body, or even manipulate the environment to make sounds and move objects.

Experiences typically caused by intruding souls include hearing voices, having odd emotions, and exaggerating problematic behavior. Other more startling examples include strange behaviors, such as the person with the intruding soul being thrown up against a wall, apparently by no one, hearing sounds in an adjoining room, and having unusual experiences in the presence of other people. Another example is of a person with a deck of cards in her hand, which streamed out to the feet of a person ten feet across the room. In another case, a patient was reported by an observer to have been lifted and pushed backward over two rows of pews in a church. These examples have been reported by reputable people, but there is no scientific way to verify or explain these reports. When "science" or scientists cannot explain or verify something like this, they tend to discount these observations as not happening rather than simply recognizing that the experience is "out of the norm."

Treatment with the Process Healing Method

Most therapists don't work with the subconscious or ask the subconscious to help problem-solve to treat trauma issues. The therapies they use usually combine dormant memories and the subconscious as part of the unconscious mind. Hypnotherapists use metaphors in their dialogue to activate old, unconscious memories, so they can deal with those memories consciously or help resolve them with hypnotic interventions.

With some hypnotic methods, therapists communicate with the unconscious by using a hypnotic technique, described by Edelstien, Rossi and Cheek as the 20-question approach, using ideomotor responses of the fingers — index finger as "Yes," thumb as "No," and so forth. These therapists use this approach to communicate with the unconscious in various ways to reveal the cause or circumstance of mental or physical issues for conscious insight and resolution or to orchestrate a hypnotic treatment of the issue.[1]

I use an approach that elaborates on Edelstien's method by removing the subconscious and dormant memories from the unconscious and communicating directly with the subconscious to assist working with and changing problematic memories. In this way, I usually avoid evoking the painful dormant or unconscious memories into the conscious experience and, most importantly, can use the full capabilities of the subconscious.

Before I continue, I am going to give you the essence of the Process Healing Method. The introduction to using ideomotor responses is presented in detail in Appendix I. With the Process Healing Method, there is both an education process and a treatment process.[2] The overall objective is to get all the patient's personality parts onto a Treatment Team. To do this, the therapist explains how the personality develops and how dissociative and compartmentalized parts are created. Then the therapist explains the procedure for treating regular and fragile parts without experiencing pain, followed by an explanation of the mechanics of joining or integrating a part with the Main Personality. After integration, all parts can get more happiness and less pain, while running the body with no conflict. This is the leverage to get parts to join the Treatment Team.

After teaching the patient's subconscious to respond to my questions with finger responses, I establish rapport with all aspects of the personality and convince them all to join the treatment team. I generally refer to the aspects of the personality as personality parts or parts as a matter of convenience because, in addition to compartmentalized parts, other memory structures apparently have language. Once all the parts become members of the treatment team, they are usually willing to give me permission to teach the subconscious how to treat them. Talking to the subconscious is usually easy. Negotiating with parts to get them to join the treatment team and to get permission to teach the subconscious how to treat the patient is a little more difficult, but it can usually be accomplished in a 90-minute session.

Some personality parts have objections to treatment. Communication with a part involves the therapist asking the part questions and waiting for the part to make a finger movement to provide one of a range of responses: "Yes," "No," "I don't know," "I don't want to tell you," and no response — "I'm not talking." The therapist identifies and explains away the objections for treatment and finally gets all parts onto the Treatment Team. This "explaining away" is called **reframing** the objections. When all the members of the Treatment Team give their permission, the therapist teaches the subconscious how to treat trauma memories, beliefs, and other problematic memories.

The next step is to test the treatment process on a phobia to show the personality parts and the patient how it works. Often the patient feels skeptical, and the successful treatment of a phobia will convince the patient and all the parts that the internal healing process carried out by the subconscious is working. The patient feels his or her phobia reduce in intensity as time passes during the treatment, which confirms the effectiveness of the method.

Let's look at the treatment of simple issues without soul attachments. Recall that the Active Experience is a construct containing all active internal and external stimuli and all active memories and emotions in the conscious and unconscious. The constantly changing environment is reflected in the activity of the Active Experience. A slight change in the situation causes a change in content and emotions in the Active Experience. This causes the creation process to create new memory structures, so any behavior is the result of a new memory with a unique memory structure. Ongoing behavior consists of a sequence of active memory structures created in a changing stimulus environment to cause the unfolding behavior. Each memory structure has a collage of triggers to activate emotions and activity in the physiology of the person, leading to the desired response. The memory and response are created at the same time. The response is created to give the person more happiness and less pain. The 10th dimension, operating to maintain coherency, manages the creation of new behavior. In my earlier book, I defined a construct — the Basic Neurostructure — as the neural mechanism for the creation of the new response. I now believe that the Basic Neurostructure is the 10th dimension.

When treating an issue in a quiet therapeutic environment, the stimulation in the Active Experience is low, and there is no issue of maintaining coherency with the environment. The patient is thinking about the issue. This means that the memory is activated in a relatively neutral environment and a new memory structure does not need to be created to accommodate a change in the situation or the condition in the Active Experience. Treatment with sensory stimulation, like tapping, results in changing the trauma structure by replacing the trauma emotions associated with the memory with the current emotions. There is an incoherency between the emotions of the trauma and the current emotions. After the change, the old memory structure is recreated with less associated pain. Then a content or emotion stimulus or the patient's intention again triggers or reactivates the target trauma memory into the quiet Active Experience. With stimulation, such as tapping, eye movement, or a subconscious treatment activity, this learning process causes the neutral or positive emotions in the present situation to gradually replace some of the painful emotions in the old, activated trauma memory structure, which is created again with the same structure and content. With continued treatment, the unchanged trauma memory structure continues to have the associated painful emotions replaced by neutral emotions. As a result, the patient experiences a gradual decrease in pain when thinking about the trauma memory.

Treatment of a trauma issue normally takes place in the Active Experience, where the subconscious and memory structure work together. The pain from a brief interval of time during the trauma is activated in the Active Experience. The pain in this interval is treated. When the pain is treated, the overall pain of the memory structure decreases. The treatment is repeated again and again, treating pain in brief intervals across the remembered trauma experience until the trauma pain is gradually removed. The pain is, therefore, treated a little bit at a time across the duration of the trauma, until none of the pain remains.

Here is the most common problem with intruding souls. When a soul is entrained to the pain of a trauma memory, it causes a barrier to treating the trauma because an active emotion triggered by the intruding soul disorganizes the Active Experience. Here's how it works. When the subconscious activates the trauma in the Personal Field of the patient, the trauma pain of the patient triggers pain in the intruding soul, which triggers additional pain into the patient's Active Experience. The pain triggered by the intruding soul is not involved in the treatment process of the subconscious because the trigger for the pain is in the soul's field. The subconscious is not treating the soul's field. When the emotions of the patient, triggered by the field, are active, they disorganize the Active Experience by creating changing conditions (see Figure 4-3). This causes emotional turmoil in the Active Experience, so it is constantly

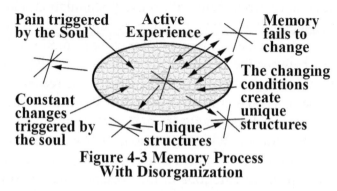

Figure 4-3 Memory Process With Disorganization

changing. The constant change causes the 10th dimension to create a series of new, unique memory structures during the treatment process. However, the patient's memory structure associated with the trauma pain is not changed. The subconscious cannot treat the emotions in the Active Experience caused by the intruding soul because the cause of the disruptive emotions is in the field of the intruding soul and not in the Personal Field of the patient.

After the subconscious learns about entrained souls and the proper ways to treat them, the subconscious can usually treat intruding souls without the therapist's support. After treating the soul, the emotions that blocked the treatment process are no longer triggered. The Active Experience is quiet, and treatment continues successfully. When barriers arise from intruding souls, treating them is generally a routine intervention after you learn the techniques to address the belief or structural complexities of intruding souls. This chapter will explain these techniques in detail.

Treating souls requires that you have contact with the patient's subconscious, or contact with your subconscious, if you wish to treat yourself. Otherwise, there is no way to communicate with the souls. If you want to treat intruding souls in yourself or others, read Appendix I. There you will be shown the steps to make contact with your subconscious. In addition, it helps to have rapport with all parts of your personality, so you will have cooperation to support treating parts and field (soul) barriers. With practice, treatment will become easier and may even become automatic for the subconscious. At that point, as you will learn in Chapter 6, your subconscious can teach your patient's subconscious all the problem-solving techniques and information needed to treat soul intrusions.

Intervention in Action: Identifying and Removing Intruding Fields

I don't think about treating intruding souls in a patient unless I find a barrier while trying to treat some memory structure. Before asking about souls, I ask the subconscious several questions about possible memory structures that could cause the barrier. When I am satisfied a memory does not cause the barrier, I ask the subconscious if a field is causing the barrier to treating the memory. I refer to souls as fields when working with patients.

In practice, I ask questions and use the patient's finger movements to communicate with his or her subconscious. I encourage patients to stay conscious and remember everything I say. In some cases, people stay conscious, remember everything I say, go home, and work with their subconscious quite effectively. Others feel that they have to go into a light trance or a deeper trance just to feel like they aren't consciously causing or influencing the responses. When they do this, they don't necessarily remember anything, but their finger responses still work well.

Below, I provide transcripts of actual interventions with patients. Read the script as if you are the therapist. The following key identifies statements during the sessions:

T: **A statement or question by the therapist.**
S: **The response by the subconscious.**
P: **The response by the patient.**

When you're talking to the subconscious, you always have to stay on your toes for responses that are incongruent with your expectations.

Some other memory structure or an intruding soul may be giving the response. Frequently, patients feel that they may be influencing the responses, but as long as the responses seem to lead to a successful treatment of issues, I feel that communication with the subconscious is undistorted. When the response doesn't fit the question, the patient's previous treatment, life history, or my intuition, then I ask one of the following questions: "Am I talking to the true subconscious?" "Am I talking to a part?" "Is this a pre-birth part?" or "Is this a field barrier?" Invariably I get a "Yes" to one of these questions.

If I'm trying to do an intervention and communication stops, I can ask, "Is this a part who wants to be treated?" When I get a "Yes," then I treat the part and go back to what I was doing. With a "No," I ask more questions to resolve this barrier to communication. If it is a soul, I treat the soul.

With some people, I can clear the field barrier without explaining what I did and continue treating the issue. After clearing the field, I ask if they felt a "swoosh" or an energy movement anywhere in their body. A surprising number of patients feel this energy shift. Then I usually ask them if they want to know what I did.

Explaining the Intervention to a Patient

When the person wants an explanation of the treatment of intruding souls or the hidden reality, here is what I say:

T: **Let me explain about intruding fields. Quantum theory says that dimensional fields in the hidden reality create our 3D-Reality. Well, we have a Personal Field in the hidden reality that starts at conception and records all of our experience — from conception until now.** (I say this while drawing something similar to Figure 4-4.) **We live in our 3D-Reality and cannot see our Personal Field because it is in the 5th dimension in the hidden reality. In fact, we can't see most of the 11 dimensions.**

The 3rd, 6th and 7th dimensions make up the structures in our 3D-Reality as we see it. All we do is bump into the structures or see photons bouncing off or emanating from the structures in the hidden reality.[3] Now, behavior and activity in our 3D-Reality are a result of changes in the 11 hidden dimensions. Our 3D-Reality reflects these new changes. This all happens more than several hundred thousand times a second, as we

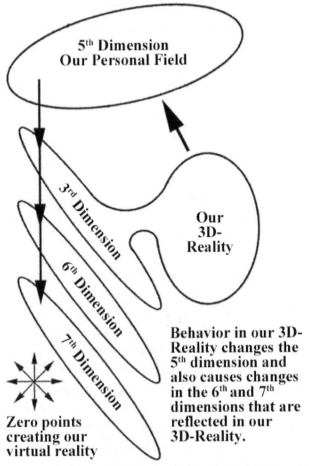

5th Dimension
Our Personal Field

3rd Dimension

6th Dimension

7th Dimension

Our 3D-Reality

Zero points creating our virtual reality

Behavior in our 3D-Reality changes the 5th dimension and also causes changes in the 6th and 7th dimensions that are reflected in our 3D-Reality.

Figure 4-4 Description of Our 3D-Reality

experience 3D-Reality unfolding.

I assume that our Personal Field is located in the 5th dimension. Our soul includes the 5th through 9th dimensions, but for our purposes here, the 5th dimension is the most important one. The field representation of all our experiences in the 5th dimension is what I call the Personal Field. It contains all of our experiences from conception until now.

I then describe the evidence for our Personal Field in the following way:

T: **Evidence suggesting the existence of our Personal Field in the 5th dimension in the hidden reality comes from an experiment carried out by the U.S. Government. In this experiment, they took a sample of cells from a subject's mouth and made a solution with them. They took the cell solution 50 miles away and prepared to record the electrical changes in the solution. They showed the subject television clips of many violent and nonviolent scenes. The electrical changes in the cell solution reflected the emotional changes in the subject caused by the** violent and nonviolent scenes. This I take as evidence for the person's emotional responses in his Personal Field traveling through space in the 5th dimension in some way to cause the reactions in his or her gum cells 50 miles away.

　　Do you now understand how we all have a Personal Field?
S: [Nods.]

　　I continue by explaining how intense emotions can lead to entraining fields:

T: **When a person dies, their Personal Field in the 5th dimension is part of his or her soul. The Personal Fields of all humans from the beginning of humankind are available in the 5th dimension. The soul or field of someone from the present or past can associate with our Personal Field. If we have trauma structures, we can have intruding fields. Fields with an emotional pattern in their trauma structures similar to the emotional pattern in our trauma structures can associate to our Personal Field.**

**　　The intense emotions associated with their trauma structures are the "glue" that enables a field to entrain. The emotions of the entrained field will increase the motivation of all the behaviors related to our trauma memories — the cause for our unwanted behaviors. The example I like to use is that of alcoholics. Sometimes alcoholics say, "I can have one drink and I am okay, but if I have two drinks, it is as if something comes over me and I have to drink everything in sight." Indeed, something did come over them. An intruding field associated with their Personal Field may have become active and literally drove (motivated) them to drink. Some fields can even create intruding behaviors like thoughts or comments or, in severe cases, take over and run the body. Usually, one can treat intruding fields easily because they want what we all want, which is more happiness and less pain. As disruptive as fields can be, I treat them with respect, because they had a hard past life. Do you have any questions?**

　　Usually after this explanation, there are no questions or objections to the notion of intruding souls or fields.

Identifying Field Intrusions

I am now going to describe the general strategy for identifying field intrusions. Intruding fields are either simple or complex. Some Personal Fields can have intruding fields from previous generations entrained to them. Simple fields are intruding souls that either do not have intruding fields entrained to them or have some fields entrained to them that want treatment. Complex intruding fields can have many generations of intruding fields, stacked like poker chips, which are either simple or complex. Invariably, some of these fields don't want treatment. Complex intruding fields are more difficult to treat.

I start thinking about the possibility of fields entrained to a patient when I run into a treatment barrier, and the subconscious is unable to treat the barrier or the issue. Other times, a symptom suggests a field because of the way a symptom is experienced by the patient. An example is when a patient describes a shift in his or her internal state that seems strange, unusual, intangible, or spirit-like, by saying something like "It just sort of moves in," "It just comes over me," or "I had a strange feeling when I was standing in that grassy field." When a patient describes an experience like this, I think that a field might be the cause.

Sometimes it is hard to distinguish between personality parts and fields. Parts get riled when you call them fields. I usually ask if it is a part first because parts are more likely to be present. If it's not a part, I ask if it is a field. If it is, I treat the field.

Here is how I treat an intruding field.

T: **Subconscious, can I talk to the field?**
S: **Yes.**
T: **Thank you for talking with me. You come from another lifetime and are still carrying the emotional pain from that lifetime. The subconscious can smooth out the emotional pain in your Personal Field, and then you can slide off into everlasting happiness. Would you like the subconscious to treat you?**
S: **Yes.**
T: **Subconscious, please treat this field and help this field slide off into everlasting happiness.**
S: **Yes.**

The patient may feel a shift in energy in some part of his or her body.

Contacting and Treating a Simple Intruding Field

Simply asking the subconscious if there is a field or field barrier present is often all that is necessary to discover whether a field is present. I try to be sensitive when treating someone, because both fields and parts can become upset when you identify them by the wrong name. When I think there is a field issue, I ask:

T: **Subconscious, is there a field present?**
or
T: **Subconscious, is this barrier caused by a field?**

With a "Yes" response, I say:

T: **Can I talk to the field?**
S: **Yes.**

Let me remind you to always treat fields with respect, regardless of their nastiness or troublesome intrusiveness. They had a hard life in their 3D existence and are still having a hard time in their afterlife. Their nastiness can be acknowledged in a positive way as an old survival strategy to handle the difficulty of their former lifetime. They deserve respect, just as anyone deserves respect.

T: **Thank you for talking to me. You came from a previous lifetime and the pattern of emotional pain you learned then is similar to the pattern of emotional pain in this person. That emotional pain you have is old pain, and the subconscious can treat your old pain so you will no longer have any pain and you can slide off into everlasting happiness. Would you like treatment now?**
S: **Yes.**
T: **Subconscious, please smooth out the pain in this field and help him or her** [the field] **to slide off into everlasting happiness.**
S: **Yes.**

At this point, many patients usually feel a "swoosh" or an energy shift in some area of the body. After a few minutes, I usually ask:

T: **Did you feel any energy movement in your body?**
P: **Yes.**

The energy movement is an experience that is not usually felt with any other intervention. This experience provides evidence that the intervention caused a change and supports the reality of intruding fields. Sometimes a patient comments about feeling lighter or more relaxed. When I get a "No," to relieve any self-judgment by the patient, I say:

T: **About half the people feel an energy shift. Others don't feel it. I never do.**

The examples below follow this general pattern. After treating several fields, the subconscious will learn the intervention, and you can then shorten your instructions to the subconscious for treating fields. These shortened interventions are metaphors for the full intervention that the subconscious can use.

Depression Caused by Father's Intruding Field

A patient's father passed away in another country and, though he felt guilty for not seeing his father before he died, the patient felt that he dealt with it well. He grieved and, after a while, his life was back to normal. The patient told me that he and his wife went camping seven months after his father's death at a location where his father used to accompany them. He said that while sitting around the campfire, he started to feel depressed. He had been thinking about his father and how his father was not there to share the camping trip.

Since that trip, he hadn't been able to work and had collected disability for almost three years. He had all the symptoms of depression — sadness, fatigue, confusion, and feeling worthless, helpless, and hopeless. He had trouble sleeping and made two suicide attempts. He was in therapy for two and a half years and went through four programs for depression. He had tried many medications with no success. Then he was referred to me.

During the initial interview, I inquired in more detail about the depression that started at the campfire. He said that he was enjoying the outing, and then a wave of depression swept over him as if something moved into him. I wondered to myself if an intruding field had brought on the depression syndrome. Using the subconscious as an ally, I treated parts that caused guilt for not visiting his father before he died.

I then asked the subconscious if there was a field present and received an ideomotor "Yes" response (a finger movement that has been defined previously). We treated the field causing the depression, other memory structures that supported depression, and additional guilt. By working with the subconscious, we determined that his father's soul had entrained with the patient's Personal Field to cause the depression.

After eight treatment sessions, the patient returned to work on a graduated schedule.

Problem-Solving Complex Soul Intrusions

Personal Fields can entrain to other trauma structures in addition to the basic trauma memory. Figure 4-5 shows the different kinds of trauma structures that can be present in a Personal Field to which fields or souls

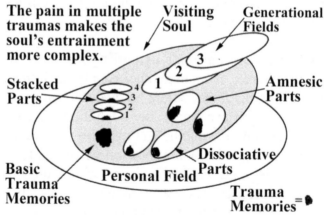

Figure 4-5 Visiting Soul Entrained with Other More Complex Memory Structures

with similar trauma structures can entrain and synchronize. These structures were described in Chapter 2. The various trauma structures include basic trauma, layered memories, dissociative parts, compartmentalized parts, stacked parts, and complex parts. In most cases, field intrusions entrained to these structures can be treated as simple field intrusions. However, the treatment of complex field intrusions becomes slightly more intricate.

Just as a person's Personal Field can have entrained souls, the entrained souls themselves can have entrained souls. I call the souls that are entrained to other souls, **generational fields** (See, 1, 2, and 3 in

Figure 4-5). One could visualize the intruding field as a beer coaster with poker chips stacked on it; the poker chips represent fields from earlier generations intruding on the most recent generation. Generational fields can cause intrusions to the intruding soul or person in the form of beliefs or running dialogues that block the field or person from wanting treatment. For example, with a ritual abuse survivor, the intrusion can be a religious diatribe providing legal reasons why the intruding soul has the right to stay attached to the patient. When the intruding soul itself has generational fields entrained and synchronized with it, they usually block the treatment of the intruding soul. Intruding generational fields can support increased anxiety, addictions, depression, phobias, physical pain, and many other issues, such as fingernail biting, hair pulling, and other behaviors in the patient.

There are other structures to which souls can associate. I have found fields associated to the subconscious, to memory structures in the Heart System, to memory structures in the Emotion System, and to other complex, unique memory structures in the Behavioral System.

In general, the treatment of generational fields is similar to the treatment of intruding fields. They usually present no problem and are easy to treat. Occasionally, when the structure of the generational field is complex, with generational fields of their own, one has to problem-solve to discover the best way to treat them. Actually, after I problem-solved and successfully treated several complex structures of generational fields, I found that my subconscious could instruct the patient's subconscious how to problem-solve and treat them. The treatment of complex fields then became relatively easy.

Sometimes a field refuses treatment. The usual cause is that he or she came from a person who was in constant pain in a previous lifetime and learned to choose to have the pain to reduce the intensity of ongoing pain. This is similar to when a runner is in a race and his or her stomach or legs start hurting. He or she can consciously choose to have that pain, and the pain goes away or reduces. In the same way, the life experience of the field taught the intruding field to believe it had to choose to have pain, so it could experience less pain. Fields with this history worry about having more pain after treatment. A simple reframe resolves this issue.

The basic strategy for treating a field is to show respect to the intruding field, to acknowledge how painful life must have been, and to educate the field about the source of his or her pain. Then I stress that his or her pain is old pain and that the subconscious can treat and remove the pain, so the pain is no longer experienced. Other barriers to treatment expressed by intruding souls are that they would die or would lose their knowledge, wisdom, and understanding of life — in other words, their history. In this case, I just remind them that they are already dead and that their soul will continue to have all their history but without the pain that they had during their lifetime.

Here is an example of the problem-solving that led me to include stacked parts (review p. 39) as one of the possible trauma structures to which intruding souls can entrain.

The patient came to me with a chronic pain in his neck. He said that he'd had it for many years. No doctor could find anything wrong, and he was at the end of his rope. After teaching the subconscious how to treat using the Process Healing Method, I problem-solved, searching for some novel structure that caused his sore neck. I didn't find one. I then asked his subconscious leading questions and found the cause was an intruding field. We tried treating the field and were unsuccessful. He felt the field leave his torso and move up over his head but then snap back into his body. I consulted with a colleague who found these fields left "footprints" as they left the Personal Field and would "follow" these footprints back into the body. This metaphor fit with what the patient had described. We tried another intervention that included removing the footprints as the field was treated. This intervention appeared to work, as his neck pain was greatly reduced.

I treated another patient who had a sore neck and found a field. I changed the intervention to have the field collect the footprints and put them in plastic bags as it left. This worked. Finally, I had the insight that the memory structure causing this particular footprint barrier was caused by stacked parts in both the patient's field and the intruding field. This new understanding fit with my theory. Since then, with several patients, I've simply asked the subconscious to smooth out the pain in the stacked parts and other structures in the intruding field, and the field quickly slipped off into everlasting happiness. This is an example of how metaphors for the same structure or issue work in treatment.

Case Histories of Treating Simple and Complex Field Structures

Below I describe a range of case histories that involve treating both simple and complex field structures.

1. Treating Simple Intruding Fields

Usually, treating an intruding field is straightforward. Again, the need to explore for intruding fields arises when there is a barrier to treating some known simple or complex memory structure or when an emotion, sensation, or thought is described that can't be explained by a memory structure. One can be alerted by the way the person describes the onset of the issue. Here is how to treat simple field barriers:

T: **Subconscious, is there a field barrier?**
S: **Yes.**
T: **Please treat the field barrier.**
S: **Yes.**

This is a brief metaphor for the whole intervention. I assume the subconscious provides the reframes presented earlier to explain the pain of the soul and the treatment process when necessary.

This next example assumes that a person's subconscious has learned the method and the reframes necessary for treating a field. When you find generational fields presenting a barrier to treating a field, the treatment only gets a little more complex.

T: **Subconscious, is there a field barrier?**
S: **Yes.**
T: **Please treat the field barrier.**
S: **No.**
T: **Are there generational fields present?**
S: **Yes.**

Note that I ask as if there is more than one generational field present. This is my first try to treat the generational field(s). I assume that it will be straightforward. I believe that this intervention uses my subconscious knowledge of the possible structures in complex generational fields and communicates with the patient's subconscious to show him or her the way to treat them.

T: **Subconscious, please treat the generational fields from the bottom up or the top down and then treat the field.**
S: **Yes.**

When the field structure is more complex or involves uncooperative generational fields, this treatment does not work. I sometimes ask if the treatment is finished or if a barrier remains.

T: Are you finished?
S: Yes.

Usually, this intervention works. If it doesn't, I problem-solve to identify the generational field causing the barrier to treatment. Occasionally, I have to identify a novel structure of generational fields. In this case, I analyze the structure and then treat it by offering treatment suggestions and follow the directions of the subconscious. With uncooperative generational fields, I reframe any considerations blocking treatment until they want to be treated. This will be covered in detail in the examples below.

2. Treating a Trauma with an Entrained Personal Field

I was treating a young woman who had been attacked and had managed to fight off the attacker. The episode terrified her, causing disturbing flashbacks and nightmares. She sought therapy to stop these intrusions.

T: **Subconscious, do you see the trauma structure causing intrusions of the memories of this physical attack?**
S: **Yes.**
T: **Can you treat the structure and do a Massive Change History and everything?**

The "Massive Change History and everything" is an intervention requested of the subconscious to treat all memories associated with the pain related to the initial trauma from the time of the trauma to the present time.

S: **No.**
T: **Is this a complex memory structure?**
S: **No.**
T: **Is there a field present?**
S: **Yes.**

T: **Can I talk to the field?**
S: **Yes.**

Sometimes I explore to find the source of the intruding field. I guessed and asked the following question.

T: **Are you the field of the perpetrator?**
S: **Yes.**

Apparently, the emotional structures of the perpetrator were similar to the emotional structures of the victim and allowed some portion of his Personal Field to entrain to the victim. (This is similar to what happens in torture settings. The fields entrained to a perpetrator or aspects of his or her own Personal Field can entrain to the Personal Field of the victim during the torture experience.)

T: **Would you like all of your emotional pain smoothed out so you can slide off and leave this young woman and return to your Personal Field?**
S: **Yes.**

I can then ask the subconscious to treat the field directly. Because I had previously shared my treatment wisdom with the patient, her subconscious will know all the reframes to convince the field to accept treatment.

T: **Subconscious, please treat this field and help him leave this young woman and slide off and return to his Personal Field.**
S: **Yes.**
T: **Please treat the trauma structure and do a Massive Change History and everything.**
S: **Yes.**

This treatment eliminated the trauma intrusions. Further therapy allowed her to comfortably confront the perpetrator, which gave her a feeling of empowerment. In most cases, confronting the perpetrator has to be carefully thought out. Usually, it is neither safe nor worthwhile.

3. Treating a Spider Phobia

I am presenting a previously described case in more detail. I had just finished teaching the Process Healing Method to a twelve-year-old child and was demonstrating the treatment process by treating her spider phobia. I asked her to imagine a tarantula on my knee to get a starting measure of her fear. It was a ten (high). I then asked the subconscious to treat the pain causing the phobia. The measure of pain got stuck at five. She had three parts that blocked the treatment. I treated the first part easily. I could not treat the second part, because a field had entrained to it.

Over half of the field barriers a therapist finds are as easy to treat as this example shows. Here is the transcript of the part of the session in which I problem-solved to discover and treat a field.

T: **Subconscious, is it safe to treat the spider phobia?**
S: **Yes.**
T: **On a scale of zero to ten, where ten is very scary, if I had a tarantula on my knee, how high is your fear when you imagine that spider?**
P: **Ten.**
T: **Subconscious, please treat the phobia.**
S: **Yes.**
T: [Waits.] **Do you feel the fear coming down?**
P: **Yes.**
T: [Waits.] **What level is the fear, now?**
P: **About a five.**
T: [Waits.] **Subconscious, are you still treating?**
S: **No.**
T: **Is there a barrier?**
S: **Yes.**

While problem-solving by guessing, I discovered that three compartmentalized parts were blocking treatment.

T: **Subconscious, do those parts want treatment?**
S: **Yes.**
T: **Can you treat the first part and do a Massive Change History and everything?**
S: **Yes.**

T: **Can you treat the second part and do a Massive Change History and everything?**
S: **No.**
T: **Is this a structured memory of some kind?**
S: **No.**
T: **Is there a field creating a barrier?**
S: **Yes.**
T: **Please treat the field and then treat the part.**
S: **Yes.**

The patient was unaware that I treated the field of an intruding soul. I completed the treatment of the remaining part and the fear of spiders decreased to about two. The patient went home and carried a daddy longlegs spider out of the house that evening without fear. (She and her mother appreciatively refer to me as Dr. Spiderman.)

4. Treating a Dissociative Experience

The patient complained of feeling "woo woo," which she described as a dissociated feeling when she was working on a computer. She felt like she was "seeing through a fog."

T: **Subconscious, is this a trauma-based condition?**
S: **Yes.**
T: **Subconscious, are there field barriers?**
S: **Yes.**

My experience with this patient was that she had many fields entrained to memory structures, so I directly asked about field barriers. (If you work with the subconscious for a while, you will learn to follow your intuition. It is as if you are receiving a cue, because the patient's subconscious is talking to your subconscious.)

T: **Subconscious, please clear the fields.**
S: **Yes.**
T: **Please treat the trauma that causes the "woo woo" and do a Massive Change History and everything.**
S: **Yes.**

The patient reported she no longer dissociated when she worked on a computer.

Notice I used the patient's words to describe her experience. The use of the words "woo woo" triggered the trauma memories associated with the "woo woo" experience she described. The active memories could then be treated.

5. Treating a Personality Shift Following an Abortion

Previously, the patient was fairly outgoing and had many friends with whom she socialized regularly. Following an abortion, she found that she tended to isolate herself and saw herself as antisocial.

Usually, great sensitivity is important when dealing with an issue of this type. Although treating this issue worked out smoothly, I might have been more sensitive. From previous case experience, I suspected that I had to work with the field of the fetus to fully treat the intense emotions following the abortion. I had already been using the Process Healing Method to treat many of her abortion-related issues. I started to treat the lingering soul of the fetus directly by asking the following:

T: **Subconscious, is the soul of the fetus still present?**
S: **Yes.**

I took a different tack on this treatment, because the intruding soul of the fetus was connected to the mother. I present this example to show an alternative way to treat a soul. In this case, I felt it important to use an intervention that would be healthy for the mother and the intruding soul. I did not want to do a fast-track, structured, field-removal intervention that is usually possible with fields.

T: **Subconscious, if Ann gives love to the fetus' soul and expresses her regret for not carrying the fetus to full term, will the fetus be willing to receive treatment and slide off Ann's Personal Field?**
S: **No.**
T: **Do we have to clear some memories first?**
S: **Yes.**

I problem-solved by making some intuitive guesses and making up the following two interventions to clear possible memory structures that might have been connected to the abortion experience. If they didn't work, I would have continued problem-solving.

T: **Subconscious, please treat the structure of beliefs, layered memories, and other memories associated with the abortion experience.**
S: **Yes.**

I noticed my intervention was not complete. I looked at my notes. By error, I forgot about possible problems in the Heart System and Emotion System, so I continued. I offered this intervention.

T: **Subconscious, please treat any trauma memories in the Heart and Emotion Systems that were caused by the abortion experience.**
S: **Yes.**

I asked the patient to experience her heartfelt regret for the abortion and her love for the fetus to whom she denied life and then made the following intervention.

T: **Ann, by your giving love and regret, the fetus may be able to receive treatment and slide off your Personal Field to find everlasting happiness. Can you give love to the fetus' soul and express your regret at not carrying the fetus to full term?**
S: **Yes.**

Ann said she could do this and felt that she could experience a clear, heart-felt expression of regret.

T: **Subconscious, please treat the field of the fetus, so he or she can slide off to everlasting happiness.**
S: **Yes.**
T: [Waits.] **Has the field of the fetus left and have we finished with the treatment?**
S: **Yes.**

This patient felt tingling in her chest and arms as the field of the fetus departed from her body. She said that she felt that a weight had been lifted off her shoulders and felt more at peace with the abortion.

I have recently read that an unborn twin — a twin who died *in utero* — can cause subtle mental issues. The field of the fetus of an unborn twin who died *in utero* can give symptoms of varying degrees of severity, such as depression, suicidal thoughts, ongoing grief, and food issues. Unless there are physical complications with the mother suggesting an unborn twin, one can never be sure that an unborn twin is the source of or contributor to a problem. The possibility of an unborn twin can be a vague, intuitive knowing of the patient.[4] It is believed that 12 to 15 percent of all births involve the death of a twin *in utero*.[5] By simply asking the subconscious, the presence of the field of an unborn twin can be discovered.

6. Treating a Field Who Refuses Treatment

There are fields who don't want treatment. These fields have had continuing, intense pain in their previous lifetime and chose to have pain in order to experience less pain. This is like choosing to have pain by biting your finger to reduce the pain of a bee sting on your big toe. Usually a simple reframe will help the field want treatment.

I contacted the field and explained how the subconscious could treat the field. Then I asked:

T: **Would you like to be treated and slide off into everlasting happiness?**
S: **No.**
T: **Did you have continuing intense pain or torture in your lifetime?**
S: **Yes.**
T: **Did you choose to have the pain to make it less painful and now believe that you have pain to have less pain?**
S: **Yes.**

I used the following reframe that is similar to the reframe I use for parts choosing to have pain in living people. It always works unless there are other barriers.

T: **Well, you learned that old pain in your previous lifetime many years ago. What is possible is that the subconscious can smooth**

out all that pain in your field so you no longer have to choose to
have it. Then, you can slide off into everlasting happiness.
**Would you like the subconscious to treat your pain now, so you
can slide off into everlasting happiness?**
S: **Yes.**

Treatment of an intruding field with this kind of barrier is usually straightforward. Sometimes there are generational fields entrained
to these fields that need treatment first. Such treatment will be discussed
in the next section.

7. Request for Treatment by Means of a Dream
The patient commented that he had had a dream since the last
session and described the dream as a conversation with his grandparents
about pain. With the dream came a feeling of being cold. We both
thought that a field might have been present and possibly caused the
cold feeling with the dream. I always reframe unusual events like this in
the positive and then wonder if a field wants treatment.

T: **Subconscious, did a field come with that dream?**
S: **Yes.**
T: **Was that dream a request for treatment?**
S: **Yes.**

A few more questions revealed that his subconscious arranged
for the dream to bring the field experience to our attention.

T: **Can I talk to the field?**
S: **Yes.**
T: **Do you want treatment?**
S: **Yes.**
T: **Subconscious, please treat this field.**
S: **Yes.**

This is an example of how easy treating intruding fields can be.
In this case, more fields wanted treatment. After each treatment, the
patient felt a tingling sensation as the field departed.

All field intrusions are not easy to treat. In the next chapter, we learn more about complex field structures that involve the entrainment of structures of fields that have been assembled over generations.

Chapter 5

Complex Field Structures

Introduction

A complex field structure is basically an intruding field with a number of generational fields stacked on it. What makes some field structures difficult to treat is that some of the fields of the stack can have one or more unique, complex field structures entrained to them. Let's start out with the basic complex field structure.

The basic complex field structure is shown in Figure 5-1. An intruding field (A) attached to the pain (black circle) in the person's

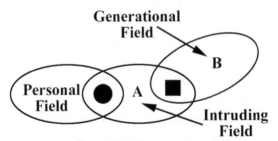

Figure 5-1 The Generational Field

Personal Field. But the field (A) is more complex because another field (B) entrained to other pain in intruding field (A) (black square) when the field (A) was living, I call field (B) a generational field to distinguish it from the field (A) intruding on the person. The treatment of a few generational fields is straightforward, direct, and usually works.

The complex structure of generational fields usually involves a structure that appears like stacked memories but consists of stacked generational fields. Each of these stacked generational fields can have their own generational fields that serve to block their treatment. Initially, I had to know the entire structure of the generational fields of a complex field intrusion to find the correct order of treatment. In other words, I had to problem-solve to identify, first, the specific structure of the stacked generational fields and then the generational fields entrained to each of stacked fields, before I could treat the field entrained to the memory structure. Now, with added experience, I can successfully treat generational fields without knowing the complete structure.

Here is an example of a complex field.

A Complex Field Structure Created by Generational Torture

Ritual abuse and mind control involve extreme physical, sexual, electrical, and drug-induced torture.[1] Survivors of torture, therefore, have many memory structures that have extreme emotional and physical pain associated with them. Since some cultures have a history of conducting ceremonial torture for thousands of years, it is not surprising to find that survivors of torture have many complex intruding fields associated with their memories. Springmeier and Wheeler note that the perpetrators of torture are aware of these complex generational fields.[2] The perpetrators know they are useful, because they prevent naïve therapists from tampering with the compartmentalized parts they have created in their victims. Usually the field intrusions found in survivors of ritual abuse and mind control are complex field structures acquired over generations and need in-depth problem-solving.

The following interesting example appeared to be a simple field intrusion. While the intervention appeared simple, the additional complexity of the treatment could have been handled by hidden communication between the patient's subconscious and my subconscious, or it could have been treated by my subconscious through surrogate treatment. I have since found a more efficient means of treating structures in torture survivors, which is described in Chapter 8. Recommended safeguards are also included.

This field had one generational structure that provided compelling, verbal intrusions of a legal-religious argument justifying her entrainment to the person. This is an example of what I found when I tried to treat her trauma structure.

T: **Subconscious, please treat this trauma.**
S: **No.**
T: **Is there a field barrier?**
S: **Yes.**
T: **Can I talk to the field?**
S: **Yes.**
T: **Would you like to have your painful emotions treated and then slide off into everlasting happiness?**

S: [The field responding.] **No. You are not going to get rid of me. I have a legal right to be here based on the authority of Lucifer. Go to Hell.**

This is the essence of a long, angry, legal-religious diatribe that justified his or her presence and blocked my attempts at removing the field. I wondered if this was a generational field.

T: **Do you have generational fields entrained with you?**
S: **Yes.**
T: **Is the generational field giving you these comments to prevent you from getting treatment?**
S: **Yes.**
T: **Can I talk to the generational field?**
S: **Yes.**

I treat these fields with respect and compose a reframe — a reinterpretation of their experience to the positive — based on what I think they experienced when they were learning the intrusive material. In other words, I make up the intervention and see if it will work.

T: **I understand that you are a highly motivated field, but the extreme torture that you experienced in a lifetime many generations ago caused this motivation. In one of your lifetimes, you learned this legal-religious argument justifying your presence under the threat of severe punishment. If you didn't give this argument, you would start feeling the remembered pain of the torture. Although that pain happened many generations ago, the pain is still present in your field. The patient's subconscious can remove this pain by smoothing it out so you will no longer have pain. Then the legal-religious argument will no longer occur and you can slide off into everlasting happiness. Would you like to have your pain removed and slide off into everlasting happiness?**
S: **Yes.**
T: **Subconscious, please treat this generational field and help him or her slide off into everlasting happiness. Then treat the field.**
S: **Yes.**

Note that I first treated the generational field before treating the field entrained to the victim.

T: **Please treat the part and then do a Massive Change History and everything.**
S: **Yes.**

This part was one of many that were treated in this difficult patient. Treatment continued with one less compartmentalized part blocking treatment or adding intrusions in the patient's experience.

Complex, Structured Field Intrusions

Two or more generations of inherited field intrusions create what I call a complex, structured field intrusion. In this example, I will show you how these structures form. The following example is of a complex structure formed over five generations. A living individual identified as "A" (see Figure 5-2a) experienced pain and fear in a severe trauma represented by the black square. Field B was attracted and entrained to this pain pattern because of a similar pattern of pain and fear in his or her field. The intrusion of B increases A's motivation for problematic behaviors based on the trauma pain and causes barriers when treating the trauma memory.

When the survivor A dies, the intruding field (B) remains entrained to the emotional structure in A's soul (Personal Field). Intruding field B is then a generational field entrained on the field or soul of A.

If the field A entrains to the emotions of a trauma memory (black circle) in another living torture survivor's Personal Field C (see Figure 5-2b), Field A carries generational field B with it (A & B). In addition, another field D entrained to the same emotion pattern in C. In general, more than one field can entrain to the same emotion pattern. In a later generation, this field C with his or her history of entrained fields can entrain to yet another victim of torture E (see Figure 5-2c). Figure 5-2d shows the complex field structure E entraining to a new survivor F in a later generation. A different trauma emotion pattern in F attracts another generational field G (see Figure 5-2d). In a later generation, the field F finds an attractive trauma emotion pattern in torture survivor H and entrains with it. Another moderately complex intruding field I also

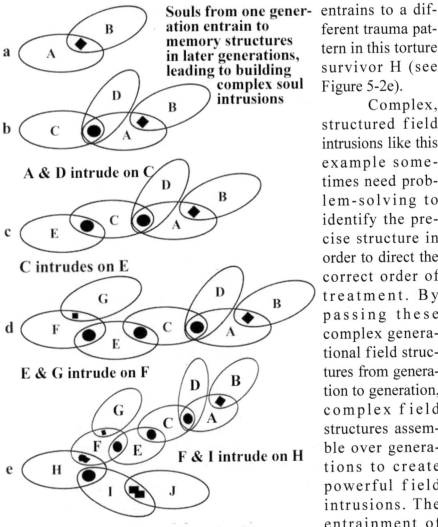

Souls from one generation entrain to memory structures in later generations, leading to building complex soul intrusions

A & D intrude on C

C intrudes on E

E & G intrude on F

F & I intrude on H

Figure 5-2 Formation of Complex Structures

entrains to a different trauma pattern in this torture survivor H (see Figure 5-2e).

Complex, structured field intrusions like this example sometimes need problem-solving to identify the precise structure in order to direct the correct order of treatment. By passing these complex generational field structures from generation to generation, complex field structures assemble over generations to create powerful field intrusions. The entrainment of these complex field structures to a compartmentalized part can serve as a complex barrier to block treatment. According to Springmeier (1996), it takes three generations of torture of ritual abuse victims to create field structures with generational fields to effectively block therapists from treating compartmentalized parts.

The following example will teach you how to problem-solve and treat complex structures. The script gives the problem-solving approach in detail to help you understand it and know how to problem-solve on your own. This example shows a structure that consists of stacked generational fields. When you feel confused and can't resolve the structure of the generational fields, always look for a more unusual structure. I have found that fields can entrain to multiple memory structures, organs, or to other people at the same time to increase the potential complexity of the complex field structures.

A Part with a Complex Field Barrier

The patient had an extremely traumatic childhood and several long-lasting physically and emotionally abusive relationships that resulted in a complex Dissociative Identity Disorder. She also had contact with people involved with ritual abuse. During her upbringing, she learned to create compartmentalized parts easily with little provocation.[3]

A strong, intelligent, protective compartmentalized part, viewed by the Main Personality as "mean," developed to protect her from aggressors and unsafe people. This protective part was successful functioning normally doing professional activities — a good businesswoman. The Main Personality was a sweet, loving woman who was close to God, from whom she gathered strength and guidance. A third major part was a delightful young child part who easily conversed with "Daddy" (Jesus) and who helped direct the course of treatment.

After treating many parts for over 23 months, the protective ("mean") and little girl parts were apparently the only remaining parts. Although both parts wanted to join with the Main Personality, I had trouble treating them for many sessions. As it turned out, the protective part had a complex field structure. Finally, the subconscious told me (by means of the patient's inner dialogue) "there was movement in the Active Experience caused by a field." This was the clue that provoked me to ask if there was a field barrier blocking the treatment of these parts.

Here is how treatment progressed:

T: **Subconscious, is there a field present causing the barrier?**
S: **Yes.**
T: **Please treat the field.**

I always try the direct approach first.

S: **I don't want to be treated.**
T: **Subconscious, is this the field responding?**
S: **Yes.**

T: **Please treat this field.**
S: **Yes.**
T: [Waits.] **Are you busy treating?**
S: [No answer]

I wasn't making any progress with the fast intervention. Therefore, thinking that this was a simple field, I presented the usual reframe by explaining the field's history and pain.

T: **Subconscious, please treat the field.**
S: **Yes.**
T: [Waits.] **Subconscious, are you treating?**
S: **No.**
T: **Are there generational fields?**
S: **Yes.**
T: **Please treat the generational fields from the bottom up or the top down and then treat the field.**

I had always used this intervention with stacked parts and tried it here with the stacked generational fields. This was before I had problem-solved a few of the structures of complex field intrusions.

S: **Yes.**
T: [Waits.] **Subconscious, was the field treated?**
S: **No.**
T: **Are the generational fields in an unusual structure?**
S: **Yes.**

You are about to read a lengthy question and answer sequence with the patient that revealed the structure of her generational fields (see Figure 5-3, next page) and how I treated them. The example shows you how to problem-solve complex structures.

First, I'll give a summary of the entire intervention. Initially, I asked if there were generational fields stacked on one another. The response confirmed that there were and with further questions, I found four fields (B through E) entrained or stacked on top of each other on top of the base field (A). I call these stacked fields rather than entrained fields because it is an easy visual metaphor for the structures.

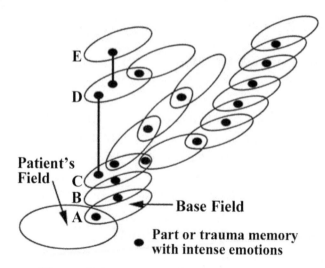

E

D

Patient's
Field

C

B

A

Base Field

Part or trauma memory
with intense emotions

Figure 5-3 A Part with a Complex Field

I tried to treat them from the top down or the bottom up. This often works. It didn't work this time, and I approached the top field (E), offered a reframe, and the subconscious treated it. I found the next field (D) to have a generational field entrained with it. The subconscious cleared the generational field and then treated the field.

The third field (C) was more complex. I found two generational fields entrained with two different traumas. I went through a similar question sequence for stacked fields and found three generational fields stacked on one trauma and seven generational fields stacked on another trauma. I was able to treat both of these stacked generational fields from the top down and the entrained field (C) with no complications. Treating the remaining generational field (B) and the base field (A) was done in the usual way. Finally, the subconscious treated the little girl part, followed by a Massive Change History and everything.

Here is the problem-solving strategy that led to the solution of treating this complex generational field structure. I just ask a question and honor a "Yes" or a "No" to confirm or reject the question — it's like the "20 Questions" game. When I am treating someone, I don't take time to write down what I do word for word. I do draw a diagram of the complex structures of fields, so I can keep track of the evolving structure. A graphic representation of the complex structure is often useful during treatment. Figure 5-3 is an example of the picture I drew as I treated this barrier.

The following example of problem-solving shows what I did with the patient over the telephone. She heard the answers in her thoughts and relayed them to me.

T: **Are the generational fields in an unusual structure?**
S: **Yes.**
T: **Are they in a stacked structure?**
S: **Yes.**
T: **Can you treat them from the top down or the bottom up?**
S: **No.**
T: **Do I have to know the structure?**
S: **Yes.**
T: **How many generational fields are stacked in the structure? I'll count.**
S: [When I got to four] **Yes.**

Figure 5-3 shows the stacked structures, b through e stacked on field a.

T: **Are there any generational fields on the top field?** (See Figure 5-3 e)
S: **No.**
T: **Can you treat the fourth stacked field?**
S: **Yes.**
T: **Please treat it.**
S: **Yes.**

The Massive Change History and everything is not necessary when treating fields because the emotions and behaviors that cause disruption in the system are not in the Behavior System or the Personal Field. Their entrainment to the Personal Field, however, allows them to activate emotions, intrusions, and behavior in the Behavior System.

T: **Can we look at the third stacked field now?** (See Figure 5-3 d)
S: **Yes.**
T: **Is there a structure of generational fields on the third stacked field?**
S: **No.**
T: **Does it have a generational field?**
S: **Yes.**

T: **Is that all?**
S: **Yes.**

I was looking for more structures at this level. I try to find all the complex structures at each level before I start treating.

T: **Please treat the generational field and the third stacked field.**
S: **Yes.**
T: [Waits.] **Are we ready to do the second stacked field?** (See Figure 5-3 c)
S: **Yes.**
T: **Is there a generational field on the second stacked field?**
S: **Yes.**
T: **Is it complex?**
S: **Yes.**
T: **Are the generational fields stacked?**
S: **Yes.**
T: **How many generational fields are stacked on the second field? I'll count.**
S: [When I got to three] **Yes.**
T: **Is that the only stacked generational field on the second stacked field?**

I ask this question before I treat the stacked generational fields to be sure that I am not missing anything at this level.

S: **No.**
T: **Is there another complex generational structure?**
S: **Yes.**
T: **Are the generational fields stacked?**
S: **Yes.**
T: **How many generational fields are stacked in this structure? I'll count.**
S: [When I got to seven] **Yes.**
T: **Are any of the seven generational fields complex structures?**
S: **No.**
T: **So, do the generational fields simply stack on one another?**
S: **Yes.**

Sometimes I try to figure out what happened during the trauma that caused an unusual structure. In addition, there could be complex structures entrained with one of the structures in the stacked structures. This would lead to more problem-solving.

T: **Are there any other generational fields entrained to the second stacked field?**
S: **No.**
T: **Are we ready to treat these structures?**
S: **Yes.**
T: **Subconscious, can you treat the stack of three from the top down, then the stack of seven from the top down, and then the second stacked field?**
S: **Yes.**
T: **Please do it.**
S: **Yes.**

I confirm the information I am getting in various ways. I am also alert for misinformation and, when I find it, I redirect the problem-solving to discover the cause and extent of misinformation. I also have to resolve the cause of the misinformation.

T: **Are there any generational fields on the first stacked field?** (See Figure 5-3 b)
S: **No.**
T: **Please treat the first stacked generational field.**
S: **Yes.**
T: **Are there any other generational fields on the entrained field?** (See Figure 5-3 a)
S: **No.**
T: **Please treat the entrained field.**
S: **Yes.**
T: **Now can we treat the part?**
S: **Yes.**

The cute part who had been helping me for months was waiting until the last part was treated. I had a lively, endearing exchange with this little part before joining her with the Main Personality. I thanked her for all the help she gave me, and she thanked me for helping all of them.

T: **Subconscious, please treat this part and do a Massive Change History and everything.**
S: **Yes.**

Another little girl, a "witty" part whom I had never met before, became active and we had fun chatting with each other. She wanted treatment, but a barrier blocked our first try. It turned out that she had a complex generational field structure that was similar to the complex field barrier of the protective part I had just treated.

T: **Subconscious, is this barrier similar to the last complex barrier we treated?**
S: **Yes.**
T: **Can you treat this complex structure just as we did the last one?**

This is an example of the subconscious repeating problem-solving and treatment strategies from a previous intervention.

S: **Yes.**
T: **Please treat the complex generational field structure, the field, and the part, and then do a Massive Change History and everything.**

I have often found that as I learn procedures and tricks for treating difficult complex memory structures or fields, the subconscious can use the procedures independently. With the subconscious treating independently, it removes the tedium of going through the treatment procedures repeatedly. After these little girl parts and the protective part were treated, I believed that the patient was fully integrated.

In truth, you never know if you have fully integrated a patient because of the possibility of dormant parts, who can activate later, or of being fooled by the last part you just treated. Additional therapy with this patient was occasionally necessary to help with issues that arose in her life experience.

Unusual Field Intrusions

Fields can entrain in other unusual ways. These unusual intrusions are not common and, in my experience, are only found in the most severely traumatized people. Occasionally, I find fields associated with other simple or complex memory structures in the Behavior System. I have seen fields entrained with parts or memory structures in the Heart System, the Emotion System, Memories I, II and III, in structures in tandem memories and ego states, and even in different organs in the body. Usually, once identified, these unusual field entrainments are easy to treat. Sometimes fields entrain with more than one structure, and I need to do some problem-solving to understand the connections before I can treat them. In practice, I seldom find these unusual examples.

I have also found aspects of the personal field of a living person to connect to another person. In a problematic case, the field connection allowed the aspect of the other person to influence my patient. In this case, the mother had verbally abused the patient for over 20 years and the connection between the mother, who was still living, and daughter was so strong that the field activity of the mother appeared to cause barriers or intrusions in the patient. The influence of the mother's field was similar to the influence shown by parts and other fields and, at the time, the possibility of this kind of field influence was unknown to me. It took months to finally discover the source of these problematic intrusions. Treating these kinds of field entrainments involves disconnecting the field from the other person — the mother, in this case — or surrogately treating the trauma and field in the person from whom the field originates.

Below are examples of unusual field intrusions.

1. Field Connected to Several People

A woman telephoned me in crisis. A part was giving her intruding comments and behaviors, disturbing her activities at work. I had had many sessions with her over the telephone. I had good contact with her subconscious and with several strong, helping parts. I immediately started problem-solving, which resulted in the following sequence of questions.

T: **Subconscious, please treat the part.**
S: **No.**
T: **Is it a complex memory structure?**

S: **No.**
T: **Is it a field?**
S: **Yes.**
T: **Can you treat the field?**
S: **No.**
T: **Does it have generational fields?**
S: **No.**
T: [Guessing] **Is it a field connection to the perpetrator?**
S: **Yes.**
T: **Can you treat this field connection?**
S: **No.**

As it turned out, the field, for some reason, had entrained to several others, including her ex-boyfriend, his mother, and the emergency medical technician who raped her. I did not identify everyone or find out how this structure came about because she was at work, and neither she nor I had the time to do this exploratory problem-solving.

T: **Subconscious, please treat and disconnect the field connected to these people.**
S: **Yes.**
T: **Please treat the field, then the part, and then do a Massive Change History and everything.**
S: **Yes.**

This resolved the issue, and she was functioning again after 10 minutes of treatment over the telephone.

2. Working with Multiple Chemical Sensitivities

I was treating a man with severe Multiple Chemical Sensitivity (MCS). He was sensitive to some chemicals that would cause respiratory problems or other allergic reactions. I had not treated MCS before and was systematically treating all the memory structures associated with chemicals, trauma, and other issues. While treating ego states that allegedly caused the man's physical reactions, the subconscious told me that they were not safe to treat because entrained fields protected them. They were not intruding souls from the 5th dimension, but were fields from another source associated with the chemical properties held in memories in the ego states. Allegedly, these fields entrained from the chemicals themselves. In this case, the subconscious was able to easily remove the fields.

T: **Subconscious, please remove all the chemical fields from the ego states.**
S: **Yes.**

The patient felt the process and described his head as stinging. I asked for a Massive Change History and everything and then treated traumas in the ego states.

In another session, I carried out the following intervention, which you will learn about further in Chapter 9.

T: **Subconscious, please contact Wisdom and ask him or her to create an intervention to remove all the memories of problematic chemicals and replace them with peace and love.**

The patient reported a noticeable energy sensation from head to toe, especially in his chest area and head. It was painful, but gradually got better.

Treatment continued for several sessions. In our last session, he thought he was 50 percent treated and was doing much better. Unfortunately, a new rug was installed in my office building, and he was no longer able to come to the office because of his sensitivity to formaldehyde. Therefore, my time with him ended.

3. Entrainment of the Perpetrator's Personal Field

A patient had received demeaning verbal abuse and life-threatening physical abuse from her mother for over 18 years. Although the daughter became successful, she was unable to make and complete plans or "to go forward in life." I worked for almost three years with this patient, treating many unusual barriers that required intense problem-solving. I frequently had no clue as to the source of the barrier, so treatment, in this case, involved identifying the premise for the barrier and the trauma causing the barrier. Later we discovered through problem-solving questions that many of the barriers were created by the trauma experience of an ancestor in a previous generation.

At this point in treatment, we had identified three self-limiting statements from her mother that my patient had internalized. Beliefs or statements learned unconsciously from someone are called introjects. These introjects, which kept perseverating or repeating, effectively stopped my patient from goal setting, planning, and moving forward in her life. She heard, "You'll never change," "You are nobody" and "You'll get worse and worse." We also identified a statement from her father that was internalized and made the perseverating process permanent. He had told her, "You're just as dumb as your mother." As her therapist, identifying these beliefs that were incorporated into her life was the hard part of the intervention. The treatment was easy once the content and structure of the barrier was identified.

It turned out that all the years of verbal and physical abuse created pain-related memory structures that were similar to the pain-related memory structures in the Personal Field of her mother. Her mother, still living, had received similar abuse as she grew up. With similar abuse histories, I believe that her mother's entire Personal Field entrained to my patient's Personal Field and was able to maintain the ongoing beliefs and provide verbal intrusions and self-organized barriers blocking her from going forward. This was treated with a direct request to Wisdom, an intervention that was unknown to me in the preceding sessions. Wisdom is further explained in Chapter 9.

T: **Subconscious, please ask Wisdom to create interventions to remove the damage in the patient caused by her mother's verbal and physical abuse that allows her mother's Personal Field to entrain to her and replace it with peace and love. Please do the same in her mother's Personal Field.**
S: **Yes.**
T: **Please do a Massive Change History and everything.**
S: **Yes.**

Now I had to remove the beliefs that were incorporated by the patient — the four ongoing beliefs that formed the barrier.

T: **Are these introjects in memory elements?**

The patient responded with what she heard. She had intrusions from Wisdom or some source of wisdom that helped with her treatment.

S: **No, it's simpler than that. Make it easier on yourself this time.**
T: **Subconscious, please remove the introjects.**
S: **Yes.**
T: **Please do a Massive Change History and everything.**
S: **Yes.**

Although she is having fewer intrusions and understands the problem better, I haven't successfully treated this patient to date. As it turned out, there were additional barriers blocking my patient from completing plans and going forward in life, which I continue to treat. However, we are being led to many esoteric interventions surprisingly consistent with her life experience. I have used a few of the interventions with other patients and found them to be effective. Some of these interventions will be described in Chapter 10.

When Fields Entrain Easily to Patients

When using the Process Healing Method in anyone with severe trauma histories, one may find the easy-creation of various memory structures. In some patients, an easy-entrainment process works with intruding fields. This makes it hard to clear all the intruding fields because fields entrain as fast as they are treated. It is a losing battle. These patients may also have beliefs that enable fields to entrain. Both of these causes for easy-entrainment of fields have to be treated.

I wondered if there was a process similar to the easy-creation of parts that was operating to cause the easy-entrainment of fields in these patients. I discovered that memories caused by unusual sequences of traumas make people easy targets for intruding fields. The trauma involves a number of structures or systems in the brain. To treat this easy-entrainment process, I had to identify the structures that facilitate easy-entrainment and request the subconscious treat these structures in the appropriate sequence.

After several failed treatment interventions, I was finally able to stop the easy-entrainment of intruding fields. The easy-entrainment of fields is learned when a trauma both damages a complexion of memories routinely used by the 10th dimension in the creation of all responses and also associates emotional pain to memories in Memories I, II, and III. These damaged memory patterns and emotional pain provide a pattern in the person that is common in many fields. This pain pattern in the patient enabled many intruding fields to entrain with the patient. Treating this problem is straightforward.

T: **Subconscious, is there a structure that causes easy-entrainment of fields?**
S: **Yes.**
T: **If we treat the complexion of trauma memories used by the 10th dimension and trauma memories in Memories I, II, and III used for this structure, will that stop the easy-entrainment of fields?**
S: **Yes.**
T: **Please treat the complexion of memories used by the 10th dimension and the trauma memories in Memories I, II, and III used for this structure in the correct order and then do a Massive Change History and everything.**
S: **Yes.**

If I had heard a "No" answer with this intervention, it would give me the opportunity to problem-solve and discover the solution either for treating the structure or for removing the barrier to treating the issue. The solution might involve other fields or involve the Heart, Emotion, Verbal, or Kinesthetic Systems in the structure. The treatment of beliefs that allow fields to entrain can be done with the Wisdom intervention.

I had originally believed that it was a complexion of memories in the Basic Neurostructure that caused the creation of behavior. However, it has become clearer that what I called the Basic Neurostructure was really the activity of the 10th dimension. A more accurate description was that a complexion of memories, which participated in this easy-creation process, was present in the memory systems listed above.

Souls Can Cause Scary Events

Another category of intruding souls is that of precocious souls, who can be scary. These souls have access to the higher dimensions and can cause physical events with and around the patient. Remember, when working with victims of extreme torture, pay attention to the considerations given in Chapter 8. Work very slowly and assess safety at each step.

I have met only two of these scary souls. These powerful souls are able to alter the basic structure of our universe to perform unusual feats. Hensley[4] describes the experiences of a musician who opened a country and western bar and nightclub in an old slaughterhouse in which, over the years after it was built, there were many severe traumas and brutal killings. At the end of his book (first edition), Hensley has 29 sworn affidavits of sightings of ghostly images, disembodied voices, roaming images, poltergeist-like phenomena, and actual physical attacks by unseen forces. The old slaughterhouse has been cited as one of the "most haunted places in America," and has been featured on several radio and TV shows.

It is well documented by Roll that angry adolescents are often found in the center of poltergeist activity. In general, people with an enormous amount of emotion, pain, or torture can attract souls who can throw them across rooms, over church pews, or against walls, or cause other unusual effects, such as throwing objects around. People with an especially painful history can attract souls that have extra-normal skills. From my clinical experience, it appears that as the pain and torture increases beyond imagination, the person's vulnerability to having these powerful souls intrude increases. Because all ages of people have experienced the movement of objects, and because Roll has found that the weight of moving objects decreases as they get farther away from the adolescent, I assume that intruding souls cause these phenomena. The fields used by intruding souls for moving objects decrease in strength, as the objects are located farther away from the location of the person and the fields.[5]

I met one of these souls while doing telephone therapy and talked to the soul for 20 minutes on two separate sessions. Both were educational talks. I made it clear that the soul did not have to talk with me. In the past, this soul had thrown the patient against a wall, had moved objects, and had caused unusual effects in nonlocal settings, like creating noises in the next room. I was cautious, respectful, and simply tried to have the soul listen to me without putting any demands on her. I gave this potentially dangerous soul, of whom the patient was terrified, as much respect as I would any patient. I explained the etiology of the soul by guessing that the soul had had a chronically painful life and had chosen to have pain. I explained the powers that she had, which involved her ability to manage the 5th, 6[th,] and 7th dimensions to alter gravity and the structure of the universe. I kept the dialogue positive with the intent to have the soul stop the intrusions, because it frightened the patient and was disturbing to others.

In the year following those two conversations, the patient did not mention any more "acting out" behavior of this powerful soul.

Afterlife

Interestingly, if intruding souls can entrain to the living soul and relate with us as we live, then when we die, other dead souls with similar qualities can probably entrain with our soul and relate with us when we are dead. If I am a person who behaves according to the rules of the universe in good ways when living, when I die, dead souls who have similar good qualities will probably associate with me and be pleasant to be with. However, if I am a mean, unscrupulous person in my lifetime, then when I die, mean, unscrupulous souls will entrain with me and I can look forward to spending a miserable time with some difficult souls. This is basically the way Swedenborg described heaven and hell in his writings in the 17th century.[6]

In the next chapter, we'll look at the nonlocal properties of the 11 dimensions, which allows for the surrogate treatment and distant healing of patients.

Chapter 6

Exploring the Properties of the Hidden Reality

The Nonlocal Capacity of the Personal Field
Nonlocality is one of the more exciting properties of our hidden or virtual reality. Nonlocality is a property of the 11 dimensions that allows the dimensional structure of an object to appear to be present everywhere in the universe. This means that a person's Personal Field can be shared with others either locally or at a distance.

Scientific research and clinical case histories have validated nonlocality. We can assume either that the Personal Field is everywhere in the universe at all times or that it can be triggered everywhere in the universe. Nonlocality makes possible the surrogate treatment of patients, which has been shown to work in surprising ways and will be described in some detail in this chapter. In addition, distant healing and prayer, as well as witchcraft and voodoo will be reviewed.

Some theorists believe that everyone's Personal Field is everywhere in the universe at the same time, as in a hologram. A hologram is a field pattern of a picture where every point in the pattern contains everything in the picture. This hologram construct has been extended to the universe to include everything created in the universe from its beginning. Physicist David Bohm has offered the theory that all the fields remain active in a hologram that is pervasive throughout the universe.[1] Pribram and Russ, and Karen DeValois carried out research that supports the theory that the brain operates in a holographic process.[2] I believe that that is true locally, but I think the assumption that the Personal Field is everywhere in the universe is too cumbersome a process for the universe. It is an assumption that is inconsistent with the simple, economical organization noted in our memory, in our behavior, and in biological structures in general.[3] If there are simple, economical approaches to behavior and processes in 3D-Reality, then there must be simple, economical processes in virtual reality.

I suggest that, while everything created from the beginning remains active in the universe, the activity is not pervasive in a hologram extending throughout the universe. Instead, the nonlocal holographic appearance is caused by the rules of the 10th dimension to maintain coherency between all things in the universe. The souls of the living and the dead are present somewhere in the hidden reality until triggered to activate locally or nonlocally by the 10th dimension to maintain this coherency. In other words, when you think of your mother, your mother's Personal Field or soul manifests in your presence.

I assume that the virtual Personal Field of a living or inert object is present locally as a hologram. The Personal Field is a hologram of field activity local to a person. Recall that memories are dormant until actively triggered by some stimulus. I assume that the universe works in the same economical way. The hologram does not extend throughout the universe. All or part of the longitudinal fields representing an object can manifest anywhere in the world when triggered into activity in some location by someone's intention and some representation of the object. The representation — a thought, an icon, a picture, or a lock of hair, for example — triggers the field into our presence in some way that is probably caused by the 10th dimension and the zero point creation process as a means of maintaining coherency. This would be more economical than having the entire history of everything in the universe represented at the same time in every point in the universe.

The assumption made here is that a person's or any object's field is available for creation in all locations in the world but has to be triggered to be active in that location. Therefore, the Personal Field of people can be triggered anywhere in the world by using their name, or some of the content of their life. For example, information in my Personal Field — my name and birth date, activities as a child, my appearance, a favorite book, a piece of clothing, in fact everything with which I've had contact — can be used by someone to intentionally trigger my Personal Field in a distant location. The identifying features of anyone can be used with intention to trigger that person's Personal Field near the person having the intention.

Recall the government experiment with human cells in which the cells responded to the emotions of the donor in another location. Similarly, a nonlocal person's Personal Field, triggered locally, establishes communication with the Personal Field of the nonlocal person. To trigger a person's Personal Field, you use a thought or an artifact that has a direct connection to the person to activate the field of that person into your field presence. Furthermore, by thinking of a geographical location or an image, you bring the field representation of the location or image into your field experience. Receiving the field and discerning information in that field takes some skill that can be inherited or in which a person can be trained.[4]

For example, when I think of Mike, my childhood friend's Personal Field is present in my location. It doesn't matter whether Mike is dead or alive. By simply thinking the stimulus "Mike," a dimensional field representation of Mike — his soul — is triggered into my presence.

It doesn't make any difference which hypothesis about nonlocality you accept when applying the properties of nonlocality in treatment, because the process of nonlocality is a fundamental property of our universe. One of the uses of nonlocal communication is between the therapist and the patient. While using the subconscious to treat my patients' issues, I have noted that the subconscious of a patient can learn to treat spontaneously and independently from his or her conscious activity. In addition, I have observed that the patient often unknowingly transfers the treatment process to family, friends, or coworkers. I believe this transferring process takes place in the Personal Field — the 5th dimension. In the same way, I have been able to transfer my treatment wisdom to my patients, both in my office and at distant locations using the Personal Field. The communication of information to someone in a different location, whether three feet away or several thousand miles away, is nonlocal communication.

This chapter approaches nonlocality initially from the research point of view. I will now review studies of the intentional influence on electrical devices and remote viewing.

Remote Influence on Electrical Devices

Robert Jahn established the Princeton Engineering Anomalies Research Lab in 1979 following an undergraduate project to study the low-level psychokinetic effects on electronic, random event generators. Over the last 25 years and more, Jahn has created a wealth of small-scale, statistically significant results that suggest direct causal relationships between subjects' intention and the distortion of otherwise random results. Other researchers discovered statistical flaws in these results.[5] Responding to these criticisms, Jahn, a scientist with impeccable qualifications redesigned his experiment. He built an apparatus using radioactive material to make random digits, 0 and 1, to see if human thought could change the randomness of the digits. The machine generated random 0s and 1s that the researchers could analyze later after the experiment to find out if the sequence remained random. They found that a person could distort the numbers produced by the machine by willing there to be more or fewer 0s or 1s so they were no longer random. This is called obtaining change by intention.[6]

Furthermore, a person at any distance from the machine could distort the randomness in the same way. Distance did not affect the person's effect on the machine. Because no known electromagnetic field could distort the random production of 0s and 1s, the following conclusion was made by the researchers. By knowing the location of the machine, a nonlocal representation of the machine was present and, by the use of intent, the person unknowingly used a field in a different dimension to distort the field of the nonlocal machine and therefore the randomness of the operation of the machine.[7] This supports the notion that there is a field in some dimension in our hidden reality that can cause these effects and that fields in other locations can be changed by intention.

Remote Viewing

Remote viewing is another form of nonlocal communication. The CIA's Stargate program trained a few people in remote viewing to help gather intelligence. They taught people to view objects remotely and allow sensory information to come through from the subconscious to the conscious mind. Remote viewers are people who can access the hidden reality to get images and other sensory information remotely from another time and place. The program ran for 25 years, until a committee decided remote viewing was not effective and ended the program in 1995. Russell Targ, who has written several books about remote viewing, discounts the ruling of the committee. His work confirms remote viewing as a legitimate area of study and has demonstrated that anyone can learn to do remote viewing. Targ & Katra (2007) have summarized many findings about the characteristics and details of remote viewing and its relationship to our reality.

David Morehouse (1996) writes about the circumstances that caused him to take part in the remote viewing project and about some emotionally moving and interesting experiences he had with remote viewing. His remote viewing skills could be used to view both current situations and situations that had occurred in the past. He describes remote viewing as traveling in what he referred to as "the ether." To view some place or person via "the ether," the researchers used geographical coordinates to approach the specific location of interest. Sometimes remote viewers used names or descriptions of objects as the matter of interest. Morehouse discovered the dangers of remote viewing when the ease of traveling in the ether went out of his control and began happening spontaneously.

People interpret their experiences in terms that fit with their life history and belief systems. For example, I question the notion of traveling in "the ether." I believe that it could be a description of the experience that fit the theory or model of the Stargate project or that that was the way that other remote viewers described their experience. I have noticed this once in my clinical practice. I have treated hundreds of intruding souls, yet only one patient always had to cough as the intruding soul left her field. I never questioned this process, but it was unusual in my experience. I believe that it was a learned response related to the expectations of the other persons who had treated her for intruding souls.

Applied remote viewing is evidence for the capacity of humans to use dimensions in virtual reality in predictable applications. Morehouse cites cases where information was obtained from a location some distance away. Contrary to Morehouse's explanation, I believe discerning or receiving information about the remotely viewed object (the details of a person or place via the coordinates on earth) is possible because cues or stimuli activate the field representation of the object in the presence of the viewer. I believe that stimuli and focused intent will mobilize the 10th dimension and the zero point activity to bring a field representation of the information or image to the remote viewer. Here is how I arrive at this interpretation.

Zero points create photons, which are absorbed immediately in a process that is beyond the scope of this book.[8] I assume that the structure of the universe, including all 11 dimensions, is created and absorbed by the same process, only to be immediately recreated, preserving any information in the dimensions. The creation process, as stated before, occurs in frames like a movie film. All objects in the universe, living and dead, can change form or position. Presenting a change in one frame causes the change to manifest in the next frame. When some experience of the representation of a distant object or location, like an icon or coordinates, is created in the present frame, its presence in the frame serves as a stimulus to trigger a field representation of the object or location in the next frame. By being trained or by natural ability, the remote viewer is then able to discern information from the local field of the distant object or location. The 10th dimension maintains coherence in the representation of the distant object within the perceptions of the viewer. Therefore, I hypothesize that the nonlocal information recreates locally in the perception of the individual, rather than the remote viewer moving to the target in "the ether."

Interestingly, the remote viewers can experience a location and then move around in the location to explore different features of the surrounding area. It is as if the viewers are using the triggers in the remote field in their presence to move around and access related views. Without triggering the remote location with coordinates or an icon of some kind, they cannot do this type of exploration. This is similar to the capacity the subconscious uses when exploring the patient's history in therapy. The subconscious cannot "perceive" the history surrounding a dormant trauma memory unless the trauma memory is triggered into the active experience. Once triggered, the subconscious can explore and identify the basis for the trauma memory and see its influence on the patient's life. It is as if the subconscious is using the same properties of the universe that the remote viewers are trained to use. The subconcious uses the properties in the active memory field as triggers for his or her exploration of the memory and the lifelong effects of the trauma. While the remote viewers record their experiences with drawings of the features they discern, my impression is that a more explicit representation of our history is available to the subconscious.

Evidence to Support Distant Intentionality

There is strong evidence supporting distant intentionality, causing change in a person's experience by intention and distant observation, The strong evidence comes from what is called a meta-analysis of a number of already completed experiments. Meta-analysis is a statistical procedure to determine the probability of obtaining the same outcome of a number of experiments if they were all repeated. Schultz and Braud (2006)[9] did a meta-analysis of 19 well-designed experiments of distant intentionality, which was measured by the changing of the target's electrodermal activity (Galvanic skin response) by a remote influencer. They also did a meta-analysis of 11 well-designed experiments of distant observation. With distant observation, an electrodermal response of the subject is obtained while a remote observer "watches" the person. This is like using a human rather than a random number generator with random 1s and 0s in the experiment described earlier.

By analyzing each of the 30 experiments separately, the experiments of both distant intentionality and observation had mixed outcomes, yet tended to support the possibility of remote influence. Each of these experiments was tested mathematically by obtaining a P value. The P value is the probability (P) of how likely something will occur and is significant or assumed true is when 5 or fewer successes are obtained by chance in 100 tries — or P is equal to or less than .05. On the other hand, the probability (P) that something will occur by chance and is not significant or assumed not true occurs when 6 or more successes are obtained in 100 tries — or P is greater than .05. The conservative level of acceptance for an outcome to be accepted as true is when the probability of the difference from chance is less than 1 in 100 (P < .01). This means that if you replicated an experiment 100 times and the outcomes were all random, there would be only 1 outcome in which the response of the targeted subjects matched the intention of the remote viewers — namely, very unlikely and can be accepted as a true event. The P values for the 30 experiments varied giving mixed outcomes.

The P values for the experiments were converted to another measure of significance (called the Z score) that allowed pooling the experiments into one grand hypothetical study to test the experimental effects. This is called a meta-analysis. When pooling and analyzing the experiments of distant intentionality and distant observation in a meta-analysis of 19 and 11 experimental outcomes, respectively, the results of each of these meta-analyses showed very significant evidence for remote influence on others. The results of the combined 19 experiments in distant intentionality showed that when the experiments are treated as one experiment, the probability of the experimental outcome to happen by chance was 7 in 10,000,000 attempts (P = .0000007). The results in the combined 11 experiments in distant observation showed that if the experiments were treated as one experiment, the probability of the experimental outcome to happen by chance was 54 in 1,000,000 attempts (P = .000054). These meta-analyses definitely confirm that intention can change the electrodermal activity or create an experience of being observed in a remotely located person.

Distant Healing

Benor (2000)[10] reviewed 61 studies of distant healing in which a healer deliberately sent a "healing" to the patient. The healers in the studies were usually professional healers. The healing was offered by intent, wish, meditation, or prayer to a person who was either in the healer's presence or far away. Some of the healers attribute the healing to spiritual agents, and others attribute it to some form of energy mediation — resolving conflicts in the energy field. Benor reviewed and discussed three studies involving physical symptoms of AIDS patients and briefly summarized the results of other studies involving distant healing on back pain, arthritis, recuperation from surgery, hypertension, anxiety, anticipatory nausea in chemotherapy, and self-esteem. A review of all the studies of distant healing on people with physical symptoms showed 12 studies supporting and 10 studies not supporting the effectiveness of distant healing on physical symptoms. These results, therefore, are leaning in the direction of supporting the effectiveness of distant healing of physical symptoms.

In the remaining experiments exploring distant healing effects, significant results were found in studies on physiological measurements on humans (all 7 supporting), on plants (5 supporting, with 2 not supporting), on bacteria (4 supporting) and yeast (all 3 supporting), on single-celled organisms (1 supporting, replication failed), on cells in vitro (all 3 supporting), on DNA (2 supporting), and in studies with animals (all 9 supporting). There seems to be strong evidence that distance healing has effects on a living subject, whether plant or animal.

Refining Research on Distant Healing

Targ (2001) reviewed the research methodology necessary to have an irrefutable research design to study distant healing.[11] Research designs for experiments of distant healing and prayer are very complex because subtle issues can cast doubt on the outcome of the research. Most of the above studies have not met the criteria laid out by Targ. However, I believe that the experiments reviewed, taken as a whole, support nonlocal communication and that a healer can exert influence on a distant person by using intention and some internal experience or dialogue.

I believe that distance healing with prayer or intent must involve an agent in the 9th dimension — assumed to be all positive human behaviors entrained on love — with healers who have the qualities necessary for it to work. Professional healers, spiritual by nature, may have the qualities needed for increasing their effectiveness with distant healing. Distance treatment doesn't necessarily work unless the right qualities of the healer are present. These qualities are love of self, others, and all things; an absence of negative self-talk and behavior; and no doubt or disbelief about the healing power of a higher wisdom. It is more likely to work with a group of individuals focusing on the same individual when the group includes some individuals who may be true "healers," whether they know it or not.

Other Examples of Nonlocality — The Dark Side

Painful emotional memories motivate "evil" behavior in the world. This is true for living beings, and this is true for intruding fields. The positive, loving aspect of this is that an individual's evil responses are avoidance responses, such as drinking, violence, and other self-defeating trauma-based behaviors. The goal of an evil response is to effectively reduce the experience of pain in the person or soul. For the "evil" individual or soul, reducing pain is the positive outcome of these avoidance responses.

Recall that the zero points simply carry any change in the current frame of 3D-Reality to the next frame of creation. The 10th dimension, which has an association with all structures in the universe, maintains coherency by making changes in the current frame of all related objects in 3D-Reality. These changes are created in the next frame by the zero points. The 10th dimension makes these changes in a way that engenders love by creating changes leading to more happiness and less pain. So fields or spirits, who appear to manifest as apparitions,[12] poltergeists,[13] or hauntings,[14] can appear stationary or moving, move objects, make noises, touch people, push people around, create illusions, and so forth, are all motivated and created by a process that is basically engendered by love.

Experiencing these paranormal events as punishing or frightening could be seen as evil that is motivated by extreme pain. Yet, the zero points and the 10th dimension working together are a creation source that engenders an apparent positive or loving process.

Though we can create pain in others by our avoidance behavior in 3D-Reality, no request by a person or soul with pain can be made of a higher wisdom, such as an agent in the 9th dimension, to hurt self or humankind. However, I believe that fields or souls with extreme pain do have access to the 5th through 7th dimensions, which allows them to manipulate emotions, thoughts, objects, and events in the 3D environment.

Witchcraft and Voodoo

Giving others pain in 3D-Reality motivates the people who practice witchcraft and voodoo. They are not able to appeal to the higher wisdom with their evil requests. When they work to harm someone, they meditate intensely on the person and appeal to spirits (fields) with similar traumas to entrain to the target person. They also use tokens — a picture, a lock of hair, a statue, some written material, and so forth — as triggers to activate and intensify the person's Personal Field in their presence. With the target's field present, they harm the person by arranging for the entrainment of fields. They probably use rituals and icons to cause specific souls to intrude. The intrusion of souls results in changes in the target's experience, behavior, and perhaps his or her environment as well.

Witches are persons who allegedly have special powers that can be used for good or evil. Witches who engage in white magic — doing good for someone — would aspire to work in the 9th dimension to cause positive change in people or situations. Nevertheless, witches usually do not have the qualities to work in the 9th dimension, so their effectiveness is restricted to the 5th through 7th dimensions, mainly by entraining fields with the target and in some cases manipulating the environment.

I believe the effectiveness of witchcraft and voodoo has a lot to do with the target person. If the target person has pain structures similar to the witch's and has fearful beliefs that engender field intrusions, the witch's fields can entrain with similar structures in the victim's Personal Field. A trauma-free person who has no fearful beliefs about fields would be hard to harm because there are few or no painful emotion structures to which a field can entrain.

The field entrained with a victim through meditation and intention is either part of the field of the witch or an intruding soul. The entrained field does not become part of the Personal Field of the victim but is simply entrained to some common trauma structure. The entrained field, nevertheless, influences the content in the victim's Personal Field by changing the 5th through 7th dimensions. This changes the emotions and behavior of the victim. When the emotions of the intruding fields are active, they increase the motivation of related avoidance behaviors, such as drinking, violence, suicide, or other self-defeating trauma-based behaviors present in the victim and in the intruding field. Again, the 10th dimension, responding to changes in the Personal Field (5th through 9th dimensions), is engendering love when creating 3D-Reality — specifically, to provide more happiness and to reduce emotional pain. Unfortunately, the behavior motivated by pain in entrained fields leads to problematic avoidance behaviors in the target.

In other cases, some witches can appeal to malevolent fields to get them to entrain to their victim. These entrained malevolent fields can cause significant changes in the target's experience and environment. Allegedly, the defense against attacks by a witch is to send heartfelt love back to him or her; namely, to meditate on the source of the spiritual attack while experiencing heartfelt love. For some, heartfelt love is a warm experience in their chest, like the love experienced for a loved one. This love triggers and entrains with structures in the witch's Personal Field and makes what the witch is doing uncomfortable and leads him or her to stop. This all takes place in the 5th dimension.

Often, the witchcraft cults work in groups to expand their effect. By working in groups, the cults take advantage of the nonlocal property of our reality. In some cults, group members have been tortured to create a particular quality in them. To do this, a person in one of these cults experiences intense abuse or torture. This trauma causes the creation of a compartmentalized part and is done in a way that connects it to a strong, self-protective heart response to the compartmentalized part. This is an experience of something like self-love that is associated with helplessness, hopelessness, and suicidal thoughts, and may be part of the process of moving the victim toward death to avoid the torture. This can be seen as a healthy, protective response in an unhealthy, life-threatening situation. With repeated torture experiences, this self-love part obtains a heightened intensity of self-love or heart response. Many participants in some witchcraft cults report receiving this "training."

When the leaders of the cult want to influence some aspect of reality, these love-trained members assemble into a group and their "love parts" are triggered into activity. All the members in the group intentionally focus on a key cult member locally or in some other location. The love, as well as the torture emotions, entrains with the key member. This key member then uses this entrained field to nonlocally alter someone's reality, as he or she desires, by focusing on the individual and the desired outcome. The outcome usually has to do with power and control over someone or something. This works in the 5th through 7th dimensions to trigger the wanted outcome and requires a lot of work for often less than spectacular results. The outcome is dependent on the intensity of the patterns of the love and trauma structures in the targeted person, and on the effectiveness of the tokens linking the key member to the targeted person. The experience of the key member, when used as a conduit for the heart energy, may be a feeling of being closer to nature or even of having an epiphany of some sort.[15]

Witchcraft and voodoo can use positive objectives consistent with the rules of the 10th dimension. However, even with positive intent, often there is an underlying need for power that taints any good intention, prayer, or meditation. The positive use of witchcraft works with positive intent. It is also possible to involve an agent in the 9th dimension to help to obtain a positive outcome. Again, witches seeking to make an impact on someone or something, whether individually or in a group, must be free of barriers to accessing the agent in the 9th dimension. They must show love for themselves and all living and nonliving things, have an absence of negative behavior and inner dialogue, and have absolute faith in the power of an agent in the 9th dimension. They must seek a goal that is in the best interests of themselves, the target, and humankind. The extent to which the witch falls short of these goals, which may be likely in most cases, is determined by the stated qualities necessary for positive work using an agent in the 9th dimension. The weak presence of the target's Personal Field can also decrease the witch's effectiveness.

Still another example of nonlocal communication is the remote creation of anesthesia.

The Remote Creation of Anesthesia

Mesmer developed a procedure for achieving electromagnetically induced anesthesia — the blocking of sensations and pain — in the early 1800s. Later, in about 1850, James Esdaile, a student of Mesmer, was a doctor who practiced medicine on peasants in India.[16] He researched the procedure, developed by Mesmer, for achieving an anesthetic effect in patients. Anesthesia as we know it, via medicine, was introduced in India in about 1847.

Here is the procedure Esdaile used to induce anesthesia in a person scheduled for an operation. He had the patient sit nude in a straight-backed chair. Then a technician would pass his hands over the patient from head to toe, about three or four inches from the patient's body. After a half an hour or up to many hours of this process, the patient would go into a deep coma. Then a doctor could perform an operation with the patient experiencing no pain. The patient would recover and heal faster than those people whose doctors had used any other available operating procedure. This means of creating a coma and anesthesia appears to have been obtained by manipulating a local electromagnetic field. During his stay in India, Dr. Esdaile allegedly treated 2,000 patients successfully using this procedure.[17]

An invited observer reported that Esdaile stood at the end of the room, 80 feet from the patient, and put the patient into a coma by looking at him and moving his hands in a prescribed way.[18] This suggests that Esdaile was using the nonlocal property of an electromagnetic field to create the coma in a patient from a distance. I believe that the process Esdaile used at a distance was different from the technician's direct use of the electromagnetic field by passing his hand over the patient. The electromagnetic field used by the technician is a field whose strength decreases with distance. Esdaile, I believe, used his Personal Field to affect the nonlocal field of the patient, which was created near him, to put the distant patient into a coma.

A Healing Exercise Using the 9th and 10th Dimensions

Accessing the 9th and 10th dimensions to obtain a change or a favorable outcome in some situation has been done in many different ways. Just as I have used Wisdom and Manager to reference these dimensions, there are scores of metaphors used throughout history that refer to these qualities of our hidden reality. In this example, the followers of Bruno Gröning access the highest dimensions by asking for God's or Bruno's help. This is an example of one group of people who have managed to find the conditions for allegedly creating positive changes in their physical and mental well-being. The following is a description of a community of these people who use a healing exercise to access the hidden reality that is consistent with the ideas expressed in this book. In any case, even though it is only validated by antidotal evidence, it is an interesting practice.

Bruno Gröning was a Christian who facilitated the healing of people with severe medical issues.[19] He credited the healing to the highest power — God. People healed in Bruno's presence, without him knowing anything about their illness or by touching them.

He gave a series of lectures in Germany in 1949. The last lecture resulted in 20,000 people showing up in a small town to hear him speak. Some people's illnesses spontaneously healed, even including some who got up and left stretchers and wheelchairs. Between then and his death 10 years later, he was fighting an injunction forbidding public lectures and healings, lodged by the German government and medical profession. Twenty years after his death, a few close followers started an organization of volunteers called the Circle of Friends.

Now, there are 70,000 members in the Circle of Friends worldwide who ask Bruno to start the "healing stream" at 9 A.M. and 9 P.M. daily. Some members meet in groups either in person or by teleconference, or at occasional large weekend conferences. It appears that as the number of members who congregate and practice the healing exercise increases, the healing stream becomes stronger, and more members experience changes. A Medical Scientific Group in the Circle of Friends with a membership of over 3,000 professionals collects pre- and post-medical reports of successful healings to validate the reported healings by this practice.

The basic home practice to create health and well-being is simple. You sit in a comfortable chair, put your hands on your lap facing up, listen and relax to peaceful music for 10 minutes, and then ask Bruno to start the healing stream to help you be physically and mentally whole. Then say "Thank you" and focus on pleasant thoughts or the sensations you might be feeling in your body. Sometimes symptoms are healed, old symptoms may appear, or current pain may increase, which are believed to be part of a regulation process that leads to healing

In all of Bruno's talks, he stressed that, in daily life, one has to keep free of negative thoughts and behaviors, to love yourself, everything, and God, and to trust and believe in the healing stream that God sends. Curiously, as an example of the unknown qualities of your hidden reality, spontaneous healings *sometimes* occur by practicing this exercise, as mentioned above, by attending an introductory meeting, a group meeting every third week, or by simply viewing his picture. He also stressed that you interpret any illness or physical problem as the regulation process, as Bruno called it.[20]

Some of the features necessary for healing in this exercise may be seen as behaviors based on faith. The key features that accompany the intention to be completely healthy are the following: the active reception and intervention of the healing stream; a lifestyle of healthy thoughts and behaviors; the love of self, others, and all things; and a trust in the creation process. The request must be beneficial to the person and humanity. It is also probable that believing that any illness or physical problem is simply the body "regulating" helps by further eliminating negativity in the person. Interestingly, Groening also asks that you give all your physical and emotional issues to him and forget about them, which further reduces negative thoughts. These key features summarize what I intend to develop below and in the next chapter, which is a model of the hidden reality that calls for these key features as a requirement for change.

Surrogate Treatment

Surrogate treatment is an intervention that uses the nonlocal property of the Personal Field. Surrogate treatment involves a therapist using a treatment intervention on a surrogate person who relates in some way to the patient. The patient can be close or distant and either aware or unaware of the treatment. The treating person may or may not have permission from the patient to treat him or her.

The primary differences between distant healing and surrogate treatment are, firstly, that a surrogate usually knows the patient or has an imagined hologram that represents the patient. This physical, personal connection is a strong trigger for the patient's Personal Field. Secondly, with surrogate treatment, there is a treatment method involved as opposed to intention or prayer alone, which is what distant healing involves. The persons attempting surrogate treatment are trained in some treatment method that seems to operate on the nonlocal Personal Field of the patient. Although there are trained distant healers, I would guess that most distant healers are not trained because the parameters for being an effective distant healer have yet to be established.

I have had five distant healing treatments performed on me and have failed to notice any change. One "healer" prescribed homework that, in my mind, would make it hard to evaluate the cause of any change in my experience — was it the healing or was it the homework? Though I am willing to try distant healing on others, my confidence in any results, positive or negative, is always clouded by not knowing the parameters of the intervention or the complexity of the situation or target person.

A few of my surrogate treatments on patients have obtained positive results. However, I think the jury is still out on both distant healing and surrogate treatment. Although there are certainly examples of significant, positive accomplishments in the literature, some of which I share here, just like conventional medicine, results, for some reason, are not always consistently obtained.

Though the reader may feel skeptical about the next two interventions presented, I believe they nicely demonstrate surrogate treatment. Case vignettes of surrogate treatment using Emotional Freedom Techniques (EFT) show frequent positive outcomes. In addition, the Family Constellation Therapy, which uses surrogates for family members in a group setting, often changes family relationships and on occasion changes the behavior of family members not present at the therapy, as well. The results presented below will help you form your own opinion about the reality of surrogate treatment and whether or not you would like to explore surrogate healing or distant healing.

Case Studies of Surrogate Treatment

Surrogate treatment involves a therapist doing a treatment intervention on a patient who is represented by someone or something — an icon — related in some way to the patient. The surrogate can be a friend of the patient or simply be the treating person. The patient can be near the surrogate or anywhere on the planet. Remember, the difference between surrogate treatment and other strategies for healing is that the therapist uses some viable treatment intervention to obtain the desired treatment goal.

The two methods of surrogate treatment mentioned above are well documented by case studies. The first studies we will look at are examples of surrogate treatment using Emotional Freedom Techniques documented on the EFT website.[21] The second study is of the Family Constellation Therapy described in a published interview with Hellinger that reveals the spiritual aspects of his phenomenological method of doing psychotherapy.[22]

1. Emotional Freedom Techniques

Gary Craig, now retired, has been spreading the word of Emotional Freedom Techniques (EFT) around the world for over 10 years. Therapists around the world found it interesting and effective. A South American researcher found that, in a clinical setting, tapping interventions — Emotional Freedom Techniques and Thought Field Therapy — were documented to get 60 to 65% positive results with 26,000 patients treated in 11 outpatient clinics over a 15-year period.[23] The results should be even better with the general public.

While EFT is a very flexible treatment intervention that can be used for just about everything, the version described here is abbreviated and is not detailed enough to use on a personal basis or as a therapeutic tool. I encourage you not to try to use it but to get the free tutorial for doing EFT found on the web at eftuniverse.com.[24]

Gary Craig shared EFT with the world by doing trainings and by selling introductory CD training disks (13 hours of video and three hours of audio) with permission to duplicate them a hundred times. Now, the three CD packages are available for rent on the eftuniverse website.[25] Also on that website are hundreds of case vignettes for many mental health issues that document the successful use of EFT in many creative and practical ways.

Both professionals and nonprofessionals who are using EFT have reported on the effectiveness of surrogate treatment on people and animals. Surrogate treatment seems to work with both physical problems and emotional issues. The percentage of successful surrogate treatments is unknown, but it is useful to review a number of cases here in which surrogate treatment did appear to work. It is interesting to note that in some of these cases the target person had an issue but did not have the intention to heal his or her issue.

I will now summarize the EFT treatment intervention, review some paradigms used in surrogate treatment, and give several case examples.

EFT is a treatment intervention that works well with distressing, unwanted personal issues. It also works well with contributing factors, called aspects, or beliefs that support the issue. Therefore, what you treat are the issues, aspects, and beliefs related to the issue.

This is an intervention where you tap on various acupressure points on your body.[26] The tapping causes the present neutral to positive emotions to replace the negative emotions associated with the issue. The mechanics of EFT involve activating the field pattern of the issue by stating the issue clearly in an affirmation and having the intention to heal it. I believe that saying the phrase representing the issue at each tapping point maintains the active field pattern of the issue or aspect during the treatment process. Since the specific acupressure points associated with the field memory of the issue can be identified by muscle testing, they appear to be in some way related to the issue. Tapping on the acupressure points disturbs the field memory of the issue and gradually causes the field of the pain associated with issue to be replaced with the field of the current neutral to positive emotions of the patient.

It can be shown that other physical interventions, such as pressing on acupressure points, or unilateral or bilateral physical stimulation, has the same effect as tapping on acupressure points. In other words, experience changes memory. The point here is that given the activation of the field pattern of the issue through intention or a verbal cue, any physical intervention — balance board,[27] singing,[28] counting,[29] chording,[30] tapping,[31] or eye movements[32] — results in a decrease in the pain associated with the issue. Because talk therapy doesn't involve intense, direct physical stimulation of the personal field, the change caused by talk therapy is slower and, perhaps, less complete.

In surrogate treatment, the Personal Field of the patient manifests in the presence of the surrogate. The surrogate's active intention to treat the issue intrudes or activates in the Personal Field of the patient to give the patient, at some level, the intention to treat the issue. While rubbing a sore spot on his or her chest under the collarbone, an affirmation and phrase is said by the surrogate that activates the issue or aspect in the Personal Field of the patient and triggers barriers to treatment. The rubbing sensation under the collarbone is associated with the barriers and learned as a trigger. Later, when tapping on the other points, the barrier in the target's Personal Field is not activated — no rubbing, and the treatment works to create change. The tapping on the acupressure points (EFT) on the surrogate stimulates the acupressure points in the Personal Field of the patient, leading to the treatment and resolution of the patient's issues in the way described — experience changes memory.

Surrogate treatment always involves having the intention to treat someone. Some EFT users obtain permission from the target person and surrogate in a formal way. Here's how it is done. The therapist usually uses muscle testing to determine answers (see p. 9). The therapist asks the surrogate if the target person is willing, able and ready to be served by the surrogate (muscle test), and then asks the person acting as the surrogate if he or she is willing, able and ready to serve the target person (muscle test). With "Yes" to both questions, the surrogate says, "My name is 'target person.'" After treatment, surrogate sessions are ended in a similar fashion by obtaining the willingness to end the surrogate session, followed by the surrogate stating his or her name. Other EFT users assume they have permission and don't ask for permission. Surrogate treatment seems to work either way.

My belief is that it is unnecessary to get permission because your intention is usually beneficial for the patient. I assume that the subconscious of the patient can block an intervention if it is unsafe or unwanted. In most cases, compartmentalized parts who don't want treatment can be treated via surrogate treatment. If you try this, it is important to ask your subconscious to ask the patient's subconscious if it is safe to treat the part.

Surrogate treatment with EFT can be carried out in two different ways. First, the surrogate treats him- or herself to treat the patient; second, the therapist treats the surrogate to treat the patient. A different affirmation is said from the usual EFT affirmation. Surrogate treatment using EFT requires the surrogate or therapist to prepare by identifying and clearly stating the target issue and, then, identifying any related aspects or beliefs related to the issue. For each aspect of the issue, the surrogate or therapist forms one or more affirmations. The affirmation consists of stating the issue or aspect followed by a healthy resolution. It is usually stated in the voice of the patient. For example, for a crying infant, "Even though I have to poo, I can remain peaceful, relaxed, and interested in other things." This affirmation states a suspected issue of the crying baby and resolves this issue with one possible, positive outcome. The affirmation involves stating the current state — the issue, aspect, or belief — followed by a resolution to achieve the treatment goal.

Now, the treating person carries out a number of cycles of EFT in his or her imagination, by physically tapping on him- or herself as a surrogate, or on another surrogate person for each aspect and the issue. The issue or aspect is summarized in the affirmation. A short phrase is obtained from the affirmation identifying the aspect and is repeated when tapping on each acupressure point. In the example affirmation, the short phrase was "having to poo." After the affirmation is said, a number of cycles of EFT are completed to treat the issue, using its short phrase with each tapping point. If for some reason the affirmations are determined to be ineffective, one can reanalyze the issue, identify other aspects of the issue, construct new affirmations, and try again.

Some of the examples of successful surrogate treatment of children are given on the eftuniverse website. These examples include children being out of control and screaming in a food court, biting a sibling or playmate, having hiccups, crying or being sick on airplanes, and a crying baby treated by a mother surrogate over the Internet. A story of a boy whose temperament changed markedly from negative to positive because of surrogate treatment is also on the website. There are more than a hundred references on the eftuniverse website of surrogate treatment of children and adults.

Below are some examples of surrogate treatment obtained from the eftuniverse website.

a. Unruly Students in a Time-out[33]

Valerie Padley was a secretary who worked in the main office of a school and was the adult present when unruly children were put in time-out cubicles. The two cubicles in the office were on the same wall as the adjoining principal's office. Some children acted out by screaming or kicking the wall. On three occasions, the secretary went into the principal's office and carried out surrogate EFT on the unruly children on the other side of the wall. Within minutes the children quieted down and, in one case, the child curled up and went to sleep.

Sample affirmations used include: "Even though I am so upset . . . so mad . . . can't stop crying . . . (or whatever fits), I can relax and be comfortable."

b. Preventing Hyperactivity During a School Play[34]

Terry Fischer was a grandmother and had a daughter with three children who lived across the country. The six-year-old granddaughter was in a play and, while attending rehearsals, the grandmother's 15-month-old grandson was hyperactive, noisy, and difficult. On the day of the play, the grandmother, who had had a year's experience with EFT, did surrogate EFT with the boy across the country in 10-minute segments, starting 30 minutes before the play and every half hour from then on. Her daughter reported that she was the only mother with a very young child who did not have to leave the play because of a disruptive child.

Sample affirmations include: "Even though I want to yell and shout and run about, I know Mommy loves me" and "I love sitting against her back or in the stroller" or "I'm calm and content." The grandmother used her intuition to create other variations of the affirmation to fit the issue and aspects.

The eftuniverse website offers many examples of treating physical problems, often to the point of complete recovery. Here is an example of treating a physical problem.

c. Surrogate Treatment of Seizures[35]

A 59-year-old started having seizures, and doctors could not find the cause. Ann Reed, a professional nurse, knew EFT and treated him as a surrogate over the telephone at the time he was experiencing the onset of a seizure. After three cycles with affirmations addressing his physical symptoms, he became relaxed with no symptoms. Then she did a number of cycles of EFT addressing the worries that the seizures caused. She was treating the aspects of the issue. After treatment, the worries were no longer an issue. The results of a later, neurological consultation to determine the cause of the seizures were negative, and the patient has had no further seizure episodes.

Sample affirmations like "Even though my arms and legs are trembling…," "Even though I have no control over my extremities…," "Even though I am afraid these seizures will reoccur…," "Even though the doctors don't know what's wrong…," or "Even though I am afraid of losing my job…" were each followed by a positive description of the desired behavior — "I will…"

Here is an example of using EFT to treat a child who was allegedly attacked by an "entity."

d. Treating an "Entity Within"[36]

Linda Compton, an EFT practitioner, received a telephone call from a grandmother whose grandson had made a marked personality change from being a happy and precocious child to an angry, incommunicative child. The practitioner had seen the child before and, at that time, he appeared to be a typical 12-year-old struggling with family changes. One issue was that he was mad at his sister and occasionally hit her. This time, when the practitioner saw him, the boy described a "madness" coming over him.

When the therapist asked about the madness, a sudden change transpired. The child withdrew, stopped talking, and cocked his head down to the side. The grandmother had reported that, whenever this occurred, the child described his experience as, "Something controls me." Further questions by the therapist failed to produce any more answers. Most of the session involved no communication from the boy, but his actions suggested internal turmoil and a battle for control. He started shouting: "He will play harder," which the therapist interpreted as an "entity" controlling the child.

Eventually, the therapist used the grandmother as a surrogate for the boy. She requested and received permission to do the treatment. Using muscle testing (see p. 9), the therapist assessed a score (0 low, 10 high) for the anger of the boy via the surrogate and found it to be 10. After four EFT cycles with affirmations, the intensity score decreased to 0, and the boy gradually transformed into a happy 12-year-old again. Questions to the surrogate revealed that the "thing" was gone. She ended the surrogacy formally by having the boy tap and say, "I am happy and joyful; I am at peace with myself now."

Sample affirmations include: "Even though I am mad . . .," "Even though I am mad at my sister, dad and mom . . .," and "Even though I am really mad at this thing that thinks it can play harder . . ." They were followed by a positive description of the desired behavior. It appears that the emotional pain in the child and possibly the entity were treated using the EFT intervention.

These vignettes demonstrate the use of the hidden reality in surrogate treatment carried out by individuals using a treatment intervention that significantly increases the likelihood of change in the target person. There are other treatment methods involving two or more participants that show the use of the hidden reality in surrogate treatment. One of the more interesting methods is the Family Constellation Method developed by Burt Hellinger.

2. The Family Constellation Therapy

Bert Hellinger is a therapist who has published more than 30 books in German (some translated into English) on various topics and the Family Constellation Therapy.[37] He simply describes the method as group work, where a group member with a problem — the patient — selects individuals from the group to represent family members. Once selected, the patient physically arranges them in a meaningful relationship to one another. After awhile, the persons selected as family members often start feeling like the persons they represent, without knowing anything about them, and often experience hidden secrets of the family. During therapy with the family group of surrogates, they sometimes show the physical and emotional symptoms of the persons they represent, such as voice changes, headaches, or saying things they don't understand.

In some groups, the therapist carefully orchestrates the interactions between the patient and the "family members." According to Hellinger, in other groups, the patient and surrogates interact to resolve issues, "as if driven by an inner force and then find a solution without any interference." He describes the dynamics of the Family Constellation Therapy and the therapist's interventions as not "self-motivated." Working with patients without fear and without personal intention allows the work of the group members and therapist to be primarily guided, as if driven, by an inner force. Hellinger believes that an unconscious collective conscious, a survival connection formed in prehistoric family groups, guides the treatment and connects all family members.

What makes this possible is that the Personal Fields of the family members come into the presence of the surrogates, causing the surrogates to experience intruding emotions or behaviors, including the thoughts or symptoms of the family members. The patient's presence and intention to change, the naming of the surrogates, the surrogates' intention to help the patient change by offering to be a surrogate for a family member, and the placement of surrogates in a constellation of the family relationships all serve as powerful icons to attract the family members' Personal Fields or souls. Sometime the family's "black sheep," even though not included in the family constellation, becomes involved in the therapy.

As a consequence of the therapy session, "changes" in a surrogate family member can create changes in the family member he or she represented. For example, after a Family Constellation session, a patient found, when she returned home, that her daughter had changed from an oppositional teen to a loving teen. Changing the daughter's Personal Field in the presence of the surrogate family member in the therapy session resulted in finding changes in her at home. The surrogates are not changed in any way other than possibly having valuable insights into their own family from the experience.

It is interesting to wonder what Hellinger's description of "something bigger" means. In this treatment, the patient is present with the Personal Fields of the family members, ancestral fields, the fields of significant others, and with strong intentions by all involved to change. In addition, there is a process in which objective truth and love are shared within the immediate and extended family members. When this is all accomplished in the treatment session, the entrained (collective) subconsciouses of all involved — the common family soul — may participate and orchestrate change for the good of the family constellation.

More Reflections on Distant and Surrogate Treatment

Although there may be trained healers who are very effective at distant healing, I believe that surrogate healing is more effective than distant healing because of two big differences.

The first difference between surrogate and distant healing is that the icon or trigger for accessing the Personal Field of the person being healed is significantly stronger when using the field of a living surrogate instead of material icons to trigger the target's field. Because there is a complexion of icons in the surrogate — memories and images — a stronger representation of the patient's Personal Field is obtained. The other difference is that, in surrogate healing, the healer or therapist is trained in some treatment method that works in standard therapy.

With EFT, the treatment procedure of tapping on the surrogate's acupressure points more reliably causes significant change in the target patient than other healing strategies. The strong presence of the patient's Personal Field enables the tapping treatment with the surrogate to impact in a similar way on the patient's Personal Field. It is as if the surrogate is tapping on the appropriate points in the patient's Personal Field. This is giving the patient experience to cause the resulting change. Other energy psychology techniques and Eye Movement Desensitization and Reprocessing (EMDR) are also viable interventions for surrogate treatment.

With the Family Constellations Method, it is the restructuring of the family system and the resolving of family schisms with objective truth, communicated nonlocally to the patient and other family members' Personal Fields, that make the changes.

With distant healing, a distant healer may have a picture or lock of hair to access the target's Personal Field. The effectiveness of the intervention generated by the healer depends upon his or her ability to access a healing agent in the 9th dimension. It is my belief that many healers do not have significant access to a healing agent because it is so difficult to clear the barriers to meet the criteria for accessing Wisdom. Very few healers, in my opinion, succeed in doing this.

Chapter 7

Interventions Using the Hidden Reality

Introduction

The properties of the personal field allow for several interesting applications of nonlocality to obtain change in patients near and far. The most convenient use of the hidden reality is the transfer of the therapist's treatment methods to a patient via the 5th dimension. Another use of the hidden reality is to use the desired behaviors in the field of another person as a template to clear barriers and strengthen the same behaviors in the patient. One can also use the properties of the personal field to treat allergies and other behavior problems that are inherited via ancestral fields. Finally, an interesting use of nonlocality is in the treatment of torture survivors (Chapter 8). In this case, surrogate fields of the perpetrators created in the presence of the survivor serve to disarm the compartmentalized parts in the programmed structure. The parts become fearful and compliant and are then easy to treat.

The information given in this chapter describes the transfer of information between people. Just by presenting this process, I believe that it is possible for the reader's subconscious to check this out by contacting my Personal Field and downloading my treatment knowledge. If you feel processing in your head as you read this chapter, or any other chapter for that matter, it is possible that your subconscious is busy at work treating some issue.

Talking to a patient over the telephone allows access to the patient's Personal Field and to his or her subconscious by bringing the patient's Personal Field into or near the Personal Field of the therapist. The therapist can then communicate all or some of a treatment method through the Personal Field to the patient. So, in addition to interventions communicated to the patient and his or her subconscious verbally via telephone, when I forget the protocol for an intervention, I frequently ask the patient's subconscious to find the protocol in my Personal Field and use it. This has usually worked. When it doesn't, I problem-solve for barriers blocking the patient's subconscious from accessing my subconscious and treatment knowledge and try the intervention again.

While exploring applications in the hidden reality, I have found that I can use the positive qualities of the Personal Field of a well-functioning friend or acquaintance of the patient as a template to obtain the same positive qualities in the patient. I use the template to first treat incompatible memory structures that block the positive qualities. Then I use the friend's template to introduce and strengthen memory structures — beliefs and behaviors — compatible with the template in the patient, thereby introducing the positive qualities. When the patient doesn't have a friend with the desired goal behaviors, I ask the subconscious to find a safe Personal Field with the desired goal behaviors. The results are often surprising because the intervention appears to work.

The examples below show the Personal Field of the therapist giving information to the patient as if the patient were in the same room. In addition, having the patient's Personal Field in your presence via a telephone call also provides "icons" in the patient to access the Personal Field of the patient's family members or relatives in the patient's ancestral history. This is important for treating issues still being caused by the parents or caused by some trauma that occurred in some past generation in his or her ancestral history.

Three examples will reveal the use of nonlocality in distant treatment using the Process Healing Method.

Giving Your Treatment Wisdom to Others

Giving your treatment wisdom to others can be an effective part of a person's therapy. Treatment wisdom in this case refers to knowledge of the treatment methodology, which involves knowing four things: the possible memory structures, the treatment interventions to treat the various structures, the problem-solving strategies, and the treatments that save time. Also included in the knowledge are treatments that allow the subconscious to carry out interventions independent of the Main Personality. This independence gives the subconscious the capacity and freedom to make positive changes in the recipient without his or her involvement.

Many readers have obtained this treatment wisdom by reading Flint (2006) or by receiving it through therapy or a mentor. When you have this wisdom, you can give your subconscious permission to share it with everyone you meet. My impression is that it is possible for one person's subconscious to have contact with another person's subconscious just in the daily course of life. I haven't ever felt a negative experience when giving away my wisdom and doubt that you will. There seems to be no danger in sharing personal wisdom with others.

Our capability of sharing personal wisdom with others in this way is not surprising. Many years ago the First Nation Elders in gatherings and in individual contacts in the mountains or on the plains used communication through the Personal Field.[1] With them, it was a routine mode of communication when encountering another person. However, most of us no longer have access to these skills, because "modern" civilization taught us not to believe or trust in this intangible means of communicating through the Personal Field.

The following case example will illustrate the quality we all have:

Early in treatment, after describing the Personal Field and the possibility of communicating through it, I determine if the patient has barriers to accepting the offer of my treatment wisdom and the wisdom of my teachers through the Personal Field. If the patient's subconscious indicates that it is okay to receive it, I give my treatment wisdom to him or her before formally teaching the Process Healing Method. When it appears the patient's system has accepted the wisdom, treating a simple phobia tests the transfer of the wisdom. Successfully treating the phobia helps the patient accept the power of the subconscious and builds trust that this unusual treatment method will work. Of course, this is not "proof" that it works, but the patient experiences changes, which validate the treatment. Repeated experiences of rapid treatment results like this among many patients validate the efficacy of the treatment by the therapist. If therapists don't try alternative methods like Emotional Freedom Techniques or the Process Healing Method, they are deprived of learning effective treatment methods.

T: [Speaking to the patient] **Let's try something. My Personal Field has my treatment wisdom. Sometimes it is possible for a person to learn my treatment wisdom just by passing it through our Personal Fields. If your subconscious decides that it is safe and acceptable for you to learn my treatment wisdom, then he or she can learn it from my Personal Field. This makes treatment a lot easier. Would you like to learn my treatment wisdom in**

    this way?
P: **Yes.**

When I get a "No" answer, I skip this approach and continue with the material presented in Chapter 3 in Flint (2006). With a "Yes," I say:

T: **Let your mind go blank or quiet without any thoughts, and when I ask, "Can I talk to your subconscious?" Do you hear a "Yes" response in your thoughts?**

When patients hear a "No" response or have no response, I sometimes repeat this introduction and question a couple of times. To put them at ease, I explain that over fifty percent of people hear a "No" response or have no response, because some aspect of them or active memory prevents the communication by the subconscious.

When patients hear a "Yes" response I continue speaking to the subconscious, assuming that the they, in fact, heard a "Yes" independent from their conscious thoughts.

T: **Subconscious, is it completely safe and acceptable with all aspects or parts of you to learn my treatment wisdom from my Personal Field?**

With a "No" or no response, I start teaching the treatment method in the usual way to educate the parts who have some consideration about receiving the wisdom. With a "Yes," I say the following:

T: **Well, I am offering you my treatment wisdom and the wisdom of my teachers.**

I usually wait for a minute or less for the information to transfer. Sometimes I ask if they feel any sensations during this time. Some people do and others don't. I usually ask the following:

T: **Subconscious, were you able to receive my knowledge?**

With a "No," I continue teaching the treatment method in the usual way. Later, when the subconscious knows the treatment process, I problem-solve and have the subconscious treat the barriers that block his or her accessing my Personal Field. Then I can offer my treatment knowledge and the wisdom of my teachers. With a "Yes," I continue.

To confirm the transfer of treatment information and validate that the subconscious can use the information, I do the following experiment.

T: **Do you have a simple phobia that you can think about that causes an experience of anxiety or fear, a phobia like spiders, rats, or public speaking?**

P: **Yes.** [Identifies a phobia]

T: **Think about the "phobia" and get the fear as intense as you can. Let's score that intensity of fear on a scale where 0 is no fear and 10 is intense fear. Do you have the fear?**

P: **Yes.**

T: **Where do you score the fear of your phobia on the scale of 0 to 10?**

S: **8.**

T: **Now ask your subconscious if it is safe to treat that fear.**

When it is not safe, find another phobia with which to experiment.

P: **Yes.**

T: **Now ask your subconscious to treat the basis for that phobia.**

I wait a few seconds and then ask if he or she can feel the emotions declining. Usually after a few moments, the fear or anxiety declines to a score of 2 or less. This is a convincing demonstration that the treatment wisdom was transferred through the Personal Field and that the patient's subconscious can use the information to treat issues from the inside. I often ask if the patients feel processing in their head and find that they do. Some patients don't feel anything, though the pain of the phobia usually decreases steadily.

At some point, the patient's subconscious will use the wisdom to start other interventions that I routinely do at the beginning of a session, such as treating barriers blocking the subconscious from independently and automatically treating issues. I warn patients that they may feel some sensations in their head or body, which are simply evidence that a treatment process is taking place. I tell them that the treatment sensations can occur at any time, day or night, because the subconscious will learn how to treat problematic issues independently and automatically. I mention that if treatment becomes too intense with a headache, dizziness, or fatigue, they can ask their subconscious to treat slower.

I explain to patients that the subconscious is a personal resource who they can use to make changes in their life. I tell them that everything I say while problem-solving and treating issues can be used by them to say to their subconscious, who will respond appropriately. I point out that it is easy to forget that they have this powerful resource. To try to help the person use these tools, I give treatment aids (see Appendix III) that outline what they will feel during treatment, directions for treating fields and issues, and brief problem-solving suggestions.

Treatment of a Patient in Another Location

The patient had pervasive fear of the unknown. She was afraid in situations where the outcome was unknown, such as when she bought a new cell phone.

Our sessions took place over the telephone. I began by communicating my treatment wisdom to the patient using the nonlocal property of the Personal Field. I frequently use this intervention to convey my wisdom and the wisdom of my teachers to a distant patient. Here is the way I problem-solved and treated the issue using the patient's subconscious, who used the treatment tools I gave to her.

T: **Can I talk to your subconscious?**

The patient feels or hears a "Yes" in her head.

S: **Yes.**
T: **Would it be okay at all levels to give you** (the patient's subconscious) **the treatment wisdom in my Personal Field?**
S: **Yes.**

With a "No" or no response, I teach the treatment process in the usual way, which resolves the barriers to talking with the subconscious.

T: **Subconscious, I am offering my treatment wisdom and the wisdom of my teachers. Please read my Personal Field to obtain my treatment wisdom and the wisdom of my teachers.**
S: **Yes.**

The following intervention is the structure procedure.[2] I frequently use this intervention when doing the Process Healing Method either in person or over the telephone. This is an example; don't worry when you don't understand the treatment intervention.

T: **Subconscious, please ask the patient's subconscious to treat the structure of fear of the unknown in the patient, and when the structure falls apart, tag and treat the memory elements in the correct order in the Active Experience using the Emotion System Procedure. For any treated beliefs, compose positive, self-empowering beliefs to take their place. Then do a Massive Change History and everything.**
S: **Yes.**

I occasionally check to see if the intervention is working.

T: **Subconscious, are you treating now?**
S: **Yes.**

In the first part of this example, I used the nonlocal property to communicate my treatment wisdom to the patient. I know this works because I have given it many times to new patients in my office or over the telephone. Usually, I immediately demonstrate that treatment method was learned and works by having the subconscious treat a simple phobia. The second part of the example demonstrates the use of the structure procedure and of what I call the Emotion System Procedure. I gave the patient my wisdom and, without giving any further details, these procedures in my treatment wisdom were used by the patient's subconscious to treat the issue. I recently found that treating the emotions in both the Active Experience and the emotions in the Emotion System and memories in Memory III associated to emotions in the Emotion System provides a more thorough treatment of the issue.

Surrogate Treatment with Wisdom

Both the patient and his mother lived across the country. The patient's mother was reactive to almost anything the patient said or did, responding always with abusive verbal behavior. The patient couldn't avoid seeing his mother, because he was a support person for her. We treated the mother with the Wisdom intervention to change her behavior. The Wisdom Intervention is explained in the next chapter.

T: **Subconscious** (patient's)**, do you have contact with your mother's subconscious?**
S: **Yes.**

Wisdom is a positive resource in the 9th dimension.

T: **Subconscious, please ask mother's subconscious to ask Wisdom to create interventions to remove the triggers for abusive behavior from all areas of the mother's brain, and to replace them with triggers for positive, self-empowering behaviors.**

This is an example of surrogate intervention using the Wisdom intervention. It is probable that along with the patient's Personal Field being present with the therapist, the entire ancestral history of the patient was present, including the mother's Personal Field. The patient reported that his mother's demeanor softened.

Using Goal Behaviors From Self and Others

Earlier in the chapter, I mentioned the use of templates. I experimented with two different sources for templates. The first was a template obtained from a time in the patient's history that had the desired outcome. The second was using the desired trait from a healthy person's Personal Field as a template for change in my patient. Using behaviors from other people's Personal Fields to introduce and strengthen desired behaviors in my patients is an interesting application of nonlocal communication. I adapted the change history intervention from Neurolinguistic Programming.[3]

When using the change history intervention with a patient's trauma, the subconscious starts treating the effects of the trauma memories from the time the trauma occurred to the present, removing the trauma-related emotions that associated with later memories. The change history intervention is a powerful cleanser of trauma and, when using the Process Healing Method, the Massive Change History procedure is requested after every intervention.

When joining the template idea with the Massive Change History procedure, I do the Massive Change History procedure first with the template used as a pattern to remove any barriers to the desired behaviors represented in the template. I assume that the template triggers memory structures that would present barriers to the desired behaviors. After this is done, the template pattern is used again to identify, introduce, and strengthen the desired behaviors in the patient. In this case, therefore, the Massive Change History procedure first uses the template as a pattern to identify and weaken incompatible behaviors (memories) and then uses the template to introduce or strengthen self-empowering behaviors (memories) from conception up to the time of treatment.

Here are some examples:

1. Using a Memory from the Past to Change Behavior

This example shows the use of a past behavior pattern in the patient as a template to obtain a desired change. Judy, 32, was recovering from alcohol and sexual addiction. She had had a difficult life and allegedly had both dissociative and manic-depressive disorders. A court ordered her to receive therapy. She was motivated and progressed well in therapy. She said that when she was younger, she could tell when she was manic and depressed but could no longer do that. She wanted to recover the ability to identify her moods.

T: **Subconscious, do you remember when Judy was able to notice the mood changes in her manic-depressive disorder?**
S: **Yes.**
T: **Please use that memory as a template to treat any barriers that block her from noticing mood changes and to strengthen behaviors that ensure that she does notice them.**
S: **Yes.**
T: **Please do a Massive Change History and everything.**
S: **Yes.**

The next week Judy reported that she was able to notice changes in her mood states.

You might wonder if the patient was only trying to please the therapist. Some of this might be happening. However, therapy is framed as a problem-solving process. Patients accept this model and are fully willing to report treatment that fails both in the session and between sessions. I always make it known that the symptom could still be untreated in dormant memories and the symptom may reappear in the future. If it does, the patient tells me and we treat it.

2. Borrowing Wanted Behavior from a Friend

In this example, I used the positive trait from the Personal Field of another person to change the behavior of the person with whom I was working. The patient was not outgoing and was uncomfortable in social situations. The desired trait was obtained from a healthy friend of the patient who had an outgoing personality and felt comfortable in social situations. I asked the subconscious to use this positive trait in the friend's Personal Field as a template for the wanted outcome. I always ask if it is safe to use the identified template.

This intervention is similar to the sentence procedure. In that procedure, by saying the sentence "I don't drink anymore," all the pro-drinking behaviors and memory structures are triggered, namely the field patterns causing these behaviors and memories to activate. Then the subconscious tags the triggered memory structures and treats them in the correct order. This reduces the motivation to drink. What happens in the template intervention is that the subconscious uses the template to trigger the field patterns of all memory elements or behaviors incompatible with the goal behaviors, tags them, and then treats them in the correct order.

In therapy, I first used the template with the Massive Change History procedure to treat all memory structures that were incompatible and caused barriers with the pattern of the template — the goal behaviors. Then I repeated the Massive Change History to have the subconscious introduce and strengthen behaviors and other memories in the patient that match the pattern of the template to obtain the goal behavior in social situations. I assessed the outcome in the next session to see if my patient noticed any change in his or her behavior in social situations, and he or she had. Below is an example of the treatment intervention on how to use the field of someone else's positive traits to change an individual's behavior. As with our example above, the goal behavior is to become outgoing and comfortable in social situations. I introduced the concepts underlying this intervention and got the patient's permission to do the intervention.

T: [Asking the patient] **Let's find a person whose Personal Field we can borrow to help you make a change in your behavior. Do you**

know a healthy person who is outgoing and comfortable in
social situations?

P: **Yes, Suzie.**

T: **Subconscious, can you access Suzie's Personal Field and identify
the part of her field that allows Suzie to be outgoing and
comfortable in social situations?**

S: **Yes.**

I suppose one could go through a ritual to get permission to
access Suzie's Personal Field, but just thinking "Suzie" accesses her
Personal Field. In theory, many people access your Personal Field daily
when they think of you. You don't know this and it usually doesn't
bother you or affect your behavior. In this case, accessing and using part
of Suzie's Personal Field as a template will not bother or affect her
behavior.

T: **I want to use that part of Suzie's Personal Field as a template
for change. Can we do that and is it safe to do?**

S: **Yes.**

With this intervention, I always ask if it is safe when I borrow a
template. I want to both protect the lender from any damage and to protect my patient from anything harmful in the lender's Personal Field. If
an intruding soul was entrained to Suzie's Personal Field, there could be
a problem. For this reason, I think it is especially important to ask about
safety when trying this intervention. When I get a "No," I ask the subconscious to find a safe and healthy person with the desired qualities.

T: **Subconscious, please do a Massive Change History and
everything and use that part of Suzie's Personal Field that
causes her to be outgoing and comfortable in social situations
as a template. Treat all memory elements from conception to
now that present barriers to behaviors prescribed by the
template.**

S: **Yes.**

T: [Waits.] **Are you finished?**

S: **Yes.**

T: **Subconscious, please do a Massive Change History and everything,
and use Suzie's Personal Field for outgoing and comfortable social**

behavior as a template to create self-empowering beliefs and behavior and to identify and strengthen all memory structures from conception to now that will provide behaviors for being outgoing and comfortable in social situations.

S: **Yes.**

T: [Waits.] **Are you finished?**

S: **Yes.**

T: **Please do a Massive Change History and everything.**

My patient's husband reported that her social behavior was much more outgoing in the following week and that friends were remarking about her positive change. There was more work to do, but the outcome of this intervention was a big step toward improved functioning.

The Treatment of Allergies

Another good example of a nonlocal intervention is in the treatment of allergies. Before I studied Tapas Acupressure Techniques (TAT), I learned a way to treat allergies by stating the name of the allergen, and then I problem-solved to localize the specific source of the trauma or conditions that created the allergy. However, Tapas developed a different way to locate the source of the allergy, although she has since simplified her treatment of allergies. By using muscle testing (see Figure 1-1, p. 8) and by asking a series of questions, one can identify the situation in which a trauma occurred to cause the allergy.[4] To identify the details about the trauma or the situation in which the allergy started requires asking the subconscious to identify which of the following options is true: the allergy started after birth, *in utero*, or in some century before birth; the particular century (counting back in time to find the century); as a male or female; as an adult or child; and on which of the six continents. This information, I believe, identifies the coordinates for the situation and the person in the ancestral field when the allergy developed. With these coordinates — similar to project Stargate — and information from our personal field, the details of the beginning of the allergy are activated in our Personal Field and can be treated. Even an inherited ancestral field originating some centuries ago can give an allergy to us.

When the allergy is learned in some ancestor's experience, it is passed down from generation to generation and is represented in a parent's Personal Field. This allergy is then transferred to the child's Personal Field at conception. Remember that our Personal Field starts by combining the mother's and father's Personal Fields. When a person is in the presence of the allergen, the allergen activates the ancestral field, which triggers the symptoms of the allergy. By stating the coordinates of the source of the allergy and perhaps with the involvement of the DNA signature of the person, the related soul, who initially acquired the allergy, will activate in the patient's immediate experience. Treating the active allergy field in the soul who acquired it and then treating the allergy in the following ancestral generations will often remove the allergy in the patient.

This allergy treatment, therefore, requires specifying the coordinates for the source of the allergy. I believe the soul at the source of the allergy activates in the local setting because the 10th dimension orchestrates the zero points with the coordinates and the DNA signature to create a representation of the soul in the patient's virtual reality. With the source identified and in the presence of the patient, the allergy can be treated with the TAT technique or by giving an intervention to the subconscious. It is important to remember that there are other sources for allergies, including trauma during this lifetime.

This strategy that worked well to find the source of the allergy was on my mind when I was working with a torture survivor. I wondered if it were possible to trigger a representation of the Personal Field of the perpetrator in the presence of a survivor to facilitate treatment. This is different from having the perpetrator entrained to a survivor's memory because it could cause disturbing emotions or behavior. Chapter 8 presents an experimental procedure to treat torture survivors. While most readers won't try this intervention, the chapter may trigger your curiosity and amazement at the innovative use of the hidden reality.

Chapter 8

Treating Torture Survivors: Using a Nonlocal Intervention

Introduction

Perhaps the most fascinating use of Personal Fields is in treating structured torture survivors who have been exposed to ritual abuse or mind control. It is important to note that this is an experimental intervention that has to be used cautiously because conditions in the therapist or a misstatement during the intervention can cause fields to entrain with the therapist. For those who have doubts about the use of torture for mind control, Google "Mind Control" and you will find many websites that describe various aspects about mind control and structured torture.

Structured torture survivors have many interrelated, complex compartmentalized parts that were created by extreme torture with pain, terror, drugs, shock, and hypnosis. When one or more perpetrators create structured memories in a person using extreme torture, the Personal Fields of the perpetrators apparently associate with or are recognizable to all the memories created during the torture. It turns out that my Personal Field, and others if needed, can safely simulate the perpetrator's field *in the presence of* the patient. With the surrogate field of the perpetrator present, the memories created during the torture become helpless and compliant — fearing punishment — and the patient's subconscious can safely problem-solve and treat the structures caused by torture with little or no problem. Although the intervention would probably work using the perpetrator's field, I thought it safer for the patient's subconscious to use my subconscious to simulate the perpetrator's field.

While I believe that all other interventions in this book are safe, the dangers involved when doing this particular intervention dictate that the procedure for this intervention must be followed precisely. A therapist attempting this intervention will need to know the treatment and problem-solving methods for working with torture patients taught in my book: *A Theory and Treatment of Your Personality: A manual for change* (Flint, 2006). The treatment is a hypnotic and memory-based method that works well with compartmentalized parts.

Caution When Working with Torture Survivors

In most cases, it is safe to work with intruding souls. I have not had any problems and know of no other persons — patients or therapists — who have had problems using this method for treating these usual intruding souls. However, one therapist had problems when working with a torture survivor. It happened when the therapist was working with structures of intruding souls in a patient who had experienced emotional and physical torture. These patients can have very strong intruding souls that are motivated by a history of enormous pain. The therapist's experience suggests that it is possible, when working with extreme trauma survivors, to have intruding souls entrain with a therapist or to trigger the therapist's trauma history. Therefore, I want to make therapists aware of a number of safeguards to take when working with intruding souls in patients with torture history.

I don't believe these safeguards are necessary for everyone, but they are worth considering:

1. It is important that trauma memories in the therapist are treated before treating patients with extreme trauma memories. If one of the interventions described later is not done properly, souls with a similar pain pattern could entrain with the therapist.

2. I believe that a therapist's beliefs could be a basis for souls to entrain with the therapist. However, the beliefs are all relatively easy to change. The belief could involve a "fear that souls could entrain" or simply a "fear about treating intruding souls (demons)." Treat all fear-based beliefs related to intruding souls before working with patients with intense trauma emotions or torture. Treatment involves simply asking the subconscious to treat all beliefs that would enable intruding souls to attach and to replace them with positive, self-empowering beliefs based on peace and love. If you are aware of the beliefs, you can assess the truth of the beliefs, on a scale of 0 to 10 (very true), before and after the intervention by asking the subconscious.

Here is an intervention using the Process Healing Method to remove the beliefs that give the grounds for souls to intrude.

T: **Subconscious, are there beliefs that could enable fields to entrain?**

S: **Yes.**

T: **Subconscious, please treat these beliefs one after the other and replace them with positive, self-empowering beliefs based on peace and love, then do a Massive Change History and everything.**

S: **Yes.**

T: [Waits.] **Subconscious, are all the beliefs treated?**

S: **Yes.**

Sometimes, a part might hold a belief that requires some problem-solving to treat.

3. Working with anyone while in a trance state also provides a basis for soul intrusions. When a therapist is doing face-to-face, remote, or surrogate work — subconscious to subconscious in a trance state — the mental state of the therapist may enable the intrusion of souls. Therefore, I don't recommend therapists work with patients with intense pain and trauma while in a trance state. A trance state is where your experience is more or less disconnected from your environment as you focus on the task at hand.

4. Doing any intervention that brings a potentially harmful intruding soul into your presence or your Personal Field is an invitation for a problematic intrusion. In the intervention for torture survivors, the therapist asks his or her subconscious to create a surrogate field of the perpetrator *near* the Personal Field of the patient. Be sure you get the wording correct — namely, create a surrogate of the perpetrator *near* the Personal Field of the patient. I believe that this is the only intervention in the book that presents a risk.

5. Finally, if you plan to work with someone who has suffered severe torture or trauma, have a colleague or minister familiar with intruding souls available as a consultant. Most likely, you will never need help, but it is good to have a colleague with whom to discuss the case and to be prepared for possible negative outcomes in yourself or the patient.

6. When working with torture survivors, retain a consultant familiar with treating dissociative disorders by contacting the International Society for the Study of Trauma and Dissociation. It is important to have a resource who is well-versed in the treatment of torture survivors.

Overview of the Uses of Torture

Many well-funded organizations around the world, such as paramilitary organizations, the military, and intelligence agencies, systematically torture people to control them.[1] The point of this immoral activity is to create people who can unknowingly become subjects in medical experiments, sexual slaves, couriers of information or drugs, assassins, or participate in other tasks that may be useful for the organization. This has been going on for hundreds of years, but in the last 90 years, both the quality and complexity of structures caused by torture have changed markedly. Techniques to carry out mind control programming with torture have become high tech, using all of our present-day electronic, neurobiological, and psychological technology.

Torture occurs when extreme emotional and physical pain is obtained by causing intense physical, sexual, or emotional damage to the victim. Systematic and repeated torture is used to intentionally create complex structures of compartmentalized parts in a child's or adult's Behavior System. In other words, programmers create many unique, complex compartmentalized parts who will be taught complex instructions, which are activated by triggers to operate and do what they want them to do. The parts are programmed by the instructions. They can run the body and carry out the learned instructions to avoid experiencing the memory of the intense pain of the torture. These are complex avoidance responses. Often the victims are completely unaware that they have these programmed structures. Different programmers create different thematic structures.

Adult survivors of structured torture are people who usually have had one or more perpetrators involved in the torture. These programmers teach them tasks, both useful in a criminal sense and protective of a unique programmed structure, while the subject is in an intense emotional trauma state.[2] Recall the creation of compartmentalized parts. Usually the torturers create compartmentalized parts embedded in a complex, metaphorical structure of memories that involves an elaborate theme, such as a castle, a pyramid, a Disney story, and so forth. The verbal instructions both control the compartmentalized part to have it carry out various tasks and to provide the metaphors and the instructions for roles in a thematic structure.

Each part in the structure has a role in the theme that is embedded in the scripts that the parts learn during the programming. They are structured like a computer game, are complex, and serve as a puzzle to confuse any therapist attempting to treat the structure — something like the Dungeons and Dragons game. These structures are difficult to treat because of their complexity and the intense motivation based on the pain memories that occurred at their creation. They behave as ordered (programmed) and are taught to resist change. The names and features of the metaphorical structures serve as triggers for different pro-grammed parts. When the therapist attempts to treat parts in the system, the parts will often trigger other parts that will block the efforts of the therapist, causing the patient to go "crazy," leave the office, threaten to kill the therapist, or to commit suicide.

Because torture usually begins early in life with extreme pain in unusual circumstances, the complex memory structures of the trauma memories can require skillful problem-solving to treat. In addition, complex fields — intruding souls with generational fields — are attracted to the intense emotion structures associated with the parts cre-ated by deliberate torture. Available complex fields, either triggered from the 5th dimension or from the perpetrator's field, entrain to the newly created trauma memories. These fields become barriers to the treatment of the compartmentalized parts. Most therapists are ignorant of or disbelieve the existence of intruding souls when treating torture survivors. However, in my experience, intruding fields are so prevalent when treating torture survivors that the torture itself is a key indicator to be on the lookout for intruding fields.

Interestingly, therapists who use EMDR may unknowingly treat intruding fields. My first ritual abuse patient who had enormous torture experiences was treated with EMDR without my awareness of intruding fields. I believe that the bilateral movement of the fingers causes activ-ity in the Personal Field, which smoothes out the pain in the fields and they depart. Emotional Freedom Techniques also works to treat intrud-ing fields — recall the surrogate treatment of the entity.

Intruding fields entrained to the patient can be quite powerful when the torture has been very complex and intense. If the therapist does not deal with fields, in most cases, there is no need to worry; how-ever, progress will be slow. If the therapist is treating fields or is using the intervention described below, the therapist should attend to the pre-cautions for treating fields in torture survivors. Most therapists who are skilled in deprogramming learn to identify a structured torture survivor and systematically dismantle memory structures part by part by using their knowledge of the structure, prayer, trance talk, and other therapeutic skills. They continue with this strategy until they fully treat the thematic structure. This can be a time-consuming, painstaking task lasting months or years.

After about 12 years of using the Process Healing Method to do this dismantling of programmed structures, I struck on another way to treat these patients that involves using the properties of the hidden reality. Here's how I figured it out. I had learned to treat allergies by having the patient create the field of the allergen by thinking about the allergen. The thought of it created a representation of the allergen that triggered the allergy response in the Personal Field of the patient. Notice the use of the nonlocal property of our Personal Field. Then I asked the subconscious to treat the memories in the Active Experience triggered by the allergen — the triggered memories that cause the allergy symptoms. When the memories were treated, in some cases the allergy symptoms no longer occurred. This approach was consistent with treating trauma without talking about content and emotions.

With torture survivors, I wondered if I could use part of the allergy approach to disarm all the protective safeguards. I speculated that the presence of the perpetrator's field in the presence of the survivor's field would cause all the compartmentalized parts created by torture to feel powerless and compliant. While they are in this state, the subconscious could systematically treat the structure using the Process Healing strategies for treating torture survivors. To use this intervention you will have to be clever with your treatment interventions or know the treatment of torture survivors indexed in Process Healing Method (Flint 2006). By the time I explore for a torture structure, the patient's subconscious already has my treatment wisdom, which includes the treatment for torture. I deliberately give all my patients this wisdom early in treatment.

It is key to remember that each perpetrator creates a unique thematic structure. The last I heard, one deprogrammer had identified 23 different thematic structures. All perpetrators create compartmentalized parts with unique names. The interrelations between the parts can be different, and the techniques to create the parts can be different. There can be more than one perpetrator creating a thematic structure. In addition, you have to be aware of programmed parts that were taught to protect the structure. When there are multiple programmed thematic structures, the different programmers interconnect these structures to "protect" their resources. The therapist has to be alert for these interconnections, because they serve as barriers to treatment. I once spent a whole session treating a structure caused by torture. At the end of the session, I said a word that triggered a reset-part who reestablished the whole trauma structure. At least that's what I thought. It might have been a backup of the entire structure that was triggered into activity. Needless to say, treating structures caused by torture can be complex and difficult.

Let's summarize here. I have found that when the subconscious of a healthy and safe person creates a surrogate field of the perpetrator *in the presence of the survivor* during treatment, its presence disarms the compartmentalized parts in the structure caused by torture. I believe the presence of the perpetrator's field puts the parts in a state of compliance because of the fear of pending torture. With the presence of the perpetrator's Personal Field and the compliance of the programmed parts, the subconscious can easily problem-solve, using the methods described in Flint (2006), and safely treat the unique complex structure of compartmentalized parts that the perpetrators created in the memories of the victim.

Recognizing Torture Survivors

Here is the way I recognize a programmed patient. The patient may be unaware that he or she was programmed. When doing therapy, I usually problem-solve and treat the problematic memory structures of the presenting issues or target issues that activate in the Active Experience. Occasionally, early in the first treatment session, I recognize signs of a programmed person. Some response of the patient alerts me to the possibility of an underlying metaphorical structure. It may be the family background, the father's vocation, a recognizable auditory or behavioral intrusion, the location where they lived as a child, or a particular phrase used in general conversation. A cue for identifying a structure caused by torture can occur when treating a compartmentalized part.

Here is an example of my first mind-control patient.

I was treating a part with EMDR and was only able to reduce the pain associated to a trauma in the patient to a score of five on a 10-point scale. As I problem-solved, the part I was trying to treat said, "I can't change, I have to have pain." I had been treating this patient for over two years and was surprised by this comment. This was a statement in the script learned by the programmed compartmentalized part. The statement was a barrier to treatment.

The following weekend, at an EMDR conference, a mentor identified the statement as revealing a programmed structure. Months later, the patient told me that in one of our first sessions, two years earlier, she had tried to show me she had programmed structures by revealing a part called "Judge." My ignorance of the various metaphors and names used in structures caused me to miss the cue. Judge is the name of a part in a ritual abuse structure referred to as Greenbaum Programming.[3]

Some patients arrive for therapy knowing that they are programmed. Other patients don't know they are programmed and, infrequently, I am alerted by some cue suggesting a programmed structure. When I am suspicious, here is how I now treat a torture survivor. I ask the subconscious a neutral question to determine if there are some metaphorical programmed structures in the patient. I try to hide my intention so I don't trigger any protective parts programmed in the structure. When I find a structure, I continue with the following intervention. The wording of the intervention is precise and must be given carefully. So when I find evidence that indicates the possibility of a complex structure caused by torture or simply have a hunch, I ask the following question without forewarning and out of context so as not to alert the parts of the structure:

T: **Subconscious, did someone teach you a complex structure for some purpose?**
S: **Yes.**

Notice I didn't use the word "torture" in the question. When I receive a "No," I put this possibility aside and continue treating the patient.

T: **Is there more than one of these complex structures?**
S: **Yes.**

Find out the number of structures by counting up until you get a "Yes" response. When there is more than one of these complex structures, I treat one structure first — the best one as determined by the subconscious. Then I ask the subconscious to use the same steps in the intervention to treat the remaining structures, one after the other, in the correct order. Be careful with the following question. One has to be precise.

T: **Subconscious, if you ask my subconscious to create a Personal Field similar to the Personal Field of the perpetrator who created the structure and placed it** *in the presence* **of the field of the patient, would you be able to treat the complex structure?**

S: **No.**

T: **Is there more than one perpetrator?**

S: **Yes.**

T: **Are there one, two, three . . .**[I count up until I receive a "Yes."]

S: [Three] **Yes.**

T: **If you asked my subconscious and the subconscious of "person a" and "person b" to create the Personal Fields of the three perpetrators** *in the presence* **of the survivor's Personal Field, will you be able to safely treat the structure?** (Person "a" is local. Person "b" is in Idaho.)

S: **Yes.**

It is important to use the wording of these interventions as written. Creating the presence of the perpetrator in the presence of your Personal Field or in your Personal Field could lead to the introjection of a problematic field that could distort your experience of life. Again, it is good to have a spiritual resource, such as a minister or therapist familiar with dissociative disorders and intruding souls, with whom you can consult about these difficult patients and can assist you if you have any problems. With a "No," I would carefully problem-solve.

To continue with this intervention, you have to know about complex structures, problem-solving, and various treatment interventions described in the Process Healing Method. The procedure that might be most important is where I ask the subconscious to copy the memories of the target structure into a safe memory area, only accessible by the subconscious, where the subconscious can safely problem-solve the treatment of the structure. During problem-solving, the subconscious can identify all the pitfalls and develop a safe treatment strategy without triggering parts, barriers, or memory activity into the patient's Active Experience. Once the problem-solving is complete and the subconscious has a safe treatment strategy, he or she can easily treat the entire structure. The treatment takes place in the Active Experience with the presence of the perpetrators' fields near the Personal Field of the patient, thus making the parts in the structure compliant. This simplifies and accelerates treatment of these difficult programmed structures.

T: **Please select the best structure to treat and ask the helping subconsciouses to create the Personal Fields of the perpetrators for this structure *in the presence* of the patient's Personal Field. Then please systematically treat the parts in the programmed structure in the correct order while being aware of all interrelated safeguards, suicidal parts, and reset parts. Do a Massive Change History and everything after each intervention.**
S: **Yes.**

If you get a "No," then I would suspect that the patient's subconscious does not have the skills — the treatment wisdom — or that there is a memory barrier or an intense field blocking the treatment. After the first intervention is done, I make the following request for the subconscious to use the same procedure for the remaining structures.

T: **Please treat all the remaining structures one after the other in the best order using the same treatment procedure.**
S: **Yes.**

I would try this with any non-fragile patient who I thought had one or more of these structures caused by torture. I have been successful with five or six patients, three of whom I treated over the telephone.

In one case, the subconscious believed I was talking about a structure caused by an abusive parent. This intervention did not work for this patient, because the structure was not formed by systematic torture. It was a memory structure in the Main Personality caused by a parent and the structure had a complexion of painful and positive experiences with the parent.

Let's turn now to one of the most conceptually interesting and powerful treatment methods — using Wisdom in treatment. The development of this treatment intervention led to an explanation of the unfolding of reality, the evolution of life and wisdom, and the mechanics of change in the hidden reality.

Chapter 9

The Spiritual Aspect of Treatment: Wisdom

Background and Intent

I discovered Wisdom after exploring many other metaphors to access help in the hidden reality. In earlier chapters, I developed the notion that zero points create our virtual reality, the dimensional activity that we can't see that underlies 3D-Reality. Recall that I assume that zero points are point sources of energy in the vacuum of the universe that create and immediately destroy photons and the dimensional structures many hundreds of thousands of times per second. My thinking evolved to the following: If zero points create the virtual reality that underlies our 3D-Reality, then why not try to directly involve the zero points in the treatment process?

The path to involving zero points directly in treatment appears to open the religious realm by explaining the unfolding of our reality. I am not attempting to undermine or explain away the basis for any religion. To my surprise, this model has led to a decidedly spiritual path that has deeply affected my life and, I might add, the spiritual lives of many of my patients. I hope these concepts will enhance the understanding and acceptance of all religions.

My intent here is to maximize the effectiveness of treatment interventions and to discover if this model of the universe can lead to new and novel interventions. This new direction of exploration led to an explanation of creation, miracles, and how to work with a source of wisdom.

The Development of a Spiritual Aspect in Treatment

My curiosity about maximizing the effectiveness of treatment interventions led to discovering what I initially called the zero point intervention. At that time, I held a different belief about the role of zero points in the creation process than I have now. My first attempt to treat with zero points was to simply create well-formed instructions for the subconscious to give to the zero points to change issues. These instructions had to include an accurate description of the issue or memory structures to be removed from the Personal Field and also had to include what to put in their place. Although creating well-formed instructions for the zero points appeared to work, the interplay between the therapist and the patient's subconscious was time-consuming. Later theoretical development suggested that this zero point intervention did not work as envisioned. The results obtained were an example of an inaccurate metaphor being used by the subconscious to get positive results in spite of my ignorance.

After experimenting with different strategies to use amassed wisdom in the 5th or 9th dimensions, I developed a construct called the 10th dimension, which I later called the Manager. All dimensions are embedded in the 10th dimension. This dimension maintains the coherency of the interactions between all objects in the universe. The 10th dimension also causes the self-organization observed in the 0th through 9th dimensions and makes changes to all related objects after the zero points recreate the dimensions.

I found that it was possible to access a source of wisdom in the 9th dimension who can cause changes in my patients. I called this agent Wisdom. After treatment by Wisdom, the 10th dimension adjusts the changes to obtain coherency within and between other objects. Wisdom — self-organized by the 10th dimension — is a process that experiences, learns, and amasses wisdom in the 9th dimension from souls entrained on love. (The reader can substitute a name that feels more comfortable as a way to refer to this source of wisdom and help.) The resulting Wisdom treatment intervention involving the zero points and the 10th dimension seemed quite powerful.

The Manager and Wisdom, as participants in change, work together to make permanent changes in the patient in our virtual reality and, therefore, in our 3D behavior. The Wisdom causes a positive change in the virtual reality (0th through 9th dimensions) of, say, an individual, and the Manager maintains integrity in the interaction of all related structures — living and inert — that results in positive change for all. It appears as if Wisdom in the 9th dimension, entrained on love, can be used for composing treatment interventions. By having the subconscious ask Wisdom to compose well-formed interventions to change problematic issues, I both saved time and obtained better interventions.

I collaborated with others to explore the limits of the use of virtual reality in treatment for a number of years. We explored the nonlocal property of the Personal Field to find a source of wisdom to help with composing treatment interventions. Recall that the Personal Field includes the 5th through 9th dimensions, but the 5th dimension is the primary memory for our life experiences in 3D-Reality. We started by exploring for wise agents of Wisdom in the Amassed Personal Field (5th dimension). Extending this exploration to its limit brought a more spiritual element into the treatment process, particularly when we looked to the source of wisdom amassed in the 9th dimension. It has been suggested that a Personal Field, living or dead, can operate in the 9th dimension when the person lives a life consistent with the laws of the universe.[1]

This chapter describes our early work with zero points, wise men, Wisdom, and the development of a spiritual aspect in treatment. It also offers interventions to remove barriers of various kinds to working in the hidden reality. The next chapter provides a number of experimental interventions using the Wisdom intervention that are useful in making subtle to significant changes in a person's life.

An Experimental Procedure

When I used the zero point intervention for the first time with a patient, I determined that it was so powerful that I had to be cautious with its use. To my surprise, the next patient's subconscious seemingly read my Personal Field and started using the zero point intervention before I had even taught any of the treatment method to that patient. The patient felt a tingling sensation from head to toe. I should have thought of this possibility, because, quite often, the subconscious starts treating barriers to independent treatment and other memory structures before I ask. It still surprises me when I teach the Process Healing Method to the subconscious and the patient remarks that he or she feels a tingling sensation from head to toe, an experience had only occasionally with the Wisdom intervention. This phenomenon of spontaneous communication between Personal Fields was confirmed by asking the patient's subconscious if he or she was using the Wisdom intervention. The "Yes" confirmed my suspicion. I have repeatedly found evidence like this for communication between Personal Fields.

The patients' experience of the Wisdom intervention is different from how they experience other interventions I use. As Wisdom changes the person's trauma memories, some people feel a tingling from head to toe, but most experience their trauma history passing through their awareness as it processes. In comparison, the Process

Healing intervention carried out by the subconscious causes sensations in the brain and different regions of the body, while the Tapas Acupressure Technique, as I use it, often causes a flooding of obsessive thoughts or images without emotions through the patient's conscious experience. The differences between these three interventions suggest the treatment processes are different, at least as experienced in 3D-Reality.

The Active Ingredients for Change in 3D-Reality

The capacity for the subconscious to work independently with interventions like this has interesting implications. Many of the various interventions that my colleagues and I conjure up while using Process Healing, tapping, or chording treatments might be variations of the same treatment process that is taking place in the virtual reality. I have concluded there are three basic active ingredients in 3D-Reality for such interventions.

The first is that the sensory stimulation approach is used in Brief Multi-Sensory Activation,[2] Eye Movement Desensitization and Reprocessing,[3] Thought Field Therapy,[4] Emotional Freedom Techniques,[5] all forms of talk therapy (works slower), and other sensory stimulation techniques. My learning theory model explains these treatments, described in Flint (1994, 2006). Basically, I argue that sensory stimulation causes a learning process that results in exchanging the painful emotions associated with the target memories for current neutral to positive emotions, thereby reducing the pain associated with the memory. Also, a neurostimulation model shown on the Brief Multi-Sensory Activation website[6] supports the view that any stimulation activates neural receptors in the brain, resulting in change. Both of these models are consistent with Freeman's observation that experience changes memory.[7] In the present model, the trauma experience activates in our Personal Field. Sensory stimulation causes the active field pattern of the target issue to gradually exchange the entrainment of the painful emotional fields in the trauma memory for the current, neutral to positive, emotional fields active in the Personal Field. This process is simple and supports Freeman's observation: Experience changes memory.

The second class of interventions includes all the touching interventions — for example, the Tapas Acupressure Techniques[8] or the Advanced Integrated Therapy.[9] Both of these interventions involve touching acupressure points or other points along the meridian lines of the body. The Tapas Acupressure Technique involves holding a pose with the ring finger and thumb lightly pressing on points on the nose slightly out from the tear ducts and with the middle finger placed between the eyebrows. The other hand cups the back of the head with the thumb at the base of the skull. The Advanced Integrated Therapy approach involves holding pressure on meridian lines (Chakras) successively from the top one down to remove emotions and from the bottom one up to strengthen beliefs. This technique is a theory-rich method dealing with core issues and beliefs. Both of these treatment methods are powerful, stand-alone, comprehensive methods used to treat many mental health issues, allergies, and physical problems.

I hypothesize that the active ingredients of these touching interventions, when combined with intending to heal and thinking about the issue, are the "out-of-phase brainwaves" coming off the fingers that are delayed by having to travel the length of the arm. The out-of-phase brainwaves on the acupressure points or meridian lines lead to neural activity creating disturbances on the synapses of the neural structure of the active issue. This disturbance, like stimulation, changes the issue. The out-of-phase brainwaves provoke a memory change in which the current neutral to positive emotions replace the remembered painful emotions associated with the memory.

In these stimulation models, the stimulation on neural-rich points on the body causes an out-of-phase stimulation of the neurostructures in dimensional activity leading to the brain centers in our Personal Field. A representation of this field phenomenon can be found as neural activity in our 3D-Reality. This stimulation causes the active field pattern of the target issue to gradually shift the entrainment of the traumatic emotional fields to the current, neutral to positive, emotional fields active in the Personal Field. Again, experience changes memory.

Thirdly, in the Wisdom intervention, an agent in the virtual reality is thought to directly act to change a person's Personal Field (5th through 9th dimensions). The desired changes made in our Personal Field by the subconscious or Wisdom, adjusted by the Manager to maintain coherency, are created by the zero points in our virtual reality. The changes are then experienced in our 3D-Reality.

My conclusion is that the all treatments carried out in our 3D-Reality cause changes in our virtual reality. Process Healing, tapping, chording — applying pressure to meridian centers — and Wisdom interventions all change the Personal Field (5th through 9th dimensions).

This change results in some measure of change that is experienced in our 3D-Reality.

Let's look, then, at the zero points as a treatment tool.

Zero Points as an Active Ingredient of Treatment

As an introduction to the use of the zero points as an active ingredient of treatment, I want to review the sequence of events that takes place in our virtual reality when we do something.

Each object in the universe, no matter how big or small, has a unique set of zero points committed to creating the dimensional structures for that object in the virtual reality. For that matter, there are millions of objects in us with unique sets of zero points that make up the human body. The zero points create and destroy all objects hundreds of thousands of times a second while preserving history and information in all the dimensions. Each object is actively represented in our virtual reality in the 0th through 9th dimensions. The activities of all apparent self-organized and inert objects in our environment — including everything that we see and do — involve changes in all the dimensions. These changes occur in the virtual reality of everything in our 3D-Reality.

As I've described before, our world unfolds like a movie, frame by frame. The frames are infinitesimal in size and time. Remember the flipbook described earlier. As the reader flips through the book, the images on successive pages gradually change to create the illusion that the characters are moving and interacting. This is similar to the frame-by-frame unfolding of our 3D-Reality.

Here is how I think it works. The living objects in our virtual reality are more or less independent of each other, with unique histories. Each living object has its own unique memories that are motivated by positive or negative emotions. When a new frame is created, there is emotion associated to many memories in a person that serves as pressure for change in our Personal Field. The memories are motivated and are related to current activity. The 10th dimension uses these motivated memories to make a change in the frame while maintaining coherency within an individual and between all related living and inert objects. The change in all related objects starts with the current state of each object, memories, and motivation, and moves to the next logical state while preserving coherency in all objects. The motivated memories in all living objects are involved in the change. So all related objects experience change to maintain coherency and to find more happiness and less pain, which can be either an assertive or an avoidance response. This is just change happening in the current frame. The zero points create the changes in all related living and inert objects in the next frame. Here is another description of the way this creation process works.

Figure 9-1 shows the unfolding reality. The zero points have just created frame "A" in virtual reality. A change in the frame (A) for some

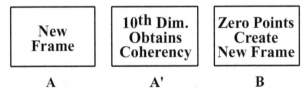

New Frame	10th Dim. Obtains Coherency	Zero Points Create New Frame
A	A'	B

Virtual Reality unfolds frame by frame. With each new frame (A), the 10th dimension honors memories and the emotions (motivation) associated with the memories of all living objects by making changes in the current frame (A') of all related objects in the universe to maintain coherency. These changes are then created by the zero points in the next frame (B) of all affected objects. The memories are amassed.

Figure 9-1 The Unfolding Reality

living object is created by the 10th dimension in frame A'. The rule for any change made with living objects in 3D-Reality is to create more happiness and less pain. Some of the object's memories and emotions are the basis for the change. At the same time, changes in the frames of all other related objects are made. This action by the 10th dimension maintains coherency among all objects, namely causing the relationship between objects to be logical, orderly, and consistent. The zero points then create the changes made in frame A' in the next frame (B), and in the next frames of all objects that were changed by the 10th dimension related to the changes in frame A'. Change in any object in the universe causes simultaneous changes in all related objects in the universe. This is incredibly complex and is managed mechanically by the 10th dimension, governed by the laws of the universe. The 0th through 9th dimensions of all objects in the universe are embedded in the 10th dimension. Because of this, one could say that interconnection is possible between all objects in the universe.

I assume that the zero points that create the change in the next frame (B) do not have access to the content of the structures in the

10 dimensions but robotically replicate all the dimensions in the next frame while maintaining the content and amassing history. The zero points and the 10th dimension existed before the creation of the other 9 dimensions, and the information in those 9 dimensions evolves as the universe evolves. The 9 dimensions are embedded in the 10th dimension, because the 10th dimension is connected to all structures via the core of the flunots (the xyzs). The 10th dimension, therefore, adjusts the universe to the changes in the frames of all related objects to maintain coherency between all objects.

After the zero points create a new frame, the 10th dimension, governed strictly by the laws of the universe, causes what is called self-organization. The core of the flunots (the xyzs) gives the Manager contact with all the objects in the universe. The Manager simply uses the amassed templates and the memories in all related objects to change the current frame in the virtual reality to obtain the next most likely response in a way that maintains the coherency with all other related objects. I believe that since we have experienced our history, we believe that we are controlling our life and causing our behavior.

The Manager uses and modifies the 0th through 9th dimensions to create our 3D-Reality (see Figure 9-2). The 5th through 7th dimensions cause the basic structure of living and inert objects. The 0th through 4th dimensions complete the objects to give the physical property to the objects that we feel and see in our 3D-Reality.

This frame-by-frame, flipbook type of unfolding of virtual reality causes the 3D-Reality to proceed according to the fixed rules of the universe. Each creation by the zero points serves to amass memories. We experience change in our 3D-Reality by amassing memories, by seeing photons emitted from or reflected off objects, or by bumping into the electromagnetic qualities of objects in the virtual reality. These are the experiences that cause learning — the creation and amassing of memories.

In short, the zero points create virtual reality and the 10th dimension is the self-organized Manager of virtual reality that maintains coherency between all objects. At this point, it appears that changes to our virtual reality lead to the recreation of the virtual reality with all the changes included, which we subsequently experience in our 3D-Reality.

The unfolding of reality in this way means that each individual's Personal Field uniquely determines the outcome of his

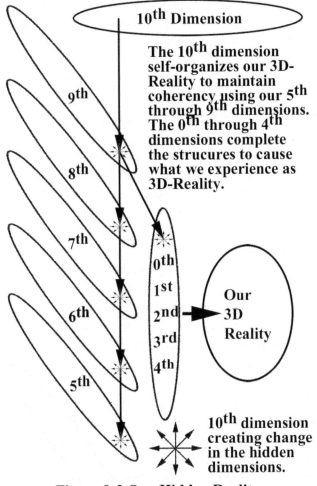

The 10th dimension self-organizes our 3D-Reality to maintain coherency using our 5th through 9th dimensions. The 0th through 4th dimensions complete the strucures to cause what we experience as 3D-Reality.

10th dimension creating change in the hidden dimensions.

Figure 9-2 Our Hidden Reality

or her experience. All the characteristics of an individual, such as mindset, intention, self, core beliefs, quirks, biases, blind spots, self-defeating behaviors, and so forth, are in the Personal Field and are presumably considered in the activity of the Manager. Each individual is different, and his or her unfolding reality is different than anyone else's unfolding reality. Because of this, everyone reacts differently in major or subtle ways. The strength of the intention of an individual and intention itself is caused by memory structures with varying degrees of motivation — memories with more or less positive or negative emotions. I don't believe that the subconscious is involved much in our daily behavior because the bulk of our uniqueness is in the 5th dimension. However, if the subconscious learns what is possible, such as what you are learning in this book, then it is possible that the subconscious will participate more in your unfolding reality. Just the fact that the subconscious can learn to treat negative issues between sessions is an argument that the subconscious can participate in your unfolding reality.

Now I will go out on a limb to explore the active ingredients for change.

The Active Ingredients for Change in the Hidden Reality

The active ingredients for change are the specific actions of the therapist, the patient, or the physiological mechanisms that cause change in the patient. For example, you could call the active sensory stimulation of the patient one of the active ingredients for change for tapping treatments and EMDR. I assume that sensory stimulation is the primary active ingredient for any change of behavior in all therapies. Creating a theory of the active ingredients for change without a behavioral intervention is an interesting challenge. All behavioral interventions involve stimulating our experience in some way, through tapping, touching, journaling, or talking, to obtain a change, such as replacing the undesired response with the wanted response or by manipulating emotions to reduce the likelihood of the response. All these sensory stimulation interventions cause changes in the Personal Field.

According to this theory, in formal hypnosis, the therapist empties the Active Experience by arranging in various ways to have the active memories go dormant. Then he or she triggers positive, healthy behaviors and beliefs with unwanted behaviors in a beneficial way to get the wanted change. The resources and unwanted behaviors, in addition to a suggested strategy for positive behavior change, causes an interaction in the hidden reality that results in the desired change. He or she may also use the dissociative process to keep the unwanted responses or emotions in the unconscious. Sometimes it appears that simply asking the hypnotized person's subconscious for a specific change results in getting the change without any apparent behavioral intervention. In addition, you will see that some of the Wisdom interventions described in this chapter are similar to prayers with no apparent behavioral intervention. In this case, the changes were not created by activity in the 3D-Reality but by changes or activity caused by Wisdom in the virtual reality.

We have all heard of spontaneous healings occurring. Quite regularly, these healings follow some appeal to a higher power through prayer. Since the zero points are assumed to recreate everything in the unfolding activity of the universe, these healings are physical changes involving some aspect of the hidden reality and the zero points. What is it about appealing to a higher power by someone with beliefs, behaviors, and faith consistent with the 10th dimension that provokes spontaneous healings?

One hypothesis is that therapeutic metaphors always create change in the Personal Field to which the Manager (10th dimension) responds by creating the best possible response to fit the metaphor. Remember that metaphors are simply words, and both loving and painful metaphors can change the Personal Field in some way to cause some change in our 3D-Reality. This is the reason positive thinking is healthy for us.

Now, when one prays, the wanted outcome is the purpose of the prayer. Most prayers by individuals for a specific outcome don't always work because the change is self-serving or the person is not a person with the necessarily qualities. For example, if a person prays that he or she won't flunk out of school, it won't work. The prayer was self-serving. However, when prayer does work, it is caused by something hidden from our behavior. Prayer by some extraordinary person will indeed create an immediate outcome. The prayer must be received and translated in some way that causes change in the 5th through 9th dimensions of the circumstances involved with the wanted outcome.

Anything we think or say is a reflection of the hidden reality. We know then that a prayer is represented in the hidden reality. Actually, the prayer happens in the hidden reality before we think it because the prayer is formed before it enters our thoughts. When a prayer is created and it works, action by the Manager and zero points make the change real in the virtual reality (0th through 9th dimensions) with all the objects involved in the wanted outcome. Because the zero points and the 10th dimension are run mechanically by the laws of the universe, I am assuming that there is a different agent that makes this change in the 0th through 9th dimensions. That is, there appears to be a translation of the prayer into change by an agent in the hidden reality. This agent can change the Personal Fields of the living and objects in the universe, which results in the zero points and Manager creating the wanted outcome in our virtual reality that is seen in the 3D-Reality — in other words, creating a miracle. The answering of a prayer, then, appears to be a change caused by an agent in the hidden reality that is manifested by the Manager and the zero points to become real in our 3D-Reality.

Here is how I believe miraculous interventions are created. Consultation with the subconscious of many patients has confirmed that the subconscious appears to run as a self-organized composite of the 5th through 9th dimensions. The subconscious is self-organized by the Manager. I believe that the subconscious can communicate with a wise agent in the 9th dimension, who is capable of causing changes in any situation or Personal Field to which the Manager and zero points respond. The wise agents are souls from the present or from previous lifetimes. This sequence of events — an agent causing a change extended by the Manager and manifested by the zero points — is caused by a request made by prayer. Not every subconscious or person can do this because his or her behavior and spiritual development may be incomplete.

The agents in the 9th dimension learned to follow the same rules as the 10th dimension that work to give more happiness and less pain. For this reason, it is necessary for the person having a desire, appealing for a change, or praying to have the required qualities — namely, love for him- or herself and everything else, positive thoughts and behavior, absolute faith that the Manager or Wisdom can heal self, others, or make changes in the world, and to be seeking an outcome that is positive for him or herself and all humankind.[10] I don't believe the strength of the desire is an important ingredient. Given the qualities, it is simply sufficient to think of the desired outcome.

A communication can take place between the subconscious and an agent in the 9th dimension to cause the changes in our Personal Field and world. In addition, it appears that a person with the required qualities can seemingly operate in the 9th dimension. His or her prayer or simple desires work directly with the help of an agent and the Manager in all dimensions to simply manifest in 3D-Reality. As the presence of the required qualities decrease in a person, the frequency of positive outcomes of the prayer and desires will decrease because of a poorer connection to the 9th dimension. A clear experience of living the required qualities is the gate to miraculous changes in our 3D-Reality.[11]

I believe the subconscious can create changes in our Personal Field, resulting in changes in 3D-Reality. Nevertheless, the subconscious initially formed from the parents' Personal Fields evolves with experience along with a person's Personal Field. This limits the wisdom of the subconscious to the experience of the person, to any wisdom acquired by inheritance, and to any entrained ancestral fields that contribute positive or negative information to the subconscious. What appears possible is that the subconscious can create change by requesting an agent in the 9th dimension to create interventions to adjust the Personal Field. While the interventions composed by an agent in the

9th dimension do not necessarily create miracles, these interventions are probably well-formed interventions that work better and faster than interventions created by the therapist and the patient's subconscious working together.

Finding a Helper in the 5th Dimension: Wisdom

For several years, I had been working with the subconsciouses of various people to try to tap into a source of wisdom. I believed that accessing such wisdom could speed up and improve the power and effectiveness of the Process Healing Method.

A collaborator and I were accessing and exploring souls of positive mystics from the middle ages, as well as many other unusual sources of wisdom. He sought out books about old mystics in a metaphysical bookstore and then asked his subconscious to help him identify the page and paragraph giving the precise statement describing the goal of a healthy mystic. Later, when we talked, he would read the paragraph, and I would problem-solve with his subconscious to clear all barriers to accessing the stated goal.

After removing the barriers (beliefs and memory structures) to reaching the goal and strengthening the qualities described by the goal, he reported experiencing results that were similar to the goals the mystics described. The goal was usually a feeling state or an experience of having some form of wisdom readily available. This goal-state experience was short-lived. Of course, there could be other explanations for his experience, such as hypnosis, hysteria, or delusions, but we obtained the goal experiences for a number of different mystics that were all different and interesting. This supported us to continue searching for a source of wisdom to help us compose interventions that were more powerful.

We began seeking wisdom in the Amassed Personal Field (5th through 9th dimensions) that consists of the Personal Fields of all living persons and the souls of all deceased persons from the beginning of humanity. Since the Amassed Personal Field has the Personal Field memories of all humans from the beginning of time, it may also have some form of collective wisdom.

Eventually, we tried to access the wisdom of God, Jesus, the Teacher of All Saints, the Akashic records, and other wise teachers of the past. We believed that the teachers of the past would be more effective than simply the wisdom entrained in the Amassed Personal Field

(5th through 9th dimensions). During this experimentation, our results did not noticeably improve.

It occurred to me that when Jung[12] was talking about the collective unconscious, he was talking about the wisdom of all who ever lived — the Amassed Personal Field. Believing that the wisdom of the Amassed Personal Field might be entrained on love, we experimented further. Was it possible that negative wisdom or memories might be excluded, leaving only true beneficial wisdom? The question was intriguing. We assumed love was the basis for the entrainment in a higher dimension and that any significant information that remained would be positive and helpful in treatment.

Eventually it occurred to me that the wisdom of every subconscious in amassed souls could be entrained and synchronized with love. Since the subconscious is usually not distorted by the experience of physical or emotional pain, I figured that the subconscious would be an unbiased resource for positive information related to treatment, healing, and behavior change.

This led to experimentation with what I came to refer to as the Collective Subconscious — the entrainment or association of every subconscious of all beings from the beginning of living organisms (see Figure 9-3). I started asking the subconscious of my patients to remove barriers to communicating with the Collective Subconscious, so that the patient's subconscious could contact and work with the Collective Subconscious. I found that engaging the Collective Subconscious to help problem-solve in treatment was worthwhile.

Figure 9-3 also describes the mechanics of change in our 3D-Reality using the Collective Subconscious. The Manager (10th dimension) orchestrates change strictly by the fixed rules of the universe, which maintains the coherency of the unfolding of 3D-Reality. The zero points manifest those changes caused by the 10th dimension. I decided that an intervention in 3D-Reality (A) could ask the Collective Subconscious (B) to cause changes in the Personal Field (C). The change would result in the response by the Manager (10th dimension) (D) and the zero points making the changes real in virtual reality (E), which the patient would experience in his or her 3D-Reality (F).

I created interventions for the removal of barriers to communicating with the Collective Subconscious. After we obtained some success with these interventions (or at least we thought they were successful), a friend gave me the five volumes of *The Lives*

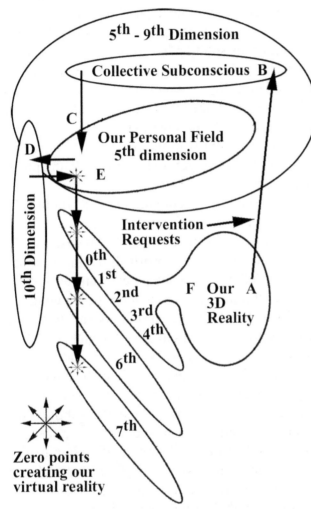

Figure 9-3 The Collective Subconscious

and Teachings of the Masters of the Far East to read. These are the accounts of 13 men who spent two and one-half years in the Far East studying with the Masters. The Masters were living a life similar to that of Jesus. They demon-strated and taught many capabilities of humans that we call miracles. These capabilities were allegedly commonplace in the past but have been generally lost to present-day humanity. These books describe the beliefs and behav-iors necessary to manifest miracles through either prayer or desire, and stimulated my interest in finding an agent in the amassed 9th dimension.

Finding a Helper in the 9th Dimension

When a person dies, his or her zero points continue to create the Personal Field. In other words, the soul of the dead person (5th through 9th dimensions) continues on forever. This means that all the amassed memories in the soul also continue forever. The Personal Field of a soul retains its apparent self-organized capability caused by the Manager and, theoretically, could be interactive in other dimensions (5th, 6th and

7th dimensions). We all know ghosts or other apparitions are not always stationary figures. They move around as apparitions that appear "solid," but they don't usually manifest as solid bodies in our reality. As mentioned before, McCall describes the haunting activity of various kinds of spirits — souls in the hidden reality — which he has traveled around the world to heal,[13] and Hensley described the intense haunting activity in a slaughterhouse in Louisiana.[14] I believe that the spirit activity described in these books is consistent with the portrayal of intruding souls described here. They show self-organized behavior, with apparitions similar to a living person.

The souls, which are primarily functioning in the 5th through 7th dimensions of the Amassed Personal Field, initially have barriers that prevent their full access or participation in the 8th or 9th dimensions. The barriers are varying degrees of being self-absorbed, having negative thoughts and behaviors, disbelief in the creation process, and an absence of love for self, others, and all things, not to mention the accumulated pain and trauma in their lives. How we live our life appears to govern the quality of our life after death.[15] This is a sobering thought. Gradually, these barriers are resolved in some way until the memory and behavior of these souls becomes more in line with the rules of the 10th dimension. As this change gradually occurs, the souls are increasingly able to operate in the 8th and 9th dimensions and positively affect the 9 dimensions in the living. The souls entrained on love amassed in the 9th dimension have the wisdom of the ages. With this wisdom, and acting as wise beings in the 9th dimension, they can make positive changes with persons and objects in our virtual reality because their behavior is motivated by love and is consistent with the rules of the universe.

Accessing the 9th Dimension: Wisdom

In our investigations, we have called this source of wisdom by many names, such as God, Creator, Jesus, Higher Wisdom, Helper, Wisdom, Gramps (author of the Lives and Teachings books), and the Masters. It probably doesn't matter what you call this wisdom, because the word is a metaphor and simply a way of labeling something so complex that it is unimaginable in our 3D-Reality. You can call it what feels most comfortable to you.

We eventually called the self-organized process of wisdom in the amassed 9th dimension Wisdom. Initially, we called this wisdom in the 9th dimension the Creator. However, Wisdom is a more neutral reference. When appropriate during therapy, I use the word Creator.

I believe that it is possible for everyone to have access to the amassed wisdom in the 9th dimension. The 9th dimension is subject to the action of the Manager, so it is self-organized. I check for barriers blocking access to the wisdom in the 9th dimension. When I find them, I ask the subconscious to clear the barriers. I feel that it is important to have the patient be able to access the wise beings in the 9th dimension. I believe that these wise beings can radically change, remake, and add to the virtual structures of the 3D-Reality to create permanent changes in the individual. The desired change made through the 9th dimension cannot be in conflict with the well-being of an individual or of humankind simply because such action would be in conflict with the rules of the universe. The intervention would fail.

I routinely ask Wisdom for help in creating interventions for change in the patient. An intervention involving the Wisdom is believed to involve changes made in the Personal Field (5th through 9th dimensions), which the Manager (10th dimension) and zero points make real in the frame-by-frame unfolding of all dimensions of our virtual reality (see Figure 9-1). We experience these changes in our 3D-Reality. Change is not immediate. Sometimes the process can last days.

The Manager is the substrate that enables the evolution of all matter, living and inert, and all wisdom that amasses and evolves over time. As living matter evolved, Wisdom itself evolved (amassed) in all dimensions. Wisdom, as we know it, started to evolve from complete ignorance at the first creation of living matter. As millennia passed, the wisdom of the living and entrained souls, and the Wisdom itself, amassed to what we have today. As we know more, Wisdom knows more.

This is also true of our physical evolution. As positive physical changes in the universe occurred following novel interactions of the living and inert objects, they were remembered in the 3rd, 5th, 6th and 7th dimensions and were more or less able to "spread the word" through procreation as our physical world evolved. This led to the gradual development of more complex structures of living organisms based on the success of novel interactions. The successful changes were preserved by the gradual amassing of increasingly complex memories of the dimensional representations of evolving species. Recall that the creation of the soul, 5th though 9th dimensions, starts at conception by the joining of the mother's and father's souls. The gradual amassing of memory is probably true of all living species. This amassing of memory accelerates the development of increasingly complex species that we see as evolution. Once a positive change has happened, it will manifest and become more evident in later generations.

Now, the Manager (10th dimension) usually causes our behavior in 3D-Reality. Our behavior is directed by our own memories and the memories of all related objects to maintain coherency within and between all related objects. These changes are made strictly according to the fixed rules of the universe. The zero points manifest these new changes in the next frame of our virtual reality, which we experience in 3D-Reality.

When we request an intervention by Wisdom with some action in our behavior (A) — say, by hearing or saying it — we make an appeal to some aspect or agent of the amassed 9th dimension (B) (see Figure 9-4). The Wisdom (B) can cause changes in 0th through 9th dimensions in our virtual field (C). The Manager (D) (10th dimension) will fine-tune the changes instantaneously in 0th through 9th dimensions of the virtual reality (E) to maintain coherency within and between all related objects. The zero points create the changes in the next frame and preserve the memory of all changes. We experience the change in our 3D-Reality (F).

The Manager (10th dimension) and zero points respond to changes made by Wisdom or 3D interventions to make the changes real and coherent in the virtual reality. Memories of changes amass normally in all dimensions.

Initially, we used the Wisdom to compose well-formed interventions to get the wanted changes in our 3D-Reality. However, for some reason, these changes were not immediate, with some of the interventions taking weeks to complete. The patients experiencing these changes were still aware of gradual, positive progress. Interestingly, the more I worked with Wisdom treating trauma memories and clearing barriers of negative thought, and so forth, the more rapid the interventions became. I take this as evidence that the amassing of more wisdom in the 9th dimension leads to faster changes. This has been observed in other treatments involving stimulation.

It is easy to hypothesize that all interventions resulting in some change of behavior modifies the virtual reality, and change in the virtual reality is reflected in our 3D-Reality. It follows that the use of the subconscious or Wisdom to create a change in our Personal

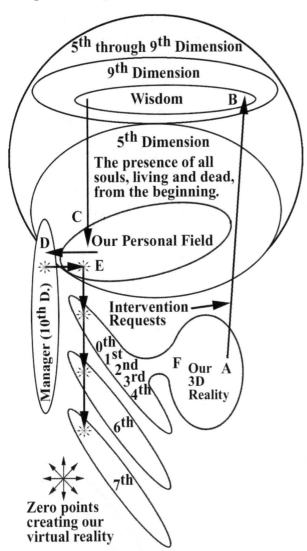

Figure 9-4 The Process in Virtual Reality

Field will change our 3D-Reality. The question is how to safely get the most desirable change with the least amount of effort.

Interestingly, when the patient making the intervention has the qualities that conform to the rules of the 10th dimension, it allows him or her to create rapid changes in 3D-Reality. I have worked with several highly spiritual persons who appeared to manifest changes in their environments simply by having the desire. It is as if they were operating in the 9th dimension. In working with my patients, I have learned to work with the 9th dimension by asking their subconscious for help to get around this issue of "being in the 9th dimension." I ask the subconscious to ask Wisdom to compose well-formed interventions. These interventions treat the patient quickly and more comprehensively.

Frankly, at this point, it is hard to know what active ingredient brings about change when I make an intervention through Wisdom. So, when I make a Wisdom intervention, I ask the patient's subconscious to ask Wisdom to create a series of interventions to remove some issue and replace it with peace and love. How do I know if it is the patient's sub-conscious asking, my subconscious asking, or if I am asking? I don't, but just go with it because it works. My wife, Jane Wakefield-Flint, is an exceptional therapist who incorporates much of this model, but with different metaphors in her treatment of patients. Could it be that her metaphors, learned by my subconscious, are the active ingredients in the change in my patients, or vice versa? At this point, in my mind, the active ingredients for change with this intervention are confounded by the properties of the hidden reality and by not knowing the specific active ingredients for change and where the subconscious or Wisdom is getting them. Thankfully, it isn't necessary to know everything about how the healing works for my patients to benefit from Wisdom's help.

Treating Barriers to Contacting Wisdom

When attempting to communicate with Wisdom, I often found a bar-rier blocking our efforts. This barrier involved beliefs that had to be identified, treated, and replaced with positive, self-empowering beliefs. Any doubt or disbelief in the form of beliefs in the patient would pres-ent a barrier to the communication of his or her subconscious with the 9th dimension.

Here are some examples of barriers and their treatment:

1. A Belief Blocking Communication

The patient made an intervention with a request to Wisdom and found the results of the treatment incomplete. We treated the same issue several times with no success. The issue was the anger connected to all memories of mother from birth to now. The patient continued to have remnants of the issue. We problem-solved and found that a belief was blocking communication with the Wisdom. In practice, I don't bother to identify the belief specifically unless instructed to do so. When the sub-conscious knows the belief, then it can usually be treated. The purpose of this belief barrier was to protect a personal issue. Here is how I cleared the barrier.

T: **Subconscious, please treat the beliefs that block the communication of treatment requests to Wisdom, so they are no longer true. Then compose and strengthen positive, self-empowering beliefs to replace the treated beliefs that will support all**

requests to Wisdom.
S: **Yes.**

I frequently check to see if an intervention is complete.

T: [Waits.] **Subconscious, have you treated the old beliefs and are the new beliefs strengthened to be 100% true?**
S: **Yes.**

2. A Field Blocking Communication

I discovered a field barrier entrained *with* the subconscious. By guessing, we found that the field interfered with the patient's communication with Wisdom because the communication involved the subconscious. We decided to clear all fields associated with the subconscious. I had done this before.

T: **Subconscious, please clear all fields associated with you.**
S: **Yes.**

Seemingly, most people have a field associated with the subconscious, which suggests that this would be a good intervention for all patients. To be thorough, we made the following intervention.

T: **Subconscious, please clear all fields entrained with any process within the body that interferes with the communication with Wisdom.**
S: **Yes.**
T: **Please do a Massive Change History and everything.**
S: **Yes.**

Treatment Interventions with Wisdom

The treatment interventions using Wisdom are all in the same format. Because of the incredible complexity caused by severe trauma, treating difficult cases can take months or possibly years using both conventional therapy and Wisdom interventions. A treatment using Wisdom is not an immediate fix, for it can take weeks to complete the treatment. Although I must say, it seems to work faster than any of my other techniques. In fact, over the course of my practice, as I mentioned before, treatment using Wisdom seems to be working increasingly faster.

When approaching an issue, I decide which intervention to use by offering options to the subconscious, such as the sentence procedure, the structure intervention, parts work, or a Wisdom intervention. As I list the options, I look for a "Yes" response. Sometimes, interventions working directly on the memory structures of some issues are better or faster than working with the Wisdom intervention. When the Wisdom intervention is preferred, I ask the subconscious to ask Wisdom to compose an intervention to handle the issue. After giving the Wisdom intervention to patients, they recognize the treatment process because the treatment experience occasionally starts with an initial physical sensation from head to toe. This is followed by the usual experience during the treatment of ongoing, fleeting, painless memories related to the target issue. Some patients have experienced these fleeting memories for several days.

The Long-Form Wisdom Intervention

After trying many different ways to get help from "higher wisdom," I considered the following intervention as the most inclusive request of Wisdom. As it turns out, as Wisdom evolves, the interventions can become less descriptive because the fine points become included in the memories of the amassed Personal Field (5th or 9th dimensions) or Wisdom. Just as I found with the Process Healing Method, the finer details of interventions no longer have to be given, but are made available with a brief treatment request with the fine details filled in with the help of Wisdom or the subconscious. For example, systematic interventions that I made five years ago using Process Healing treating complex memory structures are no longer made now because I apparently communicate the interventions to the patient's subconscious, either through my Personal Field or because they are available in the body of wisdom in the 5th or 9th dimension.

The following brief intervention includes aspects of other interventions I've previously used — a curious feature of evolving information and wisdom.

T: **Subconscious, please ask the Wisdom to compose a series of interventions to remove all dormant and active fear- or pain-based memories in any memory system, cellular memories, or fields that cause self-limiting behavior. Create and replace them with self-empowering memories that will guarantee**

achieving maximum potential. Please create fields to stop the active memories from moving and being half-active and half-dormant, so they can be treated. Do this when either awake or asleep, and repeat this intervention until maximum potential is fully obvious, available, and experienced in the patient's life.

When I give this intervention, I usually check occasionally to see if the Wisdom intervention is in progress. When it isn't, I shift into the problem-solving mode.

Examples of the Wisdom Intervention

Here are several examples of the Wisdom intervention. With all my patients, therapy included using various treatment interventions from the Process Healing Method to treat memory structures and, less often, the Tapas Acupressure Technique[16], Emotional Freedom Techniques,[17] and Eye Movement Desensitization and Reprocessing.[18]

I assume the Wisdom interventions made some impact, because the patients often reported an experience of treatment processing immediately after the intervention was given. Though some patients commented about noticeable change, my use of other interventions to deal with the same or related issues makes assessing the effectiveness of the Wisdom intervention difficult. Patients often feel the Wisdom intervention continuing for days, as indicated by the flooding of painless trauma memories, which included, in one case, experiencing hallucinations on day six.

Before most of the following interventions, I asked each patient's subconscious if the Wisdom intervention was well-formed and correctly stated, if it would be safe to do, and if the treatment would be at a comfortable level. These examples of interventions will give you a good idea of how I phrase working with Wisdom.

1. Treatment for Anxiety and Depression

A patient was referred for treatment after years of anxiety and depression. The symptoms involved feeling inadequate, emotionally stuck, and having no heart feeling for his spouse. He had many stressors, including his job, the death of his mother, his wife's anger, and a lack of passion in his life. I saw him for seven sessions.

The first session involved a clinical interview, teaching him the Process Healing Method, and conducting other initial interventions that

I do with all patients. We treated many parts and the emotion memories that supported his depression. We also did the following Wisdom interventions.

T: **Subconscious, please ask Wisdom to compose an intervention to remove all negative dormant and active predispositions in Memory II, all negative complex memory structures, all pain-related memories, all painful emotion clusters, all beliefs caused by trauma emotions, and replace them with love.**
S: Yes.
T: **Subconscious, please ask Wisdom to compose an intervention to replace all memories blocking the experience of emotions with love.**
S: **Yes.**

Following the first session, this patient used his subconscious to make regular Process Healing interventions, as well as interventions using Wisdom.

The patient returned for the next session and reported that, on the evening after the session, it "had been a ride," and he had many physical sensations. The day after the first session, he felt stronger, more composed, and was soon "back to normal." I treated many parts and other memory structures, treated DNA-related beliefs from ancestors,[19] and assigned some homework.

T: **Subconscious, please ask the Wisdom to compose an intervention to replace all trauma memories that give self-limiting emotions with self-love and self-confidence.**
S: **Yes.**

The patient said, "I felt that."

In session 3, he reported having loving, heart feelings, and being able to have a good talk with his wife about their issues. He added that he felt more adequate, less emotional, and that his anger was in the past. We treated memory structures, parts, and more issues. I did the following Wisdom intervention.

T: **Subconscious, please ask the Wisdom to compose an intervention to replace with love the emotions of all memories that have negative emotions.**
S: **Yes.**

In session four, we did general counseling and Wisdom interventions on his defensiveness and on barriers to finding time for himself. During the final three sessions, spaced roughly a month apart, his life became more positive as we focused on spiritual issues and cleaned up other problems that arose.

2. Treating Self-Destructive Behavior

This patient had bouts of anxiety caused by various situations in which he found himself. He couldn't make decisions because he became overwhelmed. He had a strong fear of failure and was "self-destructing" his relationships with his wife, his friends and at work. To activate all the self-destructive behaviors involved, I asked the subconscious to identify and tag the memories as he role-played in his thoughts the self-destructive scenarios with his wife, friends, and work. Then I requested a Wisdom intervention.

T: **Subconscious, please ask the Wisdom to identify the self-destructive behaviors, compose an intervention to remove the basis for these self-destructive behaviors, and to replace the self-destructive behaviors with positive, self-empowering behaviors.**
S: **Yes.**

The patient felt goose bumps on his neck (which felt good), an overwhelming "processing" sensation, and "flashbacks" of old memories flooding his thoughts.

T: [Waits.] **Please do a Massive Change History and everything.**
S: **Yes.**

I felt that treating trauma memories would be fitting in this case.

T: **Subconscious, please ask Wisdom to create an intervention to remove any trauma symptoms obtained from conception**

to now and replace them with peace and love.
S: **Yes.**

The patient had flashbacks of past trauma. As he remembered the circumstances and the details precisely, he felt more relaxed. I then repeated the first intervention in a different metaphor to treat the self-destructive behaviors directly. I believed that Wisdom could identify the behaviors that were self-destructive.

T: **Subconscious, please ask Wisdom to create an intervention to remove the self-destructive behaviors and compose and strengthen positive, self-empowering behaviors to take their place.**
S: **Yes.**

The patient reported feeling a huge flash of memories that rose in waves. At one point he said, "I am now coming down." He gained insight that explained some of his self-destructive behaviors. He went on with his life with fewer problems.

3. Removing Memories That Caused Headaches

T: **Subconscious, please contact Wisdom and ask it to create an intervention to remove all memories that cause headaches and replace them with love.**

The patient felt processing. The headache went away.

4. Treating the Pain Associated with Images of a Loved One's Death

A relative of a patient was killed in a severe auto accident. She had recurring intrusions accompanied by grief and pain. In this case, it was fitting to contact the Creator.

T: **Subconscious, please ask the Creator to create interventions to remove the pain from the death images and replace them with love.**

The patient had a vision of Jesus healing her memories.

5. Treating Trauma-Based Memories and Memory Structures

T: **Subconscious, please ask Wisdom to create interventions to remove all trauma-based memory structures and, when fitting, replace them with positive, self-empowering memories.**

The patent felt the processing start.

6. Treating Mean and Codependent Behaviors

T: **Subconscious, please ask Wisdom to make an intervention to remove all mean and codependent behaviors, and replace them with positive, self-empowering behaviors.**

7. Treating Childhood Trauma

T: **Subconscious, please ask Wisdom to create an intervention to completely treat the residential school memories by removing the barriers to treatment and the emotions from all residential school memories and replacing them with love.**

While this intervention had noticeable impact, there was still treatment necessary for some exceptionally difficult issues.

A Brief Summary of Wisdom Interventions

While I continue to work mostly with memory structures to treat problematic issues, I also use the Wisdom intervention in applications similar to the interventions listed on the next page. I find the subconsciouses of some patients spontaneously use the Wisdom intervention in place of what I request. Yet, with other patients, other direct interventions will often produce faster results than Wisdom interventions. For this reason, I offer the subconscious a list of treatment choices at the beginning of the session. Again, when using the Wisdom intervention, I ask the subconscious to ask Wisdom to create the intervention. After this is done successfully, I am relatively confident that the intervention will be well-formed and will work.

Here are some issues for which I used the Wisdom intervention. In all of these examples, I first inquire about safety, then ask the subconscious to ask Wisdom to remove the issue, and then make the replacement.

Negative predispositions or habits – replace with love.

Self-limiting layered and complex layered memories – replace with love.

Cellular memories with the disempowering belief – replace with love.

DNA memories with the disempowering belief – replace with love.

Structures in DNA causing chemical sensitivities – replace with love.

Self-limiting negative predispositions – replace with positive, self-empowering predispositions.

Parts and memories based on negative emotions – replace the emotions with love.

Self-limiting beliefs – replace with positive, self-empowering beliefs.

All negative physiological and emotional responses from thoughts about work – replace with love.

Pain-related behavior (or memories) – replace with positive, self-empowering behavior.

Treating Unusual Situations with the Wisdom Intervention

When I run into unusual situations or simply want to try something new, I ask the subconscious if the Wisdom intervention would work best and if it would be safe to treat with it. Occasionally, there may be a better or faster treatment, even though it is probable the Wisdom intervention would work.

Here are some examples of treating unusual situations.

1. Treating Fields with the Wisdom Intervention

The patient had fields disturbing the treatment process. I wanted to treat these fields with the Wisdom intervention because this intervention will treat most types of fields. When treating fields or parts with the Wisdom intervention, I make sure they are available for treatment because the fields or parts can resist treatment when they are cycling between active and dormant memories. This cycling problem needs to be included in the instructions to the subconscious.

T: **Subconscious, are there fields present?**
S: **Yes.**
T: **Can we use the Wisdom intervention to treat these fields?**
S: **Yes.**
T: **Subconscious, please keep the fields either dormant or active, and ask Wisdom to make an intervention to remove all the dormant and active fields and replace them with love.**
S: **Yes.**

Some of the intruding fields have to be treated individually. Some have to be treated in other ways. I had a patient who kept getting intruding fields. It occurred to me that I could treat the emotions to which the fields were entraining. I started giving the following intervention.

T: **Subconscious, please ask the Wisdom to identify all the traumas to which the fields entrain and compose interventions to replace trauma emotions with love.**
S: **Yes.**
T: **Please do a Massive Change History and everything.**
S: **Yes.**

Recall that the "everything" on Massive Change History also includes identifying and treating the emotion templates in the treated memories. This treatment has to do with stopping the reassociation of pain to the trauma memories and to prevent fields from reassociating to the pain pattern. The "Massive Change History and everything" intervention is given after all interventions.

2. Treating Trauma to Heart Memories
The patient had a torture history. Problem-solving resulted in a cue that suggested the presence of trauma in heart memories.

T: **Subconscious, should we treat the heart memories with the Wisdom intervention?**
S: **Yes.**

T: **Subconscious, please ask Wisdom to create an intervention to identify all trauma in the heart memories and replace the trauma memories with peace and love.**
S: **Yes.**
T: **Please do a Massive Change History and everything.**
S: **Yes.**

The patient felt a tingling all over her body, which she described as a change in the heart that radiated to all cells in her body.

Removing a Field Connection from Another Person

In some unusual cases, I have found that a torturer can set up a continuing nonlocal field connection between him- or herself and the victim. Through this connection, the torturer allegedly maintains some ability to provide intrusions and keep tabs on the victim. In this particular case, I was not sure if the torturer was fully aware of this connection. It may be that a compartmentalized part in the torturer preserved and used this field connection long after torturing the survivor.

T: **Subconscious, please ask Wisdom to compose interventions to change the basic chemistry of the patient, and permanently remove the link that connects the torturer with the patient.**
P: **Yes.**

The patient said it felt like a tug-of-war going on. She could almost see her torturer's face, and the torturer wouldn't let go. The patient heard many nasty verbal intrusions and said that the torturer was crying in desperation not to let go. Within moments, the intervention successfully removed the link to the torturer. I continued with the Massive Change History intervention.

Treating a Barrier in Your Personal Field

While working with a patient, he heard an intrusive voice of a helper in the hidden reality say that there was another intervention that would help people. This involved treating current and ancestral emotional and physical trauma memories amassed in the 7th dimension. Recall that the 7th dimension carries the memory for the composition of the body. Apparently, for some reason, these emotional and physical memories that amassed in the 7th dimension presented barriers to treating mental and physical issues. By treating a patient for these barriers, I was told that the patient would be able to auto-heal more easily.

T: **Subconscious, please ask Wisdom to remove the current and ancestral emotional and physical trauma memories that are amassed in the 7th dimension and replace them with peace and love.**

S: **Yes.**

T: **Please do a Massive Change History and everything.**

S: **Yes.**

Further Refinements of the Wisdom Intervention

I was told by a helper in the hidden reality, via an intrusion in the person's thoughts, that there was more to know about treatment interventions. Identifying the issue and just treating the issue does not result in a complete and pervasive treatment of the issue. There are three subtle influences that can cause an increased intensity of the emotions or behavior surrounding any issue.

The first involves a soul intrusion. Issues are usually created in some well-defined situation. All situations giving rise to problematic behavior or experience have emotions associated to the situation, as we know, but there is also a situational quality independent of the emotions. Similar, intense, well-defined trauma situations can have happened repeatedly over generations in many lifetimes. Just as souls entrain to the emotion pattern of extreme, emotional trauma, souls with experience in similar intense situations can entrain with the similar situation in the patient. These intrusions are not long-term intrusions and last only as long as the situation lasts. For example, a person of authority is angry at something that you did. Your response is to get upset and defensive. It is easy to imagine souls who have had a similar experience of being blamed and becoming upset and defensive. Therefore, one or more souls with a similar experience can entrain to the blamed person. These entrained souls may increase the intensity of the person's emotions and behavior. This is the first type of subtle influence that entrains to a person behaving in a common situation. This subtle influence can be treated.

The second is that the repeated activity of an intruding soul in some situation causes a neurological memory of the influence in a person. The neural activity caused by the intruding soul creates a memory of the response in our Personal Field. This is called a shadow memory that that can be triggered by the situation without the presence of the soul. Hence, even without an intruding soul, there is a learned, subtle influence caused by this shadow memory of the responses and emotions caused by the soul. This shadow memory can intensify or distort the behavior of the person. These shadow memories can be treated easily as well.

The third subtle influence is one of which we are all aware. This is learning from modeling. We know that when children watch other children being violent, the modeled behavior increases the probability that the observing children will show aggressive behavior in a similar situation. Imagine all the situations in our lifetime in which negative behavior is modeled to handle situations. We learn these modeled negative behaviors and emotions so that in similar or related situations these negative behaviors and emotions subtly influence our behavior. Significant components of a memory learned from modeling can trigger an emotion or behavioral tendency.

For example, a child who sees his mother being repeatedly slapped acquires fear related to the punishing hand. The child remembers this. As an adult, activities involving the hand, such as shaking hands, getting touched, or a stroke on the cheek, may trigger an experience of fear. This intrusion is similar to a predisposition that triggers fear that is related to some component of the modeled behavior, in this case the hand.

If we do not address these three subtle influences in our request for treatment, they remain untreated. To some extent, the untreated issue remains and continues to subtly distort our behavior and experience. Here is a fine-tuned intervention to treat an issue and the related subtle influences.

T: **Subconscious, please ask Wisdom to create interventions and remove** (the issue) **and any subtle influences related to this issue, and replace them with peace and love. If behaviors or beliefs were treated, then compose and strengthen positive, self-empowering behaviors and beliefs to replace them.**

For all patients at the start of a session, I like to request the following intervention.

T: **Subconscious, please ask Wisdom to repeat all previous interventions and remove any subtle influences related to any previously treated issue and replace them with peace and love. If necessary, strengthen or compose positive, self-empowering behaviors and beliefs to replace any that were removed.**

Many mental health professionals have created innovative strategies for treating issues in their patients. In the next chapter, I will reveal a number of these strategies and suggest experimental interventions using these strategies with the Wisdom intervention.

Chapter 10

Other Experimental Interventions in the Hidden Reality

Introduction

The experimental interventions given in this chapter are findings that are more recent and are primarily based on the treatment strategies of other therapists. When it is appropriate to use, I have found this first intervention to be more powerful than any of my usual interventions. The other experimental interventions are believed to treat the more or less subtle influences on our behavior and show how the Wisdom intervention can be extended to other treatment objectives. As with other interventions in this book, these are experimental interventions because there is no peer-reviewed research to validate the efficacy of the interventions. Before I use any of these interventions with a patient, I assess the safety of the intervention by asking the subconscious. After using these interventions, the patients often reflect on the treatment processing and report increased peace, relaxation, or a shift in their experience. Often, I ask the subconscious if it was beneficial to do the intervention. In most cases, the subconscious reports that the intervention was good to use.

Treatment Using Field Patterns

Treatment using field patterns is my most unusual experimental treatment intervention, however, it is one that I frequently use. It is based on the work of a healer by the name of Adam, who has the amazing ability to view the hologram of quantum information that causes physical issues.[1] He can do this when the person is in his presence or at another location. Adam talks with the person, and, once the issue is identified energetically, through seeing the quantum information (a field pattern in the Personal Field), he can then manipulate the hologram to heal the cause of the issue. This removes the physical problem or pain of the issue. This is a gradual process depending on the severity of the illness.

Adam's first healing experience was of an energy hologram showing all aspects of the body. This hologram allowed him to take a "tour" of the body and identify physical issues. The energy blockages of any physical issue appeared in the foreground of his experience. This was demanding work, but he soon learned to use this experience with no ill effects on himself.

He later discovered that he could safely manage the experience of being inside an organ in someone's body and take an internal tour. His experience was similar to looking through a microscope where you can zoom in and out, move to different depths, and to different locations. Usually he uses the physical real-time hologram and accesses locations that need healing. The healing involves identifying the hologram of the targeted physical issue, having the intention to heal, and giving information with arm movements and visualized colors that allows the targeted issue to heal. He uses different holograms for different issues. I am listing the different holograms, not for the treatment of physical issues, but to teach your subconscious what is possible for the treatment of psychological issues.

> **The energy hologram** – gives an overall energy view of the body's energy grid and flow of energy, which is useful for simple issues.
>
> **Brain signals' hologram** – is a view of the neural functions and flow of impulses on neural pathways in the brain.
>
> **Real-time physical hologram** – is a view of any organ or nerve system at the cellular level. This hologram is used for treatment or to create a treatment strategy.
>
> **The smart energy packets** – are "Pac-Man-like" robots put in by intention to treat blockages. These robots can continue for a long time after the initial intervention.
>
> **Pattern energy grid** – is like a 3D contour map that reveals the source of the disease by distortions of the grid.
>
> **Heat hologram** – used for the treatment of cancer, for which he uses colors to treat. He uses different colors to treat different problems.
>
> **Genetic hologram** – reveals genetically based diseases started by damaged genetic influences that the body believes are healthy.
>
> **Overall-view hologram** – a pre- and post-assessment of the person that should show that the intervention created health.

I was curious about whether the subconscious could see the field patterns of mental issues. I asked my subconscious and observed a "Yes." I have experimented with this treatment with a number of patients. I gave my recent learnings about Adam's work to each of them through the Personal Field. Their subconscious, then, presumably knows as much about the field pattern as I do. When working with mental issues rather than physical issues, the intention or request to treat an issue activates the appropriate field representation of the issue. The subconscious could use this representation to identify, treat, and remove the issue. I have found that it works very quickly and thoroughly. The subconscious, I believe, can operate independently and can be asked to repeat the treatment over time to obtain the desired results. Here is the way the subconscious does this intervention.

The subconscious discerns a field pattern of the psychological issue in the Personal Field of the patient. This pattern apparently includes the historical causes of the pain and trauma of the issue. The subconscious is able to manipulate the field pattern in the direction of health by treating and removing the historical causes of the issue. The subconscious can allegedly see a change in the field pattern as he or she treats the causes of the issue. The field pattern also includes later memories that are related to the trauma of the target issue. Treatment of the later memories results in changes that are similar to the Massive Change History procedure.

Patients' experiences varied during treatment. One patient felt her body contort by twisting in one direction, and by having other body and head jerks. She is a registered nurse and was able to track the activity of the treatment procedure as starting in the heart, then moving to the lower back, up the right side, to the left shoulder, up the brainstem to the midbrain, and out the left parietal lobe. She felt "wasted" for a number of hours while the treatment continued that night with other issues.

Another patient felt an uncomfortable feeling start from her head to toes immediately after the field pattern intervention was given. This continued for about five minutes. Then she said she could "feel it all" streaming out the top of her head. Testing the issue confirmed that the treatment caused positive change.

In another patient, two barriers apparently blocked the subconscious from treating the field pattern. First, there was an intruding soul that was entrained to the field pattern of the issue. The second barrier was that the patient was not involved in the treatment; namely, there was no intention by her to heal the issue. The intruding soul was assisted to leave, and the patient was asked if she intended to no longer have the problem. She said, "Yes." After these barriers were resolved, the subconscious was able to treat the field pattern.

A fourth patient, who used the intervention on herself, felt uncomfortable with the intensity of the body feelings while processing an issue. She moved to another chair and the body feeling reverted back to relatively normal. Then it became intense again, and she moved to a third chair with the same result. Some aspect of the body feelings anchored to the chair in which she was last sitting. The body feelings "remained there" while the treatment continued without the uncomfortable body feelings when she sat in another chair. She unknowingly used a hypnotic technique used by hypnotherapists who anchor the barriers to trance by having the patient sit in one chair and then, after moving the patient to another chair, the patient often easily goes into trance. The barrier to treatment remained anchored to the previous chair.

Several things need to be taken into consideration when treating with the field pattern intervention. Some issues need a more precisely stated intervention, like a regular Process Healing intervention or a Wisdom Intervention. I always ask the subconscious if the field pattern intervention is the best intervention to treat the issue and if it is safe to use the field pattern intervention.

There are at least three barriers to treatment using the field pattern intervention. First, the patient may not want to treat the issue. The intention to treat the issue must be present. Second, there may be an intruding field entrained with the target field pattern. The intruding field can be treated in the usual way. The third barrier is when a person has compartmentalized parts who obstruct the treatment. These barriers are discovered by problem-solving when the field pattern intervention doesn't work.

Here is what I say while working with patients.

T: **Subconscious, can you see the field pattern that is causing this issue?**
S: **Yes.**

With a "No," I would explore for barriers to seeing the field patterns of issues, namely intruding fields and the intention of the patient.

T: **Subconscious, is the field pattern intervention the best intervention to treat this issue?**

S: **Yes.**

T: **Subconscious, can you safely treat the basis for the field pattern, so the issue is removed?**

S: **Yes.**

With a "No," I would explore for barriers to treating the field patterns of the issue.

Sometimes there is a better intervention than using the field pattern intervention. I determine if this is the case and ask the subconscious to treat the issue in the best way.

T: **Subconscious, please treat the cause of the field pattern of the issue in the best way and when you have finished, please compose and strengthen positive, self-empowering beliefs and behaviors to replace any that have been removed.**

S: **Yes.**

The phrase "and when you are finished" is important because, if it is not included, the subconscious tries to do both incompatible interventions at the same time.

T: **[Waits.] Subconscious, would it be good to repeat this treatment a number of times?**

With a "Yes," one can determine the frequency that treatments should be repeated. In addition, by getting a score for the strength of the issue — say, between 0, untreated, to 10, fully treated — you can follow the rate of change as the treatments are repeated. I usually continue with this request.

T: **Subconscious, can you please repeat the field pattern intervention for this issue, when appropriate, until the issue is fully treated?**

S: **Yes.**

Recent Findings with the Field Pattern Intervention

I have not used the field pattern intervention enough to have a full understanding of its scope of use and possible barriers. However, here are some of my recent findings.

I have combined the field pattern intervention with another intervention used in the Process Healing Method, called the Sentence Procedure. The Sentence Procedure is one in which you say a positive sentence about the goal issue that activates parts and memory elements that block treating the goal issue. An example is "I will no longer get anxious performing." Usually, I have the subconscious "tag" (label in some way) and treat the memory elements evoked by the statement, one after the other "in the best way." I have found that the subconscious can use the field pattern of the triggered memory elements and further identify additional field patterns of other dormant memory elements or barriers to the goal issue. After ascertaining that it is safe to treat the identified field pattern, I ask the subconscious to treat it.

I have found other barriers to the field pattern intervention. One barrier was that the field pattern of the issue was too large to treat in one intervention. In this case, I asked the subconscious to partition the issue into manageable sizes and, if it was safe, to do a series of field pattern interventions, one after the other, to treat the different partitions of the issue. In another patient, the field pattern intervention had to be both partitioned and treated every other day with positive, self-empowering beliefs and behaviors replacing the treated beliefs and behaviors.

Another barrier that blocked identifying the field pattern was a number of intruding fields with different considerations about treatment. In this case, there were three groups of fields, each with different considerations — the fear of intense pain, the fear of death, and the fear of both pain and death. Once the usual reframes were used to clear these fields, the field patterns were found safe to treat and were treated.

1. Treating multiple issues

The successful treatment of one issue using the field pattern intervention leads to treating other issues with the field pattern intervention. Since the subconscious is probably aware of other issues that are problematic for the patient, I believe that the following questions for the subconscious will initiate further treatment of these issues by the subconscious using the field pattern intervention.

T: **Subconscious, are there other issues that can be safely treated with the field pattern intervention?**

S: **Yes.**

T: **Subconscious, can you treat them in the appropriate order and with each, when finished, compose and strengthen positive, self-empowering beliefs and behaviors to replace any that have been removed?**

S: **Yes.**

The following three vignettes are with a woman who I had seen once in a group setting about five years previously. The treatment session lasted less than 60 minutes and took place via telephone.[2] I treated these issues using the field pattern intervention. Other issues were treated with the Process Healing Method.

2. Treating a mother's trauma caused by her children being molested

The woman's two children had been molested, and she was constantly distraught, hypervigilant, would scream with fear, and couldn't relax with the children around. She couldn't stop thinking about the molestation, felt someone in the other room two to three times per day, and saw movements in the house leading her to call the police several times. I first did an intervention to treat the emotions connected to the molestation of her children.

T: **Subconscious, do you see the field pattern of her reaction to the molestation of her two children?**

S: **Yes.**

T: **Is safe to treat this issue using the field pattern intervention?**

S: **Yes.**

T: **Subconscious, please smooth out the field pattern of the emotions so that they remain at the right level and are not overwhelming.**

I ask for them to be treated at the right level, so her healthy protectiveness is maintained.

S: **Yes.**

After the three or four minutes of processing, she said, "I felt pain first, almost cried, then it went away. When I think of it now, it doesn't feel that bad. It is at a comfortable level."

Then, I did another field pattern intervention clearing the pain that motivates all other problematic behaviors she listed related to the molestation of her children.

T: **Subconscious, can you see the field pattern of the pain that motivates all the other protective behaviors that are problematic?**
S: **Yes.**
T: **Is it safe to use this treatment intervention?**
S: **Yes.**
T: **Please smooth out the pain in the field patterns of those behaviors. Compose and strengthen positive, self-empowering beliefs and behaviors to take their place.**
S: **Yes.**

She felt the processing and described it. She said, "It felt like my eyes went to the left with memories coming in and then the memories were going away." By questioning the subconscious, I learned it would be completed that day. I asked if there was more to do and if the subconscious knew what needed to be done. She said there was and that it was safe to do. I asked her to do it.

I asked her to think about the molestation. She said that her thoughts took off like an obsession. I usually use the TAT intervention to treat obsessions. This time I used the field pattern intervention to treat her obsession.

T: **Subconscious, Can you see the field patterns of the thoughts that she is having and is it safe to smooth them out to remove the thoughts?**
S: **Yes.**

Two weeks later, she reported that the problem behaviors were gone, and she was not thinking much about the molestation of her children.

3. Treating a memory of a violent rape

The mother had her own abuse history. She was violently raped at the age of four. I treated this next. Two other field interventions were carried out to treat the effects of the rape.

T: **Subconscious, can you see the field pattern caused by the pain from the molestation at the age of four and the pain from this trauma associated to memories throughout her life?**

This is like a Massive Change History procedure.

S: **Yes.**
T: **Is it safe to treat this pain with the field pattern intervention?**
S: **Yes.**
T: **Please treat it and give peace, love, and forgiveness to the memories treated.**
S: **Yes.**

After the treatment ended, she said, "I don't know, I just feel happiness; giggly."

When I asked her to think of the perpetrator, she felt fear and anger. I asked for the following intervention.

T: **Subconscious, can you see the field pattern of the fear and anger she feels when she thinks of the perpetrator?**
S: **Yes.**
T: **Is it safe to treat it now?**
S: **Yes.**

After the intervention, she said, "I have a good feeling, almost like when I was on antidepressants."

4. Remote treatment of a boy acting out in school

She mentioned that her son, who was five years old, was well behaved at home and in the community. However, the effects of the abuse two years earlier caused problems in other areas. It was difficult to get him to the school bus. At school, he acted out so much during recess that she was thinking of home-schooling him. We decided to try a surrogate treatment. Here is what I did.

T: **Subconscious, can you communicate with her son's subconscious?**
S: **Yes.**
T: **Subconscious, please ask his subconscious to identify the field pattern of the trauma and its effects from then until now and determine if it is safe to treat.**
S: **Yes.**
T: **Subconscious, is it safe to treat the field pattern of the trauma?**
S: **Yes.**
T: **Please treat it.**

I requested another intervention to which the subconscious said "No." Then I requested the following intervention.

T: **Subconscious, can the child's subconscious see the field pattern of the rage and anger, treat it, and then replace it with peace and love?**
S: **Yes.**

We finished the session with the following intervention. I assumed that the child's subconscious had the treatment Wisdom.

T: **Subconscious, can you ask his subconscious to ask Wisdom to create an intervention for anything that prevents him from being whole and healthy?**
S: **Yes.**

Following up after two weeks, I found the boy was showing less fear, there were no problems getting him on the school bus, and his social behavior in school and on the soccer field had improved. Eight months later, the mother said that he was getting better as time passed.

5. Treating an addiction to pornography

This intervention can be used with any addiction. The patient complained that he had a mild addiction to pornography. Occasionally he would miss work because he stayed up too late.

I first treated any ancestral fields that supported addictions of any kind. Then I inquired about field intrusions that were supporting the addiction and treated them. I used the sentence procedure to trigger all porn-related memory elements and treated the field pattern of the basis for watching pornography. These three treatments addressed the patient's motivation to watch pornography. Then I had him imagine triggers on the Internet, TV, and in magazines that caused him to want to view porn. I treated these triggers with a field pattern intervention. Teaching a belief that would interrupt the onset of viewing pornography was next. He offered the belief, "I don't want to view women in this way." Further treatment may be necessary in a later session to handle any untreated aspects of this issue that may have been dormant at the time. In later sessions, I would generally ask the subconscious to repeat these interventions and, if necessary, problem-solve to find other related issues until the subconscious tells me I am done.

The ancestral fields and intruding souls are treated by the procedures described above. I continue.

T: **Subconscious, when I say, "I am no longer going to watch pornography on the Internet," please tag the parts and memory elements that activated.**

S: **Yes.**

T: **Can you see the field pattern of the tagged memory elements and incorporate the field of all related field patterns of dormant memory elements that remain untagged?**

S: **Yes.**

T: **Is it safe to treat the field pattern of the memory elements related to watching pornography on the Internet or reading pornography in magazines?**

S: **Yes.**

T: **Please treat the field pattern.**

Now I ask the subject to think of as many of the triggers on the Internet, TV, and in magazines that led him to watch pornography or read pornographic material.

T: **[Waits.] Subconscious, please tag the identified triggers that have activated and identify the field pattern created by them and of all other dormant triggers that have occurred in the past.**

S: **Yes.**

T: **Is it safe to treat the field pattern of these triggers that initiate watching pornography on the Internet?**

S: **Yes.**

T: **Please treat the field pattern of the triggers.**
S: **Yes.**

Either of the field pattern interventions could have field barriers or the treatment target may be too large to be treated and would need to be partitioned as discussed previously. With field barriers, treat the barriers in the usual way, as field patterns.

By now, the field influences, the motivation, and the triggers to watching pornography have been treated. The next step was to install a belief to support him not watching pornography.

When treating issues, I often make a positive statement denying the issue in order to activate all the memories related to the issue — for example, "I don't feel betrayed by my parents," or "I am no longer going to use alcohol." This statement activates all parts and memory structures that are barriers to the positive statement. The subconscious can then identify the field pattern of the activated memories triggered by the statement and do the intervention.

In this case, I used the belief suggested by the patient.

S: **Subconscious, when I say "I don't want to view women in this way," please identify and treat the field pattern of all the parts and memory structures that activated.**
S: **Yes.**

Now, I do an intervention to strengthen the desired belief.

T: **Subconscious, please strengthen the belief, "I don't want to view women in this way," so it is absolutely true.**
S: **Yes.**

To test the treatment, I had the patient role-play in his mind different scenarios that had previously led him to watch pornography. The results suggested that the motivation to watch pornography was gone and the new belief was experienced as very natural to him.

6. Other Notes about the Field Pattern Intervention

When I have a list of the patient's issues to treat — for example, frustration, betrayal, lack of self-confidence, fear of working, depression, a trauma, anxiety, and so forth — I obtain direction by the subconscious and treat the issues in the best order and with the best intervention. When I use the field pattern intervention, it has usually worked as described in the vignettes. Sometimes, the treatment works very fast.

Here is an interesting direction that could be explored. I believe the subconscious can see the field patterns of the holograms and grids for accessing the physical issues listed above. It would be interesting to explore treating physical issues using the subconscious and the various holograms and grids as an adjunctive treatment to medical treatment. It is important to be sure that the requested intervention is safe to do. Of course, the approval of your patient's doctor to try ancillary treatments would be necessary.

Treating Cognitive Distortions Caused by Trauma

In Leahy's (2003) practitioner's guide for cognitive therapy techniques, he writes that cognitive distortions often underlie depression, anxiety, and anger.[3] He offers a number of interventions for treating these cognitive distortions. I read his list of cognitive distortions several times, so I knew that they were in my Personal Field. I experimented first by asking a patient's subconscious if he or she could read the list of cognitive distortions in my Personal Field. The subconscious said, "Yes." I asked if it would be good to treat any memory elements in the patient that caused the cognitive distortions. I received a "Yes" and requested a Wisdom intervention to remove the memory elements causing the cognitive distortions and to replace them with positive, self-empowering beliefs and behaviors. The patient immediately felt the process starting up. I did this with a number of other patients and also obtained positive results with them. I have yet to try it with someone with severe cognitive distortions. I think this intervention would be an interesting avenue to explore, as well.

Another way to use this list of cognitive distortions when using the Process Healing Method is to read each cognitive distortion to the patient, and ask the subconscious if the distortion is active in the patient. Note or tag each active distortion. Then read each tagged distortion, one after the other, and ask the subconscious to treat the memory elements triggered. Then for each distortion, compose and strengthen positive, self-empowering beliefs and behaviors to replace any treated memory elements, as needed. An example of using the Wisdom intervention in this way is provided below.

Here is the list of cognitive distortions:

Mind reading – You know what people think without evidence.

Fortune telling – You predict the future in negative terms.

Catastrophizing – You have a negative exaggeration of events and thoughts.

Labeling – You assign negative traits to yourself or others.

Discounting positives – You make positive claims of yourself and make others' positive claims trivial.

Negative filtering – You focus on the negative and seldom notice the positive.

Overgeneralizing – You perceive a global pattern of negatives based on a single incident.

Dichotomous thinking – You view events or people in all-or-nothing terms.

"Shoulds" – You interpret events as what should be, not what is.

Personalizing – You take too much personal responsibility for a negative event and fail to see others' responsibility or the circumstances involved in the cause of the event.

Blaming – You focus on others as the cause for hurt and refuse to take responsibility for changing yourself.

Unfair comparisons – You interpret events in terms of unrealistic standards. "Others did better; therefore, I am a failure."

Regret orientation – You focus on the idea that you could have done better in the past.

"What if?" – You keep asking, "What if something happens?" and are not satisfied with your answers.

Emotional reasoning – You let your emotions guide your interpretation of reality.

Inability to disconfirm – You reject evidence or arguments that might disconfirm your negative thoughts.

Judgment focus – You view yourself, others, and events as good-bad, inferior-superior, rather than simply describing, accepting, and understanding.

I start this intervention by either reading all of the cognitive distortions to the patient or by having his or her subconscious read them in my Personal Field. Then I do the intervention.

T: **Subconscious, can you read my Personal Field and see the list of cognitive distortions?**

S: **Yes.**

T: **Would it be good to treat these cognitive distortions in the patient?**

S: **Yes.**

T: **Subconscious, is it safe to do this intervention?**

S: **Yes.**

T: **Subconscious, please ask Wisdom to create an intervention to remove all memory elements that cause the cognitive distortions and replace them with positive, self-empowering beliefs and behaviors as needed. Then do a Massive Change History and everything.**

S: **Yes.**

I often ask the subconscious if this intervention was good to do. Patients have felt positive changes following this intervention.

Treating Behaviors Affected by Intruding Souls

Intruding souls can affect or distort behavior by increasing motivation for trauma-based behaviors or by introducing behaviors not learned by the person. Charles Kraft has written two books that have greatly influenced my understanding of intruding souls.[4] Though I ended up approaching intruding souls from a behavioral point of view, these two books educated me about the many ways that patients can be affected by intruding souls. Kraft's books also enlightened me about his Christian treatment approach for intruding souls of varying intensity, as well as mental health issues in general. He also clearly distinguishes between disruptions caused by spirits as opposed to dissociative or compartmentalized parts. He recommends collaborating with a Christian psychologist for patients with a dissociative disorder.[5] I appreciate his approach to spiritual and psychological treatment.

There is one section of Kraft's book that I want to include in this book. He has a section listing the "Function Names of Demons" that are connected to specific human functions — behaviors.[6] An intruding soul or demon can attach to a behavior and cause problems for the person. Kraft contacts them by the function name, but I identify them in a different way. I made a list of his human function names and use the list to identify intruding souls with the help of the subconscious.

Here is how I did it.

T: **Subconscious, I have a list of human functions to which fields occasionally entrain. I want to read the list to see if any fields are entrained to any of these functions. As I read each function name, I want you to indicate "Yes" if a field is entrained to the function or "No" if there is no field entrained to the function. Can I do this safely?**
S: **Yes.**

Below is Kraft's list of human functions. I read each function aloud, one after the other; I circle the function when the subconscious' response indicates that there is a field entrained to the function. Later, I contact and treat each field associated with the function, one after the other. Here is the question I ask as I proceed down the list of the various human functions.

T: **Subconscious, is there a field entrained to** (state the function)?

When I get a "Yes," I circle the function on the list and proceed to the next function. Later, I use the circled information to identify and treat the intruding field(s).

Here is the list of human functions:

Suicide	Fear of . . .	Anxiety
Murder	Pain	Worry about . . .
Violence	Dark	Lying
Deceit	Being alone	Confusion
Anger	Being outdoors	Frustration
Hate	Heights	Forgetfulness
Revenge	Inadequacy	Criticism
Bitterness	Unworthiness	Condemnation
Resentment	Perfectionism	Judgmental
Stubbornness	Shame	Faultfinding
Self-rejection	Guilt	Adultery
Fear of rejection	Embarrassment	Seduction
Terror	Sensitivity	Rape
Torment	Worry	Violence

Depression	Sickness, such as:	Need to understand
Defeat	Cancer	Rationalization
Nervousness	Arthritis	Religiosity
Doubt	Diabetes, etc.	Ritualism
Unbelief	Blasphemy	Doctrinal obsession
Skepticism	Cursing	Lust
Pride	Mockery	Sexual impurity
Arrogance	Compulsion	Adultery
Vanity	Control	Pornography
Perfection	Domination	Sexual fantasy
Insecurity	Possessiveness	Addiction
Competition	Performance	Occult spirits
Pride	Pleasing others	Cult spirits
		Any false religion

I have always found a field entrained to one or more human functions with patients with whom I have tried this intervention. In one patient with a serious disorder, I found fields entrained to twelve different functions. When I discover an intruding field, I ask if there is more than one field entrained to the human function and, when possible, treat them all with one intervention. Otherwise, I problem-solve until they are all treated.

Simple Breathing as a Trigger for Trauma

Orgone Therapy, developed by Wilhelm Reich, is a therapy for treating a person's character structure.[7] Although my experience of Orgone Therapy is grossly shy of truly understanding it, I do know that what I experienced receiving this therapy created significant, positive change in my life.

The Orgone therapist does an extensive evaluation to identify treatment goals. With the evaluation complete, therapy begins. I'll describe the therapy from the patient's point of view. The patient lies on a bed just wearing underwear and socks. He or she is instructed to breathe out with an audible sigh, like saying "Ahhhhhh" as you exhale. The therapist can hear barriers in your voice as you breathe out. The goal is to get a deep, relaxed vocalization while exhaling, free of any restriction. Unrelaxed auditory cues during exhalation are barriers related in some way to your character structure. As therapy progresses, the therapist occasionally squeezes muscles around your throat, thighs, and calves, or applies pressure to your chest. I was not told why he did what he did, but I did have images of childhood trauma occur to me, which I had not previously known. I believe that both breathing and muscle stimulation trigger trauma memories while in a vulnerable setting. It was an interesting and worthwhile therapy experience. The change that I experienced happened slowly and was subtle.

I was "directed" to look at this therapy as a useful intervention to combine with the Wisdom intervention. While I didn't do Orgone Therapy in the traditional fashion, I had the patient sit across from me with his or her eyes closed and vocalize a sigh. I believed the sigh would trigger past traumatic experiences that may be subtly influencing the patient's behavior. I simply have the patient breathe deeply with his or her mouth open, and asked him or her to vocalize "Ahaaaa" in a relaxed fashion, while breathing out. After six or seven breaths, I ask the following:

T: **Subconscious, please tag all of the memory elements or parts that were triggered by the breathing.**
S: **Yes.**
T: **Subconscious, please ask Wisdom to create an intervention to remove the negative emotions from these memory elements and parts triggered by the breathing, and replace them with peace and love. Please replace any treated beliefs or behaviors with positive, self-empowering beliefs and behaviors, and then do a Massive Change History and everything.**
S: **Yes.**
T: **Subconscious, should we repeat this intervention?**

I repeat this intervention as many times as requested. I tried this with a number of patients, and they all felt the processing begin. Further inquiry to the subconscious found that this was a positive intervention.

Treatment Using a Well-Formed Declaration
This is the first of a number of different interventions that were developed with help from Wisdom or some other source while treating a complex issue. I had been working with a patient for more than 170 sessions, treating difficult barriers that prevented her from moving forward to reach her personal and professional goals. It was a collaborative relationship

because she continued working on the issues between sessions and knew the Process Healing Method very well.

I am presenting some of the work here because it became very interesting and unorthodox. She had verbal intrusions that led us to many esoteric treatment interventions for issues that would have otherwise been untreated. I had some curiosity about the source of these helpful intrusions. One possibility is that the identification of issues and their treatment was orchestrated by some brilliant part or by part of her subconscious to keep us from discovering the core issue. Another possibility was that the intrusions were caused from the outside by an implant or some other method of manipulating her thoughts and actions remotely as an experiment by some unknown people. However, I did not detect any outside influence causing the intrusions. The third possibility, as reported by the intrusions, was that Wisdom was leading me to issues to teach me about treatment. Whatever the source of the auditory intrusions, they were helpful in therapy and guided me to new insights into the underlying conditions causing human behavior.

In this example, we were told by her subconscious that she was unable to go forward in life, in part due to some instability. She also had a constant, ongoing stream of negative intrusions that were memories created by her mother's constant tirades. This intervention — the well-formed declaration — was given after two or three sessions of therapy directed by Wisdom or some alleged helping, vocal intrusions heard by the patient. I am including a relatively detailed presentation of the interaction between Wisdom, the patient, and myself. I am doing this to alert therapists to the possibility of establishing this kind of relationship with some unknown helpful resource. This is another good example of Wisdom — or the intrusions — leading the therapist to interventions that may be useful with other issues and other patients.

Wisdom had "told" us in the previous session that the person would receive information that would direct the treatment path. As it turned out, a few days before our session, the person heard two cues: "Unwillingness to succeed and instability" and "Omnitude."

Omnitude? Neither of us had ever heard of this word, much less used it. Its meaning is synonymous with entirety. This cue is an example of intrusions she frequently had that used words or phrasing that neither of us would normally use. After a few guesses, we found the cues meant that she had an unwillingness to succeed and her instability was pervasive throughout all the cells in her body — like a part. This cellular part added to the instability. Wisdom told us that behavior by her father had caused this part and that we had to know the causes and origin of the instability to treat it. Knowing the cause and origin of a barrier was frequently necessary to solve difficult, esoteric problems and barriers caused by ancestral field intrusions.

The patient did the TAT and heard that "the flunots go out of whack." Recall that TAT is the intervention where the patient places his ring finger and thumb just above the tear duct, the middle finger between the eyebrows on the crown of the nose, and the other hand cupping the back of his or her head. This pose is useful to get cues in treatment or information about the source of trauma. What she heard didn't make sense until the next session. She learned that something unusual had caused the creation of the cellular part. Here's how it was allegedly created.

Her father worked hard and was seldom at home. When he was, he never said much. When she was three years old, her father slapped her hard. At the same time, she heard him call her "a fool" and she felt embarrassed. Prior trauma had caused an easy-creation of parts and this trauma with her father caused the atypical, cellular part and the pervasive instability. The experience caused an unusual shift in the 6th and 7th dimensions that we "wouldn't totally understand." The definition of "fool" fits many of the behaviors that this person does in many circumstances. The word "fool" implies instability and being called a fool in that situation was the cause of her instability. The inability to succeed is part of the instability.

Another "catastrophic" event occurred at age 11 when her three-year-old brother had an accident in which he lost a finger in a cement mixer. This traumatic experience solidified the presence of instability, based on the pervasive introjection of the belief that she was a fool.

Being called a fool caused structures that had to be treated first because this was the root of the instability and the barrier to going forward. I had to use a Wisdom intervention to remove the fool introjects, but Wisdom said, "Know that you have to fully remove all roots because that is the basis for the whole tree" of instability. After some guesses and redirection, we had the following intervention.

T: **Subconscious, please contact Wisdom to create an intervention to remove all roots caused by the word "fool" used in any**

context over the person's life, and replace it with behaviors showing her genius.
S: **Yes.**
T: [Waits.] **Are you processing?**
S: **Integrating. Patience please.**

When working with Wisdom, the patient often gets candid intrusions like this.

In the next session, we found the structure we had removed in the last session had automatically "re-grown." Wisdom said, "Don't be subservient, use ambience." We eventually found out that this meant to look at the Personal Field in a different way.

There was an aberration in the 9th dimension that created changes in the 6th and 7th dimensions. I asked about starting treatment and the patient heard, "No, more must be known." I asked if the 9th dimension was confused. She heard, "No. Don't consider that. Confusion doesn't exist."

More questions revealed that the problem was in the 9th dimension in her Personal Field. Recall that a person's subconscious has varying degrees of representation in the 5th through 9th dimensions. The aberration in the 9th dimensions was caused in the subconscious by the repetitive punishment that happened between ages three and six. Although there was severe punishment from birth, this particular punishment from age three to six was "emotional, and charismatic and deeper, more profound, robust, and stagnating."

The patient then had a flash intrusion, "Everything is in a bubble, all of it." This had something to do with how the subconscious believed that "everything my mother said was true." This was clarified: "All of what Mother did to her was accepted by the subconscious as true in its entirety, which resulted in creating this structure in the 9th dimension." Mother prefaced punishing comments with "Nobody more than me will . . ." and "Whatever I say is right . . ." Statements like these caused the subconscious to accept the premise that "Mother is right," which corrupted the Personal Field and altered the activity of the subconscious .

There was more: "Fear, pain, and punishment," we were told. There was conflict in the subconscious about going forward. The pain and punishment were so great that they supported a problematic structure in the 9th dimension. The field of the structure in the 9th dimension kept the inability to go forward always present.

After doing this exploration and preparation, we were finally ready to do an intervention. This may sound "out there" and implausible, but Wisdom said that the following intervention should be used. Make a clear declaration stated in the active tense. "This statement affects the 10th dimension, which operates to obtain coherency. A statement such as this creates harmony, because it is in line with a loving universe — the 10th dimension, it is positive for the person, and it is positive for humanity." Wisdom said that this intervention was used centuries ago and allegedly around the world, but not in the western cultures. This intervention using a clear declaration can be used remotely and anyone can do it.

I inquired about a Wisdom intervention and the patient heard, "Do it yourself. There is a learning curve. March forward. This is a declaration."

I asked and confirmed that this was an intervention that I hadn't used much. Wisdom said to state the wanted outcome clearly, with conviction, and assert that it is true. The intervention had to be a declaration stated in a clear and active tense, healthy for the person and humanity, and with positive effects to be experienced or produced by the patient. Here is the declaration.

T: (Person's name) **experiences being capable of moving forward in all areas of her life forever to fulfill her optimum potential.**
S: **Yes.**
T: **It is true.**
S: **Yes.**

Other declarations, such as "So it is," "So be it" or "Amen," can also be used.

This statement alters the current frame of the unfolding reality. With the positive goal stated in the current frame, the 10th dimension obtains coherency of that change with the universe. The zero points create these changes in the next frame.

Since the issues addressed by the previous week's interventions were re-created, I had to repeat the previous week's interventions.

T: **Subconscious, please repeat last week's interventions.**
S: **Yes.**
T: [Waits.] **Done?**
S: **You need a Massive Change History.**
T: **Please do a Massive Change History and everything.**
S: **Yes.**

Although I have tried the declaration intervention a few times, I have only one other case where I feel confident that this intervention produced striking results. I believe that with poorly formed declarations, the subconscious may reframe them to use local interventions or it simply doesn't do anything. Nevertheless, the intervention is consistent with the model of the universe and can be offered as an intervention using the properties of the universe. I don't know the parameters of this intervention, but will occasionally ask a subconscious if the declaration intervention is the correct treatment for the issue. If it is, I use it. I wonder if it is possible to get positive results consistently by making declaration interventions?

In the present case, as I have found with scores of other interventions, there was another barrier that was blocking the declaration intervention and the interventions of the previous week. There was a limit to what this person could do, because there was "a pure and sound belief" that caused the barrier. The belief held by a part was a childlike belief in the Behavior and Verbal Systems. Wisdom told us to find the belief and the whole barrier would "fall apart."

After 50 minutes of guessing and receiving cues, the belief was: "Mommy, I promise to do what you tell me to do." This belief held the hundreds of layered memories together that battered her with verbal intrusions. We were told that "traumatic fright" in the Emotion System motivated the layered memories. The patient heard that "asking (in the intervention) must come from a childlike standpoint, so the child part fully understands it." Here is the intervention:

T: **Subconscious, please remove the fright from all of Mommy's demands in the Verbal System and replace them with neutral emotions.**
S: **No, this is not from a child's standpoint.**

I had guessed incorrectly. Here is my next guess:

T: **Subconscious, please take away all those scary statements my mommy said to me.**
S: **Yes.**
T: [Done.] **Please do a Massive Change History and everything.**
S: **Yes.**
T: [Waits.] **Does that get rid of the barrier?**
S: **Yes.**

 The person's heart was racing, and she heard a little girl's voice saying, "Wow, I'm free. I have so many choices right now."
 To complete the treatment for this issue, we asked the subconscious to repeat the interventions we had done in the last two sessions. Months later, we found a barrier that had prevented the interventions we had been doing for years. There was still an underlying process that reversed or blocked the treatment effects having to do with making and completing plans. It was an inherited DNA pattern.

Treating an Inherited DNA Pattern

In the session after the declaration intervention, the patient found no change in going forward, but the stream of nasty intrusions had stopped. I wondered if the previous interventions had been successful and the patient heard, "Your interventions have all worked meticulously. Stop doubting yourself." So we had to identify a new target, described as "very simple, but (the treatment) must be accurate."
 Here is another example of communication via the vocal intrusion. I asked if it had to do with the initiation of behavior. The patient heard: "Inaccurate question. Accuracy is the key at this stage of the game. So please do not judge something that really isn't there. You are asking a question really not appropriate here. We understand where you are coming from, but it is in the wrong direction. You must be accurate. Please bear that word in mind from now on."
 Over the next 45 minutes, we got cues in various ways — through intrusions, using the TAT pose, and guessing. Wisdom said, "As you get to the end, it will become more and more complex." We had been working many, many sessions to give the patient the option of going forward in any area of her life. After hearing "It was a preemption inherited from mother and grandmother," I guessed correctly that it was a DNA pattern from the inception of living matter that had created the belief. In turn, the belief had created the preemption.

Nearing the end of the session, the patient repeated the TAT intervention and heard "I'm a nobody." This belief is the preemption — something like a predisposition. To remove or treat this preemption, the treatment had to proceed from the grandmother, to the mother and then to the patient. The patient heard "accuracy is required, no exception. It must be absolutely clear."

After trying several poorly formed interventions, here is the intervention I used to treat the belief entrained to a DNA pattern from inception.

T: [To the patient] **Please state the belief, "I am a nobody."**
P: **I am a nobody.**
T: **Subconscious, please remove the DNA pattern for the belief from the grandmother's cellular memories and her Personal Field. Do a Massive Change History and everything. Then do the same treatment for the mother's cellular memories and Personal Field, and then do a Massive Change History and everything. Finally, do the same treatment for the person's cellular memories and her Personal Field, and then do a Massive Change History and everything.**
S: **Yes.**
T: [Waits] **Please do a Massive Change History and everything.**

Wisdom said that this intervention was important to put in this book, because many people have a belief such as this, and when they read the dialogue, the intervention will be triggered.

Later, I expanded the Massive Change History to include removing the effects of ancestral fields on the DNA patterns and all aspects of the physiology.

T: **Subconscious, please do a Massive Change History and everything and remove, from conception to now, the distortion of all aspects of the physiology that was caused by the ancestral field and return it to normal.**

We are still continuing to treat unique barriers for going forward. These barriers are unusual, complicated, seem contrived, but always turn out to make sense and be congruent with her life history. It is as if I am being trained to treat unusual barriers that can affect human behavior.

A Conception Field Entrained to the First Cell

Apparently, a Conception Field can entrain to the first cell at conception. These self-organized fields allegedly distort the DNA throughout the brain and body. One can remove these Conception Fields by using Wisdom to treat the fields and the distortions caused in the DNA. There are two conditions for using the Wisdom intervention to treat the Conception Fields:

1. The subconscious has to be able to communicate with the Wisdom.

2. The patient must believe that the intervention will work and can genuinely make a statement to the effect that "I believe it will work."

T: **Subconscious, are there Conception Fields entrained to the first cell in conception that has distorted the patient's DNA?**
S: **Yes.**
T: **Subconscious, please work with Wisdom to create an intervention to remove the Conception Fields and all effects they caused throughout the DNA and replace it with love.**
S: **Yes.**
T: **Please do a Massive Change History and everything to normalize any distortions caused in all aspects of the physiology from conception to now.**

Fields Associated with Content — Content Fields

I received information via intrusions from Wisdom about another problematic entrainment. There are similar behaviors (content memories) that occurred in traumatic situations throughout history that entrained and are present in the Amassed Personal Field. Remember, a content memory consists of the collage of old memories that create a response — the behavior. Content memories have no emotions. The emotions are associated with the physiological activity that is associated with the memory structure (see Figure 4-1). Behaviors or content memories similar to the person's behavior in the 5th dimension — a content field — can entrain with living person's behavior to create what I call a Content Field intrusion. As opposed to soul intrusions that entrain on trauma emotions, Content Fields in the 5th dimension entrain to a similar content memory or behavior in a person's Personal Field to either distort the behavior and block or reduce the effectiveness of the treatment of that behavior.

After treating the Content Fields, one can treat trauma memory structures more quickly and thoroughly. Content Fields that entrain to the content memory structures of behavior are not self-organized. However, it appears that the Content Fields that entrain to organs and to individual cells are self-organized. Removing Content Fields is necessary for optimum effects when treating physical and emotional issues.

Here are examples of treating Content Fields:

1. Treating Content Fields and Traumas

The content memory of an experience created by intense trauma is the anchor to which a Content Field with similar content can entrain. The following intervention, by the subconscious and Wisdom, first identifies all healthy memory structures that have been damaged by Content Fields, then creates an intervention to remove the Content Fields, and finally removes the trauma. It is important to phrase this intervention in a way to put any self-organized memory structures off guard.

T: **Subconscious, please work with Wisdom to identify all the damaged memory structures. Then identify the Content Fields and traumas entrained to the memory structures, and create interventions to remove the Content Fields and the effects of the trauma and replace them with love.**

S: **Yes.**

T: **Please do a Massive Change History and everything.**

2. Field Viruses and Physical Illnesses

If a person has a physical illness, he or she should be under medical care before trying this intervention. This intervention should support medical care and not be the primary intervention. When a field virus entrains to the content of a physical memory, it is believed to contribute to the creation of physical illnesses, such as breast cancer. The field virus entrains to the memory structure of the cells of an organ in the Personal Field. Because the field virus entrained to the organ appears to be self-organized, it attacks the organ and distorts its memory structure. The distorted cells in the organ lead to illness in the body. To treat an illness, one has to identify and remove fields from the organs that cause the physical illness, and then repair the fields representing the memory structure of the diseased cells.

T: **Subconscious, please work with Wisdom to identify the patterns of the field virus entrained to memory structures causing the physical illness in the [organ]. Create an intervention to remove the field virus from the memory structures and repair the memory structures in the organ to a normal state.**
S: **Yes.**

Removing Barriers that Distort the Activity of the 10th Dimension

The Wisdom told us that there could be barriers in the Personal Field (5th through 9th dimensions) that distort the action of the Manager (10th dimension). Unusual field barriers entrained to one or more dimensions in our Personal Field decrease the effectiveness of the Manager. These field barriers cause the creation of rapidly oscillating changes in the virtual reality. The following Wisdom intervention will clear both Content Fields and other field barriers that interfere with the activity of the Manager.

T: **Subconscious, please contact Wisdom and ask Wisdom to identify the field barriers in the Personal Field that undermine the effectiveness of the Manager, and create an intervention to remove all identified field barriers and Content Fields in the Personal Field and replace them with love.**
S: **Yes.**

Treatment of Unconscious Negative Verbal Dialogue

Bruce Lipton writes and talks about the benefits of positive thoughts in obtaining a healthy life.[8] He believes that positive unconscious thoughts create positive results like those obtained with a placebo.[9] When you take a placebo, you start a positive unconscious dialogue that has a positive effect on that particular issue. You get better. On the other hand, he reasons that unconscious negative thoughts must have a negative influence on our health, maybe even propagating unhealthy behavior or physical illness. He calls it the *nocebo* effect.

While working with a patient on hair pulling, I had been able to greatly reduce the numbers of hairs pulled, but I hadn't figured out how to stop it totally. I tried to experiment with this notion of positive and negative unconscious dialogue. I routinely had the subconscious treat the unconscious memory elements, behaviors, or statements supporting the patient's hair pulling. This time, I attempted a field intervention by asking the subconscious if she could see the fields of unconscious negative dialogue supporting hair pulling. I found that she could see them in a field pattern and that it was safe to treat. I asked the subconscious to treat the field pattern of the negative dialogue.

When finished, I asked if all the unconscious negative dialogue with respect to hair pulling was treated. She said "No." I problem-solved and found that the negative dialogue was in some split-off system fragments. Apparently, the negative dialogues were dissociated and their presence in the system fragments kept the information from the subconscious. The subconscious had to look in the system fragments to see them. In Flint (2006, pp. 278-281), I gave the rationale for split-off system fragments. I describe a treatment intervention to consolidate them into one split-off system, and then join the resulting structure with the Behavior System. Then the subconscious could see the field pattern of the negative dialogues that were formerly occurring in the system fragment.

T: **Are there negative dialogues that support the issue?**
S: **Yes.**
T: **Can you see the field pattern of the negative dialogue and is it safe to treat?**
S: **Yes.**
T: **Please treat the field pattern of the negative dialogue and do a Massive Change History and everything.**
S: **Yes.**
T: [Done.] **Are there system fragments with negative dialogue in them?**
S: **Yes.**

The treatment of system fragments involves consolidating fragments that were created by the same trauma. Then these consolidated system fragments are then joined Into one system fragment. This

fragment is then joined with the Behavior System. The following intervention does all of this in one intervention.

T: **Please consolidate the groups of system fragments and join
   them with the Behavior System.**
S: **Yes.**
T: **Can you see the field pattern of the negative dialogue and is it
   safe to treat?**
S: **Yes.**
T: **Please treat it and do a Massive Change History and everything.**
S: **Yes.**

While this appeared to reduce the frequency of hair pulling,
there was more work to do.

I used this intervention with another patient. He was fighting a
genetic disease common to his home country. Many had it and had died
at a young age. He had had two siblings recently die from this genetic
disease. Much of the treatment with him had to with ancestral influences on his thinking and health. Common among his countrymen was
an unconscious belief, "I was born to die." This was treated. We
removed the negative dialogue and then consolidated system fragments
and treated the negative dialogue that was operating in the system fragments. The next week, he experienced remarkable changes in his behavior and health. He was able to talk to family members without becoming
disturbed and experiencing a reoccurrence of symptoms, something he
had not been able to do in years.

Treatment from a Higher Realm

I don't know what to make of the following observations. This seems
significant to me, although I have only seen five examples of this phenomenon. I am describing this here so that the readers can make their
own discovery of what might be possible.

The patient and his support person, in his words, had a connection to the spiritual realm. I was treating him. We were problem-solving
to determine a treatment plan for his "core issue." At one point, he said
that "a little part, who didn't want anything, was taken out into the light
and his 'core' was free." The patient also said that he could see flashes
of light occurring in different places in his brain during the treatment. I
asked his subconscious if a treatment process caused this, and he heard

a "Yes." Because the subconscious can independently start any treatment used by the therapist, I usually ask which intervention was causing this experience of flashing lights. I went through a list of all my treatments to identify the intervention, but found none.

Finally, I asked if I caused this intervention. The answer was "No." I then asked if any of the interventions that I have used in the past caused this intervention; another "No." I asked if I could learn and teach this intervention to others and received a "No." I was told that this intervention was initiated by another source — a higher dimension — and it could only occur in persons with strong connections to the other dimension. The intervention came "when the situation was ready for it." At that time, I named the cause for change the Higher Realm.

I had had a patient on the preceding day who had a similar experience of flashes of light during a treatment process. I asked if the same process caused this experience. This was confirmed and it said that the other patient also had good connections to the higher dimension; "she has a natural ability to make a spiritual connection."

A third patient experienced swirls of colors that were said to be caused by this same healing process. She said it looked like the swirling, colored lights on the midway of a carnival. Allegedly, it was the activity of the Higher Realm. I asked if I could now ask the Higher Realm to treat an issue. She heard "Yes." Following my curiosity, I found that the Higher Realm was not the 9th dimension. It was apparently the Manager who operated with some other information to make changes in the patient. I asked if the Manager could treat the list of issues written on my treatment notes. The answer was "No." Good try, but no success.

Another patient felt her little finger itching and heaviness in her chest. They were allegedly caused by an intruding soul and a part, respectively. I tried to treat the part and field in the usual ways. It didn't work. I asked if the "Realm" could please treat the part and intruding soul. After a short period, the heaviness in the chest left and the itch in the finger went away. I am currently experimenting with this intervention to explore the parameters of it — namely, whether it will work with anyone.

Further experiments with the Higher Realm were tried by appending, "With the help of the Higher Realm," onto different interventions. I tried it with the TAT intervention to treat obsessive thoughts. The treatment produced intruding lights in the experience of the patient. I have also appended it to the Massive Change History intervention.

I believe that most of these interventions would have worked in any case.

My understanding is that this "Higher Realm" intervention is possible with all those people who have a spiritual connection to the higher dimensions and are led to this option. It is not an intervention that they do by choice. The patient's subconscious intends to obtain the goal behavior. In the right circumstances with persons with a good connection to the higher dimensions, the person's subconscious is accessed and the Manager changes the person's issue in his or her Personal Field to maintain coherency between the subconscious and the patient's Personal Field. This change causes the change in 3D-Reality. With this intervention, the patient experiences swirling colors or white lights flashing.

Another explanation for how this intervention works is that this is an example of treatment wisdom accumulating in the 9th dimension. It appears that the experience and discoveries of many therapists are building on their previous experience. This results in previous interventions becoming unnecessary. I think this has been the experience of many therapists using Energy Psychology techniques. It is certainly my experience.

The interventions offered in this chapter are all experimental and the subconscious should always be asked if the intervention is safe to use with yourself or another person before applying the intervention.

Summary

This book develops a model for understanding the hidden reality — the dimensional structures causing all that we see and do in our 3D-Reality. The theory of the hidden reality connects our understanding of the quantum or subtle influences that can affect what we experience in our 3D-Reality. It explains the mechanics and treatment of demons and ancestral influences. The model offers an explanation of nonlocal phenomena, such as surrogate healing and prayer. It leads to a number of experimental interventions to treat trauma-based memories and unwanted beliefs that are problematic in our lives. The theory, really a collection of metaphors like all theories, can very well enrich your understanding of life.

Initially, the goal of this book was to present a rational basis for understanding and treating demons and fallen angels. I wrote it to explain the unknown influences of the hidden reality in a way that mental health professionals would understand. The reason we can't usually see demons is that they behave in the spirit world of the hidden reality. I started by giving some vignettes of research that were explained as fields in the hidden reality. Then, I offered clinical vignettes that involved working with intruding souls in the hidden reality and other vignettes describing communication with patients through the hidden reality in the clinical setting.

As the basis for understanding the mechanics of intruding souls, I gave a brief outline of the development of the personality using a model based on the assumption that the content of memories causes behavior. It was necessary to give this background to understand some complex memory structures found in people with severe trauma histories. Intruding souls — demons and fallen angels — attach to the pattern of pain associated with different trauma or memory structures in the living person.

To explain intruding souls, I described a physics model based on a string theory I adapted to fit my clinical experience gained over many years. The model defines 11 dimensions (0 to 10). Our soul consists of the 5th through 9th dimensions that amass important information from our lifetime. The 5th dimension — the Personal Field — was most prominent in explaining soul intrusions, because the Personal Field preserves all our life history. The Personal Field of a deceased person can contain intense pain in a pattern of memory structures that matches the same intense pain memory structures of a living person. The similarity of memory structures with intense pain can lead to a soul intrusion — the entrainment or attachment of the soul to our Personal Field.

The 6th and 7th dimensions preserve the memory of our physical being. The 8th dimension is a transition dimension leading to the 9th dimension. The 9th dimension is all Wisdom from the beginning of humanity associated with love. The 0th through 4th dimensions have to do with completing our physical structure and communicating within the body, which gives us our experience and behavior in 3D-Reality.

The nonlocal property of our Personal Field was explored. I discussed various healing methods and prayer to show the reality of nonlocal communication or distant healing. Several studies confirming the possibility of communicating with others and healing were presented. Examples were given that included vignettes of surrogate treatments using Emotional Freedom Techniques and the Family Constellation Therapy. A description of communicating with the Personal Field in treatment sessions was described.

For the first time in psychology, a physics theory led to a treatment intervention that turns out to be powerful. The basis for this theory is that unique groups of zero points — point sources of energy — create dimensional structures for all aspects of our 3D-Reality. I assume that, like photons, the dimensional structures are removed rapidly, only to be recreated while preserving history. This suggests that our 3D-Reality unfolds much like the frames in a movie, with our history amassing at all levels. The theory hypothesizes that the 0th through 9th dimensions are embedded in the 10th dimension. The role of the 10th dimension, the Manager, in the creation process is to ensure coherency between all living and inert objects as our reality changes from frame to frame. This is based on fixed rules of the universe that take memory of the living into account — the memory amassed in what I call our Personal Field. These rules manage reality, giving all living beings more happiness and less pain.

It was shown that the 9th dimension, containing all positive experiences from the beginning of humankind based on love, could be accessed with the metaphor Wisdom. The intervention is prayer-like, in which the subconscious asks Wisdom to create an intervention to resolve the issue. Other experimental interventions using Wisdom are described in the closing chapter. The most interesting and powerful is the extension of healing physical issues by changing field patterns (quantum information), a practice discussed by Adam (2003), to the treatment of mental issues. The subconscious can see field patterns of a mental issue and, when safe, effectively treat the mental issue by treating the field pattern.

Appendix I

Meeting Your Subconscious

Introduction

Based on my experience of working with hundreds of patients, I am convinced that we all have a subconscious — a part of ourselves who is free from pain and trauma and can actively heal painful memories. Many patients who come to me are already aware of this part of themselves. Others develop an awareness of this part as we work together. Whatever their experience, they each have an inner part who was there from the beginning of life. I believe that the subconscious operates as a composite of the 5th through 9th dimensions, so it is independent of the Personal Field and free of emotions. This part can serve as an ally in solving problems in treatment and can learn how to treat your trauma memories.

Some people call their subconscious their inner self, angel, field, inner spirit, core, power animal, guide, or higher self. I call it the subconscious because it is a neutral term and seems fitting, since I define the conscious and unconscious as active memories. Be clear that the subconscious is not in the unconscious. Just as the subconscious plays an important role in treatment in the Process Healing Method, he or she also plays an important role in treating intruding fields, ancestral fields and cellular memories that subtly affect our behavior. The subconscious is your contact with Wisdom, who is also an ally in treatment.

This appendix will provide a method for you to contact and communicate with your subconscious. These directions are an abbreviated version of the instructions given in Chapter 3 of *A Theory and Treatment of Your Personality: A manual for change*. The brief instructions here are not intended to organize your inner world or teach you the treatment process. However, many readers should be able to get in touch with their subconscious after having read this. This will meet your needs if you are curious or want to be able to treat basic issues. Readers who have moderate to severe trauma may have parts or memory structures that will block these instructions to communicate with the subconscious.

If you are not able to communicate with your subconscious and want to negotiate with your inner world to obtain communication, then read the full instructions in my book mentioned previously.

When working with the subconscious, there are barriers that can undermine the impact of the subconscious. For example, intruding fields can entrain with the subconscious. In addition, sometimes our memories are fragmented by trauma or circumstances, which can cause activity that undermines the effectiveness of the subconscious. In Appendix II, I include interventions for removing intruding fields and subconscious fragments that affect or distort the activity of the subconscious. These interventions are useful for persons who are exploring the presence of fields or have issues they want to treat. I will describe treatment approaches for these barriers and give several examples of each. With this information, once you have success in contacting your subconscious, the treatments described in Chapters 4 through 10 will be easier to carry out.

Many people will be successful in communicating with their subconscious by using one of the methods to be described. However, others may have unknown memory structures with painful emotions that present barriers to communication with the subconscious. This is completely normal. The easiest and most respectful approach for communication with the subconscious is to use the complete educational approach outlined in the book presenting the Process Healing Method; however, I estimate that about half the population will have barriers when they try to contact their subconscious. Unless you have a torture history, nothing in this book is dangerous for you or your subconscious when used correctly. If you find a barrier just continue reading and try to contact your subconscious later, after following the suggestions here in Appendix I or in Flint (2006).

Before You Start

Read the following carefully to protect you from any negative outcomes. In most cases, it is unlikely there will be a problem. Trauma-based aspects and the subconscious will not usually do anything that will hurt the Main Personality of the reader, especially when the parts know what is happening. It also might be useful, before reading this section, to read Appendix III-5 to see if you can download my treatment wisdom.

Before continuing, I want you to pay attention to your emotional state and internal conversations. If you have a severe trauma history, known or unknown, I feel confident that you will know by some emotion, be it fear or anxiety, or by an internal voice, that you are threatening some aspect of your internal world. If this happens or if you have any reservations, stop reading and find a therapist before continuing. This protective awareness is also necessary for anyone who you try to help to access his or her subconscious.

You can always talk to the subconscious. There is no way to block this communication. The subconscious is always awake and is aware of everything. However, arranging communication with the subconscious via finger responses when there is a barrier can be difficult. Making contact with the subconscious has to be approached by giving respect to all aspects of your personality. Now, I want to remind all of the aspects or parts, you may have, that treatments by the subconscious presented in this book are very respectful. The treatment of intruding souls, a respectful intervention, can only help create a happier internal world. The Wisdom intervention is a treatment that will only work if the treatment is good for you and your world. Parts or memory structures with valid objections to any treatment can block the communication with the subconscious and the requested treatment. Therefore, all active parts and aspects have control over the treatment process.

However, in Appendix III-5, there is a suggestion for downloading my treatment knowledge and instructions for treating parts and all memory structures. I am confident that any parts or aspects who are uncomfortable with this action have the capacity to block both the downloading of information and treatment requests. If contact with your subconscious is blocked or the downloading of treatment knowledge or treatment of parts is blocked, it is completely normal. Your parts and aspects are protecting you and themselves.

Intruding fields can affect some or all aspects of your personality. When content or emotions activate an intruding field, the emotions triggered by the intruding field will add to the emotions that motivate the active memory. This can distort the active memory in a negative way. Active fields can provide intrusive behavior, such as verbal intrusions, body sensations or even behavior that can be problematic for the Main Personality. Treating these intrusive fields reduces pain and problems for parts and the Main Personality and increases your self-control. Sometimes, compartmentalized parts can't tell the difference between activity in the Active Experience caused by a part and activity caused by an intruding field. Luckily, the subconscious can usually tell the difference. However, the activity is a barrier to treatment because the emotions caused by the field destabilizes the Active Experience and has to be treated first in a different way. It is in the best interest of all parts and other aspects of the personality to support the removal of intruding fields.

Why Communicate with the Subconscious?

To begin, communication with the subconscious is necessary to make it easy to communicate with and treat intruding fields. The description of the interventions involving communication between the therapist (reader) and the subconscious is presented in script form. I have written it in this format to model the therapeutic method to both teach the reader how to communicate with the subconscious and to give the reader experience directing a treatment process. If there is no need for the treatment, and you fail to communicate with the subconscious, nothing is lost. However, clearing disruptive intruding fields always has positive outcomes. The script shows who is communicating with capital letters on the left side. Here are the definitions of the capital letters used in the script.

> T: **A statement or question by the therapist or reader.**
> S: **The response of the subconscious or field.**
> P: **The response by the patient or client.**

    I wrote the instructions to communicate with the reader. If you are a therapist, it should be easy to convert the instructions or scripts to use in a dialogue with a patient.

    I start by saying the following to the reader and all compartmentalized parts and other aspects who are active, so they will understand your or my intentions and not be fearful.

> T: **I am going to talk through the Main Personality to all aspects of your personality. I want to let you know what I am doing. I am looking for intruding fields that may be causing problems in day-to-day behavior. Once I identify an intruding field, then the subconscious can smooth out the emotional pain in the field of the intruding field, and it can slide off into**

everlasting happiness. This will remove any problem caused by the intruding field, such as intensifying problematic responses or contributing unusual verbal intrusions or behavior.

Communicating with fields requires the reader to have a clear line of communication with the subconscious. There may be parts present who fear allowing the reader or therapist access to the subconscious. Treating fields is much different from treating parts and memory structures. The subconscious will work with the fields in the 5th dimension and will not bother any of your memory structures. I want to reassure you that no parts will be directly treated, and an effort will be made to not disrupt you in any way. The Wisdom treatment has the potential to make significant changes, but this will only happen if it is healthy for the person and healthy for the world. Valid objections to any treatment will be respected.

There is a positive consequence of treating intruding fields. Any memory or behavior to which an intruding field was entrained will have less motivation or problematic experiences after treatment. With less motivation, the experience of emotions and some behaviors will become less problematic. Any intervention to free the subconscious to talk with a higher wisdom or to treat intruding fields will automatically be made gently with the permission of all relevant parts. With this said, we will now set up communication with the subconscious. Do you have any questions?

Usually, the people don't have any questions and pass into a light trance state because the concepts presented are so novel to them.

Communicating with the Subconscious

There are three means of communication with the subconscious that I prefer. The first is to use the muscle responses of the fingers. Trained hypnotherapists use the finger response technique in some interventions. This is a technique, described by Edelstien, that was used for uncovering information from his patients. The finger movements used for communicating with the subconscious are called ideomotor responses. Either the person or the therapist can define the meaning of finger responses. Second, a pendulum can also be used to communicate with the subconscious. With the pendulum, the subconscious can cause fine muscle responses to get the pendulum to move in different directions to communicate. I will tell you more about this later. The third way to communicate with the subconscious is to quiet your mind and listen for an internal response. I'll first explain communicating with the subconscious using finger responses.

1. Communication using finger responses

T: **Now I am going to try to communicate with your subconscious. Please lay your hands, palms down, next to you, on your knees, or in front of you on a table. Let them relax. I am going to ask some questions while you remain relaxed. Be curious about the process and see if a finger response will occur. Don't make conscious finger movements. Concentrate on leaving your hands relaxed and flat because no response is also a response. First try with your eyes open and if that doesn't work, try with your eyes closed. Be as relaxed as you can. With the Process Healing Method, patients often put themselves into a light trance to allow the subconscious to move the fingers. By doing this they eliminate their own tendency to respond. A light trance won't work here because you might not feel the finger response, and I won't be with you to see the movement. Therefore, putting yourself into a light trance will not work when you are working alone. The goal is for you to be able to ask questions of your subconscious or intruding fields and see or feel the answer with a finger response.**

　　The first goal is to have you experience the involuntary finger responses caused by the subconscious. This makes communication easy. Many will only feel a sensation in one of the fingers. With practice, the sensation or movement will be clear to you and you can effectively communicate with the subconscious. When it does not work, you will have to communicate in another way.

　　The script below involves reading questions and answers. After you read a question, wait a while and you may feel a response or a tickle in one of your fingers. Wait up to 30 seconds, because different people respond at different rates — some quickly and some slowly. If you feel a tickle or a sensation, then move your finger so you can see it. Some therapists think that it

is good to let the patient define the responses. I don't do this, because I have many patients, and having different responses for different patients would tend to confuse me.

Therapist-defined responses
This is my preferred approach when I am working with someone.

T: **Subconscious, let's define the index finger for "Yes," the thumb for "No," the little finger (pinkie) for "I don't know," and the middle finger for "I don't want to tell you." Now move your fingers on both hands as I read the responses. Raise the "Yes" finger. Move both index fingers up and down several times. Raise the "No" finger. Move your thumbs. Raise the "I don't know" finger. Move your little fingers, and the "I don't want to tell you" finger. Move the middle fingers. In addition, no movement from any finger is the response "I don't want to talk to you." So it is important to leave your fingers relaxed, and be curious about which finger is going to move; in other words, let your subconscious or a part do the talking.**

Now, try it out to see if you can communicate with the subconscious.

T: **Subconscious, please show me a "Yes" response.**

You are expecting some activity in one or both index fingers. Wait a full 30 seconds to see if there is any form of movement or sensation in either index finger following the question. Sometimes, the fingers on both the right and left hand will move or have sensations. When this happens, I always wonder if a prebirth part is moving one of the fingers. Prebirth parts often learn to shuttle information from the subconscious to the conscious experience. Because of their perceived function, it seems natural for them to try to communicate when you are trying to communicate with the subconscious.

S: **Yes.** [Oh, what luck, the index finger moved.]
T: **Thank you. Subconscious, please show me a "No" response.**
S: [No response or wrong finger]

Remember, you should move any fingers in which there are sensations; if there is no response or sensation, problem-solve as follows:

T: **Is there a part blocking communication?**
S: [Waiting 30 seconds, no response]

Restate your plan to not teach the subconscious how to treat trauma directly, that trauma will be removed only by Wisdom. The subconscious will only treat intruding fields. Try again and continue to problem-solve.

T: **Is there a part blocking communication or deliberately not moving the fingers?**
S: **No.** [Thumb moves.]

I want to be sure that the thumb was the "No" response.

T: **Thank you. Subconscious, please show me a "No" response.**
S: **No.** [Thumb moves.]
T: **Thank you. Subconscious, please show me the "I don't know" response.**
S: **I don't know.** [Little finger moves.]
T: **Thank you. Subconscious, please show me the "I don't want to tell you" response.**
S: **I don't want to tell you.** [Middle finger moved.]

With any of the above questions, if there is no response or if the wrong finger moves, problem-solve by asking questions. Then say the following:

T: **Thank you. "No response" is a response in itself. I interpret "No response" as the response where no fingers have sensation or move. When the ring finger moves, I interpret this as somewhere between "I don't want to tell you" and "I don't know."**

Sometimes, you will have to remind yourself to not move your fingers voluntarily and to remain relaxed and curious about whether a finger will move. Other times, when you don't feel a response, look for a sensation in one of the fingers. Sometimes, you may see a tendon in the hand moving. If nothing works, repeat the entire script of instructions for the finger responses. Reaffirm that you will treat no parts or memory structures directly, so there is no need for fear about emotional flooding. Emphasize to yourself or to your patient that you are simply trying to communicate with the subconscious. If you make no progress, try asking the subconscious to define his or her preferred responses.

Reader-defined responses

Some readers may like to have their subconscious define their own responses. First, read the introduction material and then follow this procedure to help your subconscious define his or her responses.

T: **Subconscious, I am going to ask you to communicate with me by moving my fingers. Please show me a "Yes" response.**

Wait about 30 seconds. Some responses are quick and others are slow. If you get a response, write down the response and the name of the finger, and continue.

T: **Subconscious, please show me a "No" response.**

Usually, a different finger will give you a sensation or will move. Write down which finger signaled a "No." Now, do the same with the following two questions:

T: **Subconscious, please show me an "I don't know" response.**

Write down this response and go on to the next question.

T: **Subconscious, please show me an "I don't want to tell you" response.**

You should have four unique finger sensations or responses that you can use to help you problem-solve any issues that may arise.

Then, to educate the person about "no response," say:

T: **No response is a response in itself. I interpret no response as "I'm not talking."**

When there is a combination of responses, there is a mixed message, with several parts responding. A mixed message requires problem-solving, which will be discussed later.

If you try to get a response several times by waiting the full 30 seconds and find it not working, reread the preceding section presenting the procedure to teach therapist-defined finger responses to the subconscious. If you make no progress with ideomotor responses, try to communicate with the subconscious with a pendulum.

2. Communicating with a pendulum

The second way to communicate with the subconscious and aspects of the personality is to use a pendulum. Find an object like a 5/16 self-locking nut (my preference for personal use) and tie a green string to it — green symbolizes health. The string can be any color or even dental floss. Actually, anything can serve as a weight. Make the string about three to four inches long. Now, while holding the pendulum still, and concentrating to keep it still, ask your subconscious the questions given previously for patient-determined responses; for example, "Subconscious, please show me a yes." After each question, wait until the pendulum moves in some direction. My pendulum moves out and back for a "Yes," sideways for a "No," clockwise for "I don't know," and counterclockwise for "I don't want to tell you." If it is stationary, it may mean some part is blocking the response. The pendulum doesn't work with everyone. Artists and technicians with well-developed, fine muscle control of their fingers may not have success with this approach. However, sometimes it just takes practice to get responses with a pendulum.

3. Communicating with Internal Responses

The third way to communicate with the subconscious is by looking for a visual or auditory response in your thoughts. Some people can imagine a pad or chalkboard in their mind and have their subconscious write a "Yes" or No" on it. Others ask and get an auditory "Yes" or "No" responses in their thoughts. I prefer the finger approach, but if you are working on your own, try to get conscious contact with the subconscious. If you form pictures in your conscious mind easily, see if your subconscious can write on a blackboard, a tablet, or a computer screen. Imagine a blackboard in your thoughts.

T: **Subconscious, please write a "Yes" on the blackboard.**

If you see a "Yes," play with it by making it brighter and dimmer just to develop the awareness that you can control the image. Imagine a slide control on your wrist, where you slide it in one direction to make the image brighter and slide it in the other direction to make the image dimmer. Then ask for a "No" and the other responses, "I don't know" and "I don't want to tell you." If you get these responses easily and clearly, then this means of communication will work well for you.

If it is hard for you to form pictures in your mind, try to communicate with the subconscious through auditory responses by quieting your thoughts and asking for a response in your thoughts. Quiet your mind, ask the following question, and listen for a "Yes" or a "No."

T: **Subconscious, please give me a "Yes" in my thoughts, so I can hear it.**

If you hear the "Yes" response, see if you can reliably tell the difference between your own thoughts and the subconscious. Explore asking your subconscious for the other responses — namely, "No," "I don't know" and "I don't want to tell you" — to see if auditory responses will work for you to communicate with the subconscious.

Sometimes people get extra communication from the subconscious by picturing or hearing detailed responses to questions. If you are lucky, though not many people have this capability, the subconscious can explain or direct the treatment in sentence form by writing directions on a blackboard in your imagination or by giving you words or phrases that you can hear. The subconscious can also be humorous.

Problem-solving

The problem-solving solutions offered address problems obtaining contact and communicating with the subconscious. For your information, when I use the word "parts" to refer to barriers, I use it as a general term to refer to any aspect of you who presents a barrier. You start problem-solving when you get responses that are inconsistent with your expectation or are out of context: for example, "I don't want to tell you."

The response "I don't want to tell you" usually arises when some aspect or part has concerns about what you are reading or asking. This might be caused by intense emotional memories or a memory that would re-traumatize you if you became aware of it. Other causes for this response are handled in *A Theory and Treatment of Your Personality*.

Here, you can restate your intentions and reassure the part that you only want to communicate with the subconscious for the purpose of communicating with fields to help them leave the body, and to communicate with Wisdom. Point out to the parts that they can always block communication if anything you read or attempt to do frightens them.

Resolving Mixed Messages

Resolving mixed messages has to do with experiencing more than one finger response, like a "Yes" and "No," at the same time or responses that don't seem to be correct. There are several causes for mixed messages. Different responses at the same time could be a compartmentalized part and the subconscious both responding. A second response could be a part who has intense pain and is fearful of treatment or who has awakened after the presentation of all the information. Parts who have been asleep don't know what is going on. Their considerations can often be resolved by restating the treatment information.

On the other hand, when the response just doesn't fit, a prebirth part could be responding.

I usually inquire about parts who have just awakened first.

T: **I notice a multiple response. Is there a part who has just awakened causing this response?**
S: **Yes.**

I have found that making the following request saves time.

T: **Would you all be willing to talk to the subconscious to find out what is happening here, and then let me talk directly to the subconscious?**

With a "Yes," I wait a few minutes and ask to talk with the subconscious again.

With a "No," I continue in the following way:

T: **Are these parts threatened by what they have read because they have massive trauma pain?**

With a "Yes," I continue:

T: **The goal here is to communicate with the subconscious, to make a connection with a source of Wisdom, and to teach the subconscious to treat intruding fields to remove their negative influence. We will try not to treat or trigger your pain. You can always block any form of communication with the subconscious if you become alarmed by what is happening, either while the book is being read or upon hearing a request that frightens you. Would you be willing to allow me to continue to talk to the subconscious?**
S: **Yes.**

With a "Yes," I thank the parts and continue communicating with the subconscious. With a "No," I try some of the other means of communication with the subconscious. If you have had some severe trauma in your life, the barrier to talking with the subconscious will be resistant to change. The parts have some considerations about experiencing treatment. You will have to work through the barrier by reading and using the methods in the Process Healing book or by finding a therapist to treat the traumatic memories.

Prebirth parts sometimes cause the mixed responses or give misleading responses. In either case, I directly inquire about prebirth parts. Here is what I do:

T: **Is this a prebirth part trying to communicate?** *or*
T: **Am I talking with a prebirth part?**

With a "No" response, go to the section above, where we had trauma parts causing the barrier, and see what you can do. With a "Yes," I say the following to try to get cooperation with the prebirth part.

T: **As a prebirth part, you probably served the reader well by relaying information from the subconscious to the Main Personality. You have probably done a good job. However, what we are trying to do here requires direct communication with the subconscious, because the subconscious is the only part who can detect and treat intruding fields or communicate with Wisdom. Would you be willing to allow me to talk directly with the subconscious?**

With a "No," I suggest re-reading Appendix I again to this point to see if you get a positive outcome. If you try several times and don't get a positive outcome, you may have to work with suggestions in the Process Healing book or find a therapist to work with the barriers.

With a "Yes," try again to communicate with the subconscious.

When You Need Further Skills for Self-Treatment

Intruding fields are present in many people who have a trauma history. Some of the interventions for intruding fields are given in Appendix III. The interventions for treating intruding fields given in Chapters 6 and 10 require the subconscious to know more about the treatment of trauma. Not having contact with your subconscious won't be a bother when you are reading the book. You'll be able to learn how I conceptualize intruding fields. However, if you believe you have a trauma history with intruding fields and want to do the treatments, you will need to communicate with your subconscious and teach your subconscious the treatment metaphor. The Process Healing book provides all the information you need to get all aspects of your personality on a Treatment Team, to communicate with the subconscious, and to teach the treatment process. It also has strategies to treat complex memory structures.

Subconscious Responses Are Not Always True

An important skill involves being alert for deception when communicating with your subconscious. A response from the subconscious or muscle testing of any kind is not always true. Be skeptical. It is always possible for a prebirth part, a compartmentalized part, or a field, not to mention the patient or a therapist, to cause an incorrect response to questions asked of the subconscious.

Summary

In this appendix, I described several different ways to communicate with your subconscious. By communicating with your subconscious, you will have the means to problem-solve and treat intruding fields and possibly behavioral issues using Wisdom as an ally in treatment. If you are not able to communicate with your subconscious, read my book, *A Theory and Treatment of Your Personality: A manual for change* (2006) for help with removing barriers to communicating with your subconscious.

Appendix II

Treating Barriers to Treatment in Your Personal Field

Introduction

When trying to communicate with the subconscious, you will get a true response, no response, or a false or distorted response. Here is an example of getting a false response. After a sequence of apparently effective treatment interventions with a patient, an inconsistency led me to discover that a part had been responding as if she were the subconscious. The part did this to get my attention. She wanted to be treated. By not recognizing that I was being fooled, I lost a half hour of treatment time.

In another case, I failed to get communication with the subconscious because fragments of the subconscious were blocking communication. Therefore, you have to stay on your toes to be aware of any unusual or inconsistent responses by the subconscious. When you find inconsistent responses, a distortion, or a barrier, the material in this appendix may be useful to you. I am providing this advanced material to give you an understanding of possible problems. If you have read Flint (2006) or if Appendix III-5 works for you, you will be able to carry out the treatments.

This Appendix will give several examples of barriers that either block communication with the subconscious or disrupt the activity of the subconscious. I'll start by describing barriers that block or distort communication with the subconscious. Prebirth parts and compartmentalized parts are the usual barriers that do this and are easy to treat. I will give an example of treating a barrier caused by a complex part. Next, I will describe subconscious fragments and fragments associated to layered memories as sources that can distort communication with the subconscious.

In addition, there are several ways the subconscious can be damaged. While rare, two examples will be given to alert you to this possibility. Since beliefs can serve to distort or block access to the subconscious or to Wisdom, I'll give some treatments for belief barriers. Finally, an intervention to clear barriers to enable independent and automatic treatment of fields will be presented.

Barriers Blocking Communication with the Subconscious

There are a number of barriers that can block communication with the subconscious. This problem is infrequent. However, sometimes parts or intruding fields present barriers to communication. There are several other barriers that are caused when complex memory structures are created. The part him- or herself can be damaged by trauma in unusual circumstances that clouds the subconscious' perception. The following are interventions that resolve these barriers.

1. A part pretending to be the subconscious

One often finds prebirth or trauma parts who are responding for the subconscious and giving misleading information. I usually ask if I am talking to a prebirth part and get a valid answer. Prebirth parts are usually honest and accept treatment easily. When it is not a prebirth part, I ask if it is a part. When I still can't tell if I am talking to the "true" subconscious, I use the following approach to confuse the part and get an answer from the subconscious.

T: **Am I talking to the "True" subconscious?**

Then, before I get a response, I immediately deny that I am asking the question and continue with three our four out of context comments of irrelevant observations like:

T: **I am not going to ask that question because it's raining today and I tracked mud into my office and didn't notice until I turned the lights on because I was so preoccupied with my keys.**

Then, I get the accurate answer to the question by saying:

T: **But, if I did ask that question, would the answer be true?**

This usually confuses parts and intruding fields but not the subconscious. If a part or field is masquerading as the subconscious, the answer given by the subconscious will be "No." Then, I problem-solve and use the strategies described here or in Flint (2006) to treat the part. Otherwise, with a "Yes," I assume I was talking to the "True" subconscious.

A surrogate subconscious part is a more complex barrier for communicating with the subconscious than a trauma or prebirth part. Occasionally, I find surrogate subconsciouses in torture survivors that were created to block a therapist from using the subconscious when treating the patient. Perpetrators of torture deliberately create surrogate subconsciouses — a part named "subconscious," to confuse the therapist. I get around this by asking to talk to the true subconscious or some other metaphor for the subconscious, such as the nerd, master mechanic, primal subconscious, and so forth. This usually works because it doesn't trigger and activate the surrogate subconscious. I inquire about a structure caused by torture and, if necessary, continue with the intervention for these structures. People with ritual abuse and mind control often present the problem of surrogate subconscious parts. It is worthy information for the reader to know, so he or she can be aware of surrogate subconscious parts as a possible problem.

2. Fragments of the subconscious

Other complex structures can interfere with communication with the subconscious. For example, just as compartmentalized parts can be formed under extreme trauma, the Behavior System can be fragmented to form what I call an Independent Behavior System. These systems can be created early in life by unusual conditions caused by the overstimulation of the Active Experience of the fetus or child. Without treating Independent Behavior Systems, attempts to treat problematic behaviors can be fruitless. Subconscious fragments in these Independent Behavior Systems interfere with communicating with the true subconscious. Treatment of these systems is described in Flint (2006). Initially, they were relatively difficult to treat, but now, I never have to treat Independent Behavior Systems. This is an intervention, like many others, that is apparently automatically carried out by the subconscious because the procedure is in my subconscious or in the Wisdom of the universe.

Another barrier for the subconscious is that fragments of the subconscious can associate *to* Layered Memories. Under some circumstances, Layered Memories are created with a fragment of the subconscious layered *to* the memory structure. A barrier arises for communicating with the subconscious when these subconscious fragments activate when attempting to access the subconscious. These active fragments block communication with the subconscious.

The following examples describe treating subconscious fragments created by Independent System fragments and subconscious fragments associated *to* layered memories.

a. Treating fragments of the subconscious

Usually, subconscious fragments are simply dormant or active like any other memory. I have found that subconscious fragments are created in the following way. Just as trauma can cause compartmentalized parts of the Main Personality, other unique, early traumas can split the Behavior System to cause system fragments. With this splitting of the Behavior System, fragments of the subconscious are also created. The presence of subconscious fragments becomes a barrier to communicating with the subconscious and to independent, automatic treatment. The subconscious can usually treat these fragments easily.

T: **Subconscious, are there any fragments of the subconscious that are blocking independent, automatic treatment?**
S: **Yes.**
T: **Please treat all subconscious fragments and join them with you.**

I don't know if there is any treatment involved. Remember, these are treatment metaphors that have some connection to reality, but exactly what that is, I don't know. All I know is that these treatments appear to work in most cases. When they don't, I problem-solve.

S: **Yes.**
T: [Done.] **Please do a Massive Change History and everything.**

b. Subconscious fragments on layered memories

Layered memories are memory structures that have another memory structure associated *to* them rather than *with* them. When a memory structure associates *to* the base memory structure, you cannot treat the memories associated *with* the base memory structure. In some circumstances, a subconscious fragment can split off to create a layered memory. A subconscious fragment layered *to* a memory not only stops the treatment of the base memory, but it also becomes problematic when one tries working with the subconscious. One can treat a subconscious fragment, join it with the subconscious, and then treat the base memory in the following way. This treatment resolves the problem of subconscious fragments.

T: **Subconscious, are there any subconscious fragments layered to memories?**
S: **Yes.**
T: **Can you treat them safely?**
S: **Yes.**
T: **Please treat all subconscious fragments causing layered memories and join them with you. Treat the layered memories and then do a Massive Change History and everything.**
S: **Yes.**

There can be more complex barriers that interfere with communication with the subconscious. These can be unusual parts structures in the Behavior System, such as parts who only say "No," or parts who only say "Yes," or other unusual structures. These require the problem-solving methods described in Flint (2006).

3. Field intrusions entrained with the subconscious

As with any structure in the Personal Field, intruding fields can entrain with the subconscious. Treating intruding fields has been easy and straightforward. Here is the intervention to treat intruding fields entrained with the subconscious.

T: **Subconscious, please treat all fields that have entrained with you and help them slide off into everlasting happiness.**
S: **Yes.**
T: [Waits.] **Did that work?**
S: **Yes.**

If this doesn't work, you have to problem-solve and look for complex fields. Other unusual field phenomena can undermine the effectiveness of the subconscious.

4. Barriers in the subconscious that undermine treatment

Here are two examples of barriers in the subconscious that undermine treatment. One barrier is caused by emotions associated with the subconscious. This is a barrier I once created by mistake and had to treat the subconscious to resolve the issue. I mention this here so you don't repeat my mistake. It is unlikely that you'll run into this barrier, but it is good to be aware of the possibility and to know that it can be treated. The other barrier is a problem caused when an unusual circumstance damages the subconscious so the subconscious, itself, appears as a predisposition for anxiety in creative situations.

a. The subconscious with emotions

The subconscious does not usually have emotions associated with him or her. This apparently allows the subconscious to work in the Active Experience and allows the subconscious to problem-solve the cause for active trauma memories. I found out that when emotions are associated with the subconscious, the clarity of perception and capacity to problem-solve is reduced. One time, I unintentionally caused the association of emotion memories with the subconscious. The patient's subconscious was cooperative with treating complex behavior structures. I was learning a lot about dissociation, compartmentalization, and how the brain worked. I thought it might help my learning if the subconscious could talk directly with me by running the body. In one session, I asked the subconscious to run the body, so I could speak directly with her. In the next session, I discovered the subconscious was not as perceptive to the inner dynamics as she had been previously. While running the body, she had acquired emotions associated with her field structure in the hidden reality. The emotions that associated with the subconscious were the cause of the barrier to clarity when problem-solving issues. Here is how I treated that barrier in the subconscious.

T: **Subconscious, are emotional collages associated with your field?**
S: **Yes.** [Interestingly, the "Yes" response was this woman's arm flopping straight up off her leg.]
T: **Can I treat these emotional collages associated with you?**
S: **Yes.**

At the time, I did Eye Movement Desensitization and Reprocessing with the subconscious and removed the emotions associated with the subconscious. Though my experiment was unfortunate, it became useful and instructive. Sometime later, I had a patient who had another therapist invite the subconscious into her body to converse. Again, I had to ask the subconscious to remove the emotions associated with her.

T: **Subconscious, please treat these emotional collages associated with you and do a Massive Change History and everything.**

In general, this intervention, as simple as it seems, will remove the emotions that reduce the helpful capacity of the subconscious.

b. The subconscious as a predisposition for anxiety

With unusual conditions in intense traumatic situations early in life, the subconscious can be damaged. Here is an interesting barrier that is instructive. This barrier modifies the activity of the subconscious itself. The issue that led me to problem-solve was this. The patient said that he experienced anxiety when he was recognized as being creative. This experience of anxiety also happened in situations where he received comments about his initiative or creativity or when he simply thought about selling his art, an act implying that he was creative.

By asking the patient leading questions, his subconscious revealed that it had associated with anxiety when he was seven years old. Some people believe that the subconscious helps in creating responses to novel situations or when there is confusion. The patient's father punished his novel, risk-taking behavior in a situation that involved his creative activity. This punishment traumatized the subconscious process actively involved in the creative process. The anxiety was caused by the punishment associated *with* the subconscious process. This all takes place in the hidden reality, because I believe that the subconscious is a field process — a part of us in the 5th through 9th dimensions. My guess is that the subconscious entered the Personal Field to assist with creativity and picked up the anxiety emotions. This is similar to when I invited the subconscious into the body to speak to me.

Later, in similar creative or confusing situations, when the subconscious activated, the patient experienced the anxiety associated with the subconscious. This is the reason it looked like a predisposition. This apparent predisposition was the anxiety associated with the subconscious when the situation triggered the subconscious to make creative or novel responses. This response of the subconscious influenced all systems of brain activity served by the subconscious and may have been a significant cause of this patient's pervasive personality problems.

There were allegedly 32 of these predisposition-like emotional experiences attached to his subconscious, each with unique triggers relating to a creative situation. These predisposition-like responses of the subconscious led to avoidance responses, such as "not helping out, not doing things, shirking chores, setting up others to do things," and so forth. These experiences were the cause for procrastination, feeling ashamed, nervous associations, and the belief "nothing will work for me."

You might wonder how this came about with this person and none of the others I treated. This person had severe trauma, if not torture, in his first two years and lived in a dysfunctional family. I believe some unusual situation resulted in something like the easy-creation of triggers and anxiety associated with the subconscious.

Here is how I treated these 32 predisposition-like structures in the subconscious.

T: **Subconscious, please treat all barriers or introjects in your memory safely, one after the other.**
S: **Yes.**
T: [Waits.] **Subconscious, please do a Massive Change History and everything of all memories that related to this intervention with the memories of the subconscious and the Main Personality. Then, please smooth out the Personal Field.**
S: **Yes.**

At that time, I was experimenting with the intervention, "Please smooth out the Personal Field," that I thought was useful. Later, I doubted the usefulness of this intervention. It sounded "woo woo." However, I asked the subconsciouses of many patients if this intervention was good to do and always got support for doing it. I don't do this intervention anymore with my patients. I believe that it is an intervention that is passed on through the Personal Field and is automatically carried out by the patient's subconscious. Try it with yourself. Do the intervention and ask your subconscious if it was useful to do. This offers some support for doing this intervention.

5. Treating beliefs that undermine communication

Beliefs can undermine communication with the subconscious and your ability to access Wisdom to treat your own and others' emotional and physical issues. Wisdom is an intelligent resource in the 9th dimension that can facilitate treatment (see Chapters 9 and 10). These undermining beliefs can be treated, as well. If you have not read Flint (2006) or downloaded my Treatment Knowledge, some of the following interventions may not work. However, the subconscious can reword the interventions to get help from Wisdom, who has all the information necessary to do these interventions successfully. Remember, the 9th dimension is accumulating all the positive experiences of humankind that are associated with love, so the target issue and treatment metaphor are metaphors that will activate the correct intervention.

Here are eight interventions that will remove belief barriers to improve your access to Wisdom.

T: **Subconscious, after each of the following interventions, please do a Massive Change History and everything with the memories from the trauma to now, including memories in the ego states, and the tandem memories. Treat any related shadow memories and remove the emotion templates from the treated memories.**

T: **Subconscious, please treat the structures of memories, layered memories, parts, parts with layered memories, and parts with layered memories associated with predispositions that block my ability to fully treat others and myself.**

T: **Subconscious, using the sentence procedure, "I know I can treat myself and others," please tag and treat the beliefs that activated that are barriers to fully treating others and me, so they are false. Then compose and strengthen positive, self-empowering beliefs to replace them.**

T: **Subconscious, please do the Sentence Procedure with "I have no doubt or disbelief when I do any treatment involving the Wisdom." Tag all activated memories, layered memories, parts,**

parts with layered memories, and parts with layered memories associated with predispositions, and treat them slowly and safely with love and respect.

T: Subconscious, please treat all structured memories that project skepticism and disbelief about the use of Wisdom and replace the changed memories with self-empowering beliefs.

T: Subconscious, please treat any field structures related to my Personal Field that block working with Wisdom when treating my own or other people's physical or emotional issues.

T: Subconscious, please treat any ancestral fields from my mother or father causing doubt and disbelief when accessing Wisdom.

T: Subconscious, when you are finished with these interventions, please do a Massive Change History and everything with the memories, ego states, and tandem memories, and treat any relevant shadow memories.

6. Enabling the subconscious to treat intruding fields automatically

The subconscious can treat intruding fields automatically. Sometimes, though, when the subconscious attempts to treat an issue, there are barriers that block the treatment. To free the subconscious to treat independently and automatically, I always use the Massive Change History intervention to treat all memories involved with receiving or asking for treatment from birth to the present. When the subconscious initiates treatment, these memories activate to present a barrier to treatment because their activity disorganizes the Active Experience. These are memories of every time you went to your mother or father, doctor, dentist, and so forth, for help or treatment of any kind.

The second barrier blocking independent treatment is that most people have predispositions, which are triggered whenever a painful memory activates in the conscious experience. This predisposition dissociates the painful memory to the unconscious, which allows a comfortable experience without pain in a generally negative environment. The subconscious has to treat these predispositions for dealing with active painful memories, because the activity of the predispositions disorganizes the Active Experience and blocks treatment.

With this in mind, I discovered that similar barriers could prevent the subconscious from automatically treating intruding fields in the Personal Field. Here are the interventions for enabling the subconscious to treat intruding field barriers as they arise in the healing process. This intervention involves treatments explained in Flint (2006).

T: **Subconscious, please do the sentence procedure with the belief "I can treat all intruding fields that associate to parts and other structures in my Personal Field." Then tag the memories, beliefs, and parts that activated and treat them in the correct order.**

This sentence triggered all memory structures that present barriers that stop the subconscious from treating intruding fields automatically and independently.

T: [Done.] **Subconscious, please treat any predispositions in the Memory II that might prevent the treatment of intruding fields.**
T: [Done.] **Please do a Massive Change History and everything with all memories touched by these interventions.**

Summary

In this Appendix, I described several different barriers blocking or distorting communication with your subconscious. I offered treatments for these barriers and other barriers caused by beliefs. I described the treatment of barriers that prevent the subconscious from independently and automatically treating intruding fields. The interventions in this Appendix require that you use the Process Healing Method. If you suspect that some of these barriers or other barriers are present in you, consult *A Theory and Treatment of Your Personality: A manual for change* (Flint, 2006) to learn the tools to understand and carry out these interventions. Otherwise, find a therapist who is willing to problem-solve to help you meet and communicate with your subconscious.

Appendix III

Treatment Aids

1. What You May Feel During Treatment
2. Directions for Treating a Field
3. How to Use Your Inner Wisdom
4. Problem-Solving Barriers to Treating Fields
5. How to Use Your Subconscious to Treat Yourself
6. Problem-Solving Barriers to Treating Parts

1. What You May Feel During Treatment

With any intervention, you may feel some symptoms of the issue being treated during the treatment process. Occasionally, these symptoms may seem unpleasant and perhaps frightening. However, before you see a doctor, ask your subconscious if a treatment process is causing the unpleasant or frightening experience. If the symptoms are caused by the treatment activity of the subconscious, either relax or ask the subconscious to process the issue more slowly, so you do not experience the symptoms so intensely.

a. Treatment of intruding souls

Immediately following the treatment of intruding souls, some readers may feel an energy sensation or swoosh arise from somewhere in your body, like from your torso, your back, or the back of your neck. It is also normal not to feel an energy sensation.

b. The Wisdom intervention

The Wisdom intervention can work quickly with few treatment symptoms or take a week or more with the continuous or occasional experience of symptoms. Some people feel a tingling from head to toe immediately following the intervention. Sometimes people feel sensations in their chest, stomach, or brain. Once this intervention begins, it will continue until it is completed.

The most common symptom of treatment is that the person has a constant experience during the treatment process of intrusions or thoughts of past memories associated with the treatment goal. The intrusions can be uncomfortable because they are sad memories but without any emotions associated with them. When you are uncomfortable with these intrusions, you can do something else to keep your mind busy so you don't experience them.

c. Process Healing

This treatment process is safe, but there can be periods of discomfort caused by trauma symptoms or fleeting memories triggered by the treatment process. During the treatment, some people experience headaches or different brain sensations like numbness, flashes of pain, tingling feelings, lightness in your head, and so forth. You may even experience flu-like symptoms. Just let the symptoms come and go. If the processing gets too intense, with a headache or extreme fatigue, ask your subconscious to treat more slowly. If an image is scary, ask your subconscious if this is a memory that is being treated. If it is not, ask your subconscious to treat it.

Since the subconscious is taught to treat negative emotions and is free to treat independently, you may feel the treatment process start any time of day or night. Therefore, when you are not sure why you have an intense feeling like fatigue or headache, before you call your physician, ask the subconscious if an active treatment process is causing the feeling or headache.

During active processing by the subconscious, there is apparently no danger in driving or operating equipment, but to be on the safe side, ask your subconscious to ensure your safety by not treating while you are cooking, operating equipment, or driving.

2. Directions For Treating a Field

Establish rapport with your subconscious as described in Appendix I. The presence of a field is suggested if you have a barrier to treatment, chronic issues, or changes in experience that seem to just "come over you" for no reason. In these circumstances, I ask my subconscious if a field is causing the issue or experience. If I get a "Yes," I proceed as follows:

T: **Can I talk with the field?**

S: **Yes.**

T: **Thank you for talking to me. You came from another lifetime and the pattern of emotional pain you learned then is similar to a pattern of emotional pain in me. That emotional pain you have is old pain, and the subconscious can treat it, so you will no longer have pain, and you can slide off into everlasting happiness. Would you like treatment now?**

S: **Yes.**

T: **Subconscious, please smooth off the pain in this field and help him or her slide off into everlasting happiness.**

S: **Yes.**

This is when you might feel some energy shift in your body.

Sometimes intruding fields lived a lifetime where they experienced continuous punishment and ongoing pain. They found that if they chose to have pain they would experience less pain. They formed the belief that they had to have pain to reduce the intensity of pain. Because of this belief, they may have a resistance toward treatment, which serves as a barrier to treatment. So, when the treatment fails, try the following.

T: **Subconscious, does this field choose to have pain?**

S: **Yes.**

T: **Can I talk to the field?**

S: **Yes.**

T: **In a previous lifetime, you had continuous ongoing pain and you learned to choose to have pain because it felt better. What is possible is that the subconscious can smooth out all that old pain in your field, so you no longer have to choose to have it. Then, you can choose to have happiness and slide off into everlasting happiness. Would you like the subconscious to treat your old pain now so you can slide off into everlasting happiness?**

S: **Yes.**

Sometimes there are other barriers to the treatment, such as fear of losing one's knowledge, fear that the internal social dynamics will get disrupted, fear of dying, or fear of not being able to protect the patient. The reframes for dealing with these issues usually resolve these barriers.

Another barrier to treating the intruding field could be caused by additional generational fields associated with the attached field. With luck there is only one generational field blocking treatment. To find out, ask to talk to the generational field and then try the interventions just given. If the generational field blocking the treatment has a complex field structure, then you have to refer to Chapter 5 in this book for the treatment procedure.

3. How to Use Your Inner Wisdom

These instructions assume you have established a connection to your subconscious. The subconscious is that part of you who has been with you from the beginning. He or she operates as an associate of the 5th through 9th dimensions, so it is relatively independent of the Personal Field and free of emotions. It can also be called the Innerself, Higher Self, your Spirit Animal, the name of a spiritual guide, or the name of an ancestor. In addition, the subconscious usually has a connection with Wisdom, which allows your subconscious to choose the Wisdom intervention. Here is the shortest intervention:

T: **Subconscious, please safely treat this issue in the best way.**

Because your subconscious may choose one of three or more different treatment interventions, you may feel one or more of the following experiences: a sensation like warmth, numbness or tingling in your head or body, painless thoughts streaming through your consciousness, or an experience of mild but annoying visual or auditory memories from past traumas. If the treatment experience becomes too intense, try asking the subconscious to slow down the process. With the Wisdom intervention, it usually runs its course, so do something to distract you from the intruding memories.

Here is a more direct way to treat an issue by using Wisdom:

T: **Subconscious, please ask Wisdom** (Jesus, the Creator, Grandmother, ancestors, Spirit) **to safely remove all the emotions associated with** (an issue) **and replace them with peace, love, and compose positive, self-empowering beliefs and behaviors to** replace any beliefs or behaviors treated, so I can reach my true potential.

If you try an intervention and it doesn't appear to work, try this:

T: **Subconscious, please problem-solve and safely treat any barriers preventing this issue from being treated and then repeat the treatment.**

4. Problem-Solving Barriers to Treating Fields

Problem-solving a barrier first requires you to ask questions to determine the cause of the barrier. When there is a field or a single generational field barrier refusing treatment, explain the advantages of treatment and the treatment process for treating fields. In most cases, you may have to explain how the field learned to choose to have pain to experience less pain. Point out that the subconscious can remove that old pain from the past, so he or she no longer has to choose it, and then assist the part to slide off into everlasting happiness. Less frequently, fields have a fear of death, of losing their history, or that the pain will be too great during treatment. Simple reframes will generally remove these barriers.

If you find the generational field has a complex structure and the treatment in Chapter 5 fails, problem-solve by asking questions to determine the number of layers on the intruding field and the number of layers on each layer. In other words, the structures are usually stacked, one on top of the other like a coaster with poker chips stacked on it, each chip representing a field from a different generation. Occasionally, a generational field in the stack includes its own complex generational field structure, like another coaster with poker chips. Diagram the structures of all complex entrained fields and then treat the fields stacked on the base field from the top down, one at a time, problem-solving and customizing the treatment at each level.

5. How to Use Your Subconscious to Treat Yourself

If you read Appendix I and were successful in communicating with your subconscious by one of the suggested methods, this section will explain how to use the subconscious to treat yourself. Remember that I described the experience of downloading my treatment knowledge to people in my presence and across the country. Try this. See if your subconscious can download my treatment knowledge and the wisdom of my teachers.

T: **Subconscious, can you read author Flint's Personal Field and download his treatment knowledge and the wisdom of his teachers?**
S: **Yes.**
T: **Is it safe to download this information?**
S: **Yes.**
T: **Please do it.**

With a "No," ask your subconscious if there are any barriers for doing this. The barriers can be in your memory system or intruding fields. Re-read Appendix II. If this fails to resolve the problem, you may have to read the Process Healing book (Flint, 2006). If they are intruding fields, re-read the appropriate sections in Chapters 4 and 5 of this book.

The hardest part of treating yourself is remembering to do it. Find some way to remind yourself that your subconscious can treat most issues that arise during the day.

Try this brief intervention first. While thinking about the issue — say, a simple phobia — simply ask your subconscious: "Please treat this issue," or just say "Treat it," or "Fix it." Usually, when there is no particular treatment barrier, the subconscious treats the issue, and you will feel the emotions associated with the issue gradually decrease. Otherwise, if this intervention doesn't seem to work, here is another approach to treat a more complex issue.

1. Identify the issue or emotion. Then ask the subconscious: "Is it appropriate and safe to treat this issue now?"
2. If "Yes," then ask, "Are there any parts that have to be treated associated with this issue?"
3. If "Yes," ask, "Should these parts be treated first?" If "No," go to line 7; otherwise, proceed to line 4.
4. Ask, "Is it safe to treat the parts now in the best way, one after the other?"

5. With a "Yes," say, "Please treat these parts one after the other in the best order and best way, and treat the effects of each part from the time of its trauma to now."

6. After the parts are treated, continue with line 7 or complete the treatment on line 9.

7. "Please treat the memory structures associated with this issue one after the other in the best order and best way." After the memory structures are treated, go to line 8.

8. Now, treat the Main Personality. "Please do a Massive Change History and everything in the Main Personality and other memories that were influenced by the emotions of this issue."

    After this is complete and if the parts have not been treated, go back to line 4; otherwise, continue to line 9.

9. Ask the subconscious if he or she has finished treating this issue. If "Yes," ask for a Massive Change History and everything and go on to the next issue. If "No," ask questions to problem-solve.

If the expected outcome of treatment is not experienced, ask: "Subconscious, is there a barrier blocking the treatment of this issue?"

With a "Yes," ask: "Subconscious, can you treat the barrier and then the issue?"

With a "No," you can explore for fields and repeat the question.

If you want a complete description of problem-solving and treatment, obtain the book, *A Theory and Treatment of Your Personality, A manual for change*, which gives detailed strategies for treating barriers and a lot more interesting treatment strategies.

6. Problem-Solving Barriers to Treating Parts

If you have studied the Process Healing Method or have received the Process Healing Method from the author Flint through the field, the following interventions may work to remove treatment barriers. When you are working with finger responses:

a. First, ask your subconscious to contact Flint's subconscious to get help in resolving the barrier to treating the issue. If your subconscious reports receiving the information, ask him or her to treat the issue or barrier safely, in the best way with complete respect.

b. A part won't talk (no finger response): Ask if the part wants more satisfaction and less pain. If "Yes," ask if it wants to receive treatment now to remove the pain.

c. A part wants treatment now: Ask the subconscious if it is acceptable to all aspects of your personality and safe to treat this part now.

d. There is a conflict between parts: Ask the parts to resolve the conflict by drawing straws or negotiating.

e. A part awakens: Ask if he or she wants to be treated.

f. Ask if the part has massive pain and is afraid of treatment. If "Yes," ask the part if he or she is willing to talk to the subconscious and find out about the treatment for fragile parts. After waiting a short while, ask the subconscious if the part is willing to be treated as a fragile part.

g. If any part does not want treatment, ask if he or she is willing to get all the information from the subconscious, so he or she has the information to make an informed decision about being treated. Usually, the parts will be willing to be treated after they speak with the subconscious.

Appendix IV

Virtual Reality and Psychospirituality

Structure	Physics in Virtual Reality	Psychospiritual Functioning
Zero Points	A given. Creates the physical and spiritual unfolding universe.	Creates the frame-by-frame unfolding of our virtual and 3D-Reality.
0th - 4th dimensions	Particles, subatomic particles, structures, molecules, protons, neutrons, electrons, all used to communicate within the body.	Fills in the details of the structures caused by the 5th through 7th dimensions in our virtual reality to give us the 3D-Reality.
5th - 9th dimensions	Memory of the physical and experiential actions, which are used in maintaining coherency in the universe.	The soul. The closer one models the fixed laws of the universe and shows love and respect for the greater good, the more his or her presence is in the 9th dimension. Nonlocal healing.
5th dimension	Serves to amass experience in each and all souls from the beginning. Evolving content.	Amasses everything in the living soul. Records what our brain and body do and experience from conception to death.
6th and 7th dimensions	Memories of components and assembled structures in virtual and 3D-Reality.	Involved in the mind-body connection and in psychological or spiritual interventions leading to physical change.
8th dimension	Involved in the transition from the 5th dimension to an expanded presence in the 9th dimension.	Wisdom of souls entrained on emotional pain and love move toward the 9th dimension by resolving pain memories in the 8th dimension.
9th dimension	Experience of souls from the beginning entrained on love and free of emotional pain. This Wisdom evolves over time.	The treatment process consults with the evolving Wisdom — an old soul. As treatment solutions to problems evolve, they become part of Wisdom. Souls in the 9th dimension can change the 0th through 8th dimensions.
10th dimension	Maintains coherency of the activity of all living and inert objects in the universe based on fixed rules. Uses the memories in the 5th through 9th dimensions. All dimensions are embedded in the 10th dimension.	The outcome of the rules is interpreted as an apparent, constant expression of love in both beneficial and harmful behaviors — beneficial leads to getting more happiness; harmful leads to avoiding pain, both loving outcomes.

Notes

Acknowledgements
1   Anonymous Person. personal communication, 2002-2003.

Introduction
1   Kaku, M. *Hyperspace: A scientific odyssey through parallel universes, time warps, and the 10th dimension.* (New York: Anchor, 1994), p. 314.

2   Cranwell, J. C. *Spatial Dimensionality,* (1998i). Retrieved on May 12, 2010, from http://www.gootar.com/gravityboy/docs/dimen.html

3   Craig, G. Retrieved on September 9, 2010, from http://www.eftuniverse.com

4   Hellinger, B. Retrieved on May 12, 2010, from http://www.familycon-stellations-usa.com/hellinger.html

Chapter 1
1   Fleming, T. *How To Do TAT with a Stressful Event That You Experienced.* (TAT International, Redondo Beach, CA: Author). Retrieved free on May 12, 2010, from http://www.tatlife.com

2   Edelstien, M. *Trauma, Trance, and Transformation: A clinical guide to hypnotherapy.* (New York: Brunner / Mazel, 1981), pp. 53-54; Pulos L. Workshop on Ideomotor Questioning. (Workshop presented at the General Meeting of the Canadian Society of Clinical Hypnosis (British Columbia Division). Vancouver, BC, 1994).

3   Oglevie, S. & Oglevie, L. Working with Cult and Ritual Abuse, (Workshops presented at the Elijah House, Mission, BC, 1995, 1997).

4   Kaku, M. *Hyperspace: A scientific odyssey through parallel universes, time warps, and the 10th dimension.* (New York: Anchor, 1994), p. 314.

5   Fleming, T. *You Can Heal Now: The Tapas Acupressure Technique (TAT).* (TAT International, Redondo Beach, CA: Author, 2008).

6   Dickason, C. F. *Demon Possession & the Christian.* (Wheaton, IL: Crossway Books, 1987).

7   Cranwell, J. C. *The Flux Particle Theory 101* (1998i-viii). Retrieved on May 12, 2010, from http://gravityboy.gootar.com/

8   McTaggart, L. *The Field: The quest for the secret force of the universe.* (Hammersmith, London, UK: HarperCollins, 2001), pp. 88-91.

9   McTaggart, 2001, p. 91.

10   Kraft, C. H. *Defeating Dark Angels: Breaking demonic oppression in the believer's life*. (Ann Arbor, MI: Servant Publications, 1992); Kraft, C. H. *Deep Wounds, Deep Healing: Discovering the vital link between spiritual warfare and inner healing*. (Ann Arbor, MI: Servant Publications, 1993).

11   McTaggart, 2001, pp. 77-78.

12   Pearsall, P. *The Heart's Code*. (New York: Broadway Books, 1998), p. 43.

13   Pearsall, 1998.

14   Pearsall, 1998, p. 7.

15   Gardner, M. *Fads and Fallacies in the Name of Science*. Rev. ed. (Mineola, NY: Dover, 1957), Chapter 24.

16   McTaggart, 2001, p. 101.

17   Sheldrake, R. *Dogs That Know When Their Owners Are Coming Home: And other unexplained powers of animals*. (New York: Random House, 1999), pp. 30-31.

18   McTaggart, 2001, pp. 188-190.

19   Adrian, P. personal communication March 23, 2003.

Chapter 2

1   Bartlett, F. C. *Remembering: A study in experimental and social psychology*. (London, UK: Cambridge University Press, 1967), Chapter 10.

2   Flint, G. A. *A Theory and Treatment of Your Personality: A manual for change*. (Vernon, BC: NeoSolTerric Enterprises, 2006), p. 3.

3   Flint, 2006.

4   Freemen, W. J. The Physiology of Perception. (*Scientific American*, Vol. 264, 1991), p. 84.

5   Bartlett, 1967, p. 197.

6   Lankton, S.R. & Lankton, C. H. *The Answer Within: A clinical framework of clinical hypnotherapy*. (New York: Brunner/Mazel, 1983).

7   Stone, H. & Stone, S. L. *Embracing Ourselves: The voice dialogue manual*. (Novato, CA: Nataraj Publishing, 1989), pp. 13-15.

8   Stone, & Stone, 1989, pp. 13-15.

Chapter 3

1   Lipton, B. *The Biology of Belief: Unleashing the power of consciousness, matter, and miracles*. (Santa Rosa, CA: Elite Books. 2005), p. 172.

2   Ho, M. *Living with the Fluid Genome*. (London, UK: Institute for Science in Society, 2003), p. 13.

3   Cranwell, J. C. *Spatial Dimensionality*. (1998i). Retrieved on May 12, 2010, from http://www.gravityboy.gootar.com/docs

4 Cranwell, J. C. personal communication, July 13, 2007.

5 Flint, G. A. *A Theory and Treatment of Your Personality: A manual for change*, (Vernon, BC: NeoSolTerric Enterprises, 2006), p. 338.

6 Bearden, T, Correspondence, May 27, 2008. Retrieved on May 12, 2010, from http://www.cheniere.org/correspondence/052708.htm

7 Cranwell, 1998i, p. 3.

8 Bearden, T. E. *Excalibur Briefing: Explaining paranormal phenomena.* (Bakersfield, CA: Cheniere Press, 2002), p. 144.

9 Cranwell, 1998vi, pp. 1-2.

10 Cranwell, 1998iii, p. 1.

11 Cranwell, 1998i, p. 2.

12 Cranwell, 1998ii, p. 3.

13 Cranwell, 1998ii, p. 3.

Chapter 4

1 Edelstien, M. G. *Trauma, Trance, and Transformation: A clinical guide to hypnotherapy.* (New York: Brunner/Mazel, 1981), pp. 57-60; Rossi E. L. & Cheek, D. B. *Mind Body Therapy: Methods of ideodynamic healing in hypnosis.* (New York: Norton, 1988), pp. 16-19.

2 Flint, G. A. *A Theory and Treatment of Your Personality: A manual for change.* (Vernon, BC: NeoSolTerric Enterprises, 2006), pp. 47-48.

3 Bearden, T. E. *Oblivion: America at the brink.* (Bakersfield, CA: Cheniere Press. 2005), p. 144.

4 Hayton A. (Ed.) *Untwined: Perspectives on the death of a twin before birth.* (St Albans, Herts, UK: Wren Publications, 2007), pp. 1 – 6.

5 Boklage, C. E. Frequency and Survival: Probability of natural twin conceptions. In Hayton A. (Ed.) *Untwined: Perspectives on the death of a twin before birth.* (St Albans, Herts, UK: Wren Publications, 2007), p. 95.

Chapter 5

1 Sachs, A. & Galton, G. (Eds.) *Forensic Aspects of Dissociative Identity Disorder.* (London, UK: Karnac Books, 2008); Noblitt, J. R. & Perskin-Noblitt, P. (Eds.) *Ritual Abuse in the Twenty-First Century: Psychological, forensic, social, and political considerations.* (Brandon, OR: Robert Reed Publishers, 2008); Noblitt, J. R. & Perskin, P. *Cult and Ritual Abuse: Its history, anthropology, and recent discovery in contemporary America.* Rev. ed. (Westport, CT: Praeger Publishers, 2000); Ross, C. A. *Bluebird: Deliberate creation of multiple personality by psychiatrists.* (Richardson, TX: Manitou Communications, 2000); Rutz, C. *A Nation Betrayed: The chilling and true*

story of secret cold war experiments performed on our children and other innocent people. (Grass Lake, MI: Fidelity Publishing, 2001).

2 Springmeier, F. & Wheeler, C. *The Illuminati Formula Used to Create an Undetectable Total Mind Controlled Slave, Vol. 2.* (Clackamas, OR: Published by author, 1996), p. 290.

3 Flint, G. A. *A Theory and Treatment of Your Personality: A manual for change.* (Vernon, BC: NeoSolTerric Enterprises, 2006), pp. 265-267.

4 Hensley, D. *Hell's Gate: Terror at Bobby Mackey's Music World.* (Parker, CO: Outskirts Press, 2005).

5 Roll, W. G. Poltergeists, Electromagnetism, and Consciousness. *(Journal of Scientific Exploration,* 2003, *Vol. 17),* pp. 75-86. Retrieved on May 12, 2010, from http://www.scientificexploration.org/journal/jse_17_1_roll.pdf

6 Van Dusen, M. *The Presence of Other Worlds: The psychological/spiritual worlds of Emanuel Swedenborg.* (New York: HarperCollins, 1975).

Chapter 6

1 Talbot, M. *The Holographic Universe.* (New York: Harper Collins, 1992), p. 32.

2 DeValois, K. K., DeValois, R. L. & Yund, W. W. Responses of Striate Cortex Cells to Grating and Checkerboard Patterns. (*Journal of Physiology,* Vol. 291, 1979), pp. 483-505, Referenced in Talbot, 1992, p. 28.

3 Bartlett, F. C. *Remembering: A study in experimental and social psychology.* (London, UK: Cambridge University Press, 1967), p. 197.

4 Morehouse, D. *Psychic Warrior.* (New York: St Martin's Press, 1996), p. 3.

5 McTaggart, L. (2001). *The Field: The quest for the secret force of the universe.* (Hammersmith, London, UK: HarperCollins), pp. 112-115.

6 McTaggart, 2001, pp. 212-215.

7 McTaggart, 2001, pp. 188-190.

8 Bearden, T. personal communication by email, October 30, 2008.

9 Schlitz, M. & Braud, W. (2006). *Distant Intentionality and Healing: Assessing the evidence.* Retrieved on May 12, 2010, from http://www.noetic.org/research/dh/research/DistantIntentionality.pdf

10 Benor, D. J. (2000). *Distant Healing.* Retrieved on May 12, 2010, from http://www.noetic.org/research/dh/research/DistantHealing.pdf

11 Targ, E. F. Research Methodology for Studies of Prayer and Distant Healing. (*Complementary Therapies in Nursing & Midwifery,* Vol 8, 2002), pp. 29-41, Retrieved on May 12, 2010, from http://www.noetic.org/research/dh/research/ResearchMethodology.pdf

12   Belanger, J. *Our Haunted Selves: True life ghost encounters*. (Franklin Lakes, NJ: New Page Books, 2006), pp. 75-113.

13   Roll, W. G. Poltergeists, Electromagnetism, and Consciousness. (*Journal of Scientific Exploration*, Vol. 17, 2003), pp. 75-86. Retrieved on May 12, 2010, from http://www.scientificexploration.org/journal/jse_17_1_roll.pdf

14   Belanger, J. *Our Haunted Selves: True life ghost encounters*. (Franklin Lakes, NJ: New Page Books, 2006); Hensley, D. *Hell's Gate: Terror at Bobby Mackey's Music World*. (Parker, CO: Outskirts Press, 2005).

15   Anonymous, personal communication, July, 2007.

16   Pulos, L. Mesmerism Revisited: The effectiveness of Esdaile's techniques in the production of deep hypnosis and total body hypnoanaesthesia. (*American Journal of Clinical Hypnosis*. 1980, p. 206-211), p. 207.

17   Esdaile, J. *Mesmerism in India and Its Practical Application in Surgery and Medicine*. (London, UK: Solis, Andrus & Sons, 1849).

18   Esdaile, 1849, pp. 255-257.

19   Circle of Friends: A review. Retrieved on May 12, 2010, from http://www.bruno-groening.org/english/ueberblick/defaultueberblick.htm

20   Flint-Rajkumar, S. This description refined with consultation. personal communication by email, November 20, 2009.

21   Craig, 2008. Vignettes retrieved on September 9, 2010, from http://www.eftuniverse.com

22   Hellinger, B. Lectures and Articles (see Taipei and Taiwan lectures). Retrieved on May 12, 2010, from http://hellinger-sciencia.com/Index.php?id=119

23   Andrade, J, & Feinstein, D. *Preliminary Report of the First Large-Scale Study of Energy Psychology*. Retrieved on May 12, 2010, from http://www.eftuniverse.com/Research/andradepaper.htm

24   *Jumpstart Your Health with EFT*. Retrieved September 12, 2010, from http://www.eftuniverse.com/index.php?option=com_subscribe&Itemid=17

25   Rent EFT CDs. Website retrieved on September 12, 2010, from http://www.eftuniverse.com/index.php?option=com_content&view=article&id=2736&Itemid=3152

26   Flint, G. A. *Emotional Freedom: Techniques for dealing with emotional and physical distress, Rev. Ed.*. (Vernon, BC: Neosolterric Enterprises, 2003); Craig, G. *The EFT Manual*. (Fulton, CA: Energy Psychology Press, 2008).

27   Bradshaw, R. One Eye Integration website, Retrieved on May 12, 1010, from http://oneeyeintegration.com

28   Southerland, C. *About BMSA*. Retrieved on May 12, 2010, from

http://www.bmsa-int.com/index.php?option=com_content&task=view&id=12&Itemid=30

29   Ochberg, F. *An Interview with Frank Ochberg, MD, on Post-Traumatic Stress Disorder.* Retrieved May 12, 2010, from http://www.mentalhelp.net/poc/view_doc.php?type=doc&id=28780&w=9&cn=109

30   Clinton, A. *Discovering Seemorg Matrix: A journey in healing.* Retrieved on May 12, 2010, from http://www.seemorgmatrix.org/ArticlesWebPage/SeemorgMatrixWork.html

31   Craig, G. (2008); Callahan, R. *Tapping the Healer Inside: Using Thought Field Therapy to instantly conquer your fears, anxieties, and emotional distress.* (New York: McGraw-Hill, 2002).

32   Shapiro, F. *Eye Movement Desensitization and Reprocessing: Basic principles, protocols and procedures.* (New York: Guilford Press. 2001, 2nd Ed.).

33   Vignette retrieved on September 12, 2010, from http://www.eftuniverse.com/index.php?option=com_content&view=article&id=247:surrogate-eft-calms-kicking-and-screaming-students&catid=9:children-adolescents&Itemid=204

34   Vignette retrieved on September 12, 2010, from http://www.eftuniverse.com/index.php?option=com_content&view=article&id=314:surrogate-eft-benefits-both-mother-and-child&catid=9:children-adolescents&Itemid=231

35   Vignette retrieved on September 12, 2010, from http://www.eftuniverse.com/index.php?option=com_content&view=article&id=3347:successful-surrogate-eft-for-s46:mental&Itemid=2947

36   Permission granted by Linda Compton, Personal Life Consultant, Richmond, CA, Compdreams@aol.com, the case study retrieved on September 12, 2010, from http://www.eftuniverse.com/index.php?option=com_content&view=article&id=290:angry-young-boy-overcomes-an-qentity-withinq-using-surrogate-eft&catid=9:children-adolescents&Itemid=512

37   Hellinger, B. (2001). Bert Hellinger Lectures and Articles (see Taipei and Taiwan lectures). Retrieved on May 12, 2010, from http://hellinger-sciencia.com/index.php?id=119; Hellinger, B. (1999). Unraveling Family Secrets. Interview by Humberto del Pozo in Santiago de Chile in September, 1999. Retrieved on May 12, 2010, from http://www.familyconstellations-usa.com/interview.htm; Hellinger, B. (2001a). Family constellation for teachers–Taipei University. Lecture given at the Department of Education of Taipei University on October 10, 2001. Retrieved on May 12, 2010, from http://hellinger-sciencia.com/index.php?id=125; Hellinger, B. (2001b). Introduction to Family

Constellations. Lecture given in Taipei on October 11, 2001. Retrieved on May 12, 2010, from http://hellinger-sciencia.com/index.php?id=126

Chapter 7

1 Adrian, P. personal communication, August, 2003.

2 Flint, G. A. *A Theory and Treatment of Your Personality: A manual for change.* (Vernon, BC: NeoSolTerric Enterprises, 2006), pp. 222-223.

3 Rice, J. & Caldwell, L. Master Programmer. Trained and certified at The Neurolinguistic Programming Center for Advanced Studies, Corte Madera, CA, 1986.

4 Fleming, T. *TAT Professional's Manual.* (Redondo Beach, CA: TATLife, 2007).

Chapter 8

1 Ross, C. A. *Bluebird: Deliberate creation of multiple personality by psychiatrists.* (Richardson, TX: Manitou Communications, 2000); Shelfin, A. W. & Opton, E. M. Jr. *The Mind Manipulators: A non-fiction account.* (New York: Paddington Press, 1978); MKULTRA, BLUEBIRD and STARGATE Projects. Download 20,000 pages of declassified CIA mind control documents from the US Government for $30. Instructions retrieved on May 12, 2010, from http://www.wanttoknow.info/mindcontrol10pg#ciadocs

2 Karriker, W. *Morning, Come Quickly,* (Catawba, NC: Sandime Ltd, 2003); Hersha, L., Hersha, C., Griffis, D., & Schwarz, T. *Secret Weapons: Two sisters' terrifying true story of sex, spies, and sabotage.* (Far Hills, NJ: New Horizon Press, 2001).

3 Hammond, D. C. *Greenbaum Speech* (formerly called Hypnosis in MPD: Ritual Abuse), delivered at the Fourth Annual Eastern Regional Conference on Abuse and Multiple Personality, Thursday June 25, 1992, at the Radisson Plaza Hotel, Mark Center, Alexandria, VA. Retrieved July 1, 2012, from http://cassiopaea.org/2010/09/17/the-greenbaum-speech/

Chapter 9

1 Spalding, B. T. *The Lives and Teaching of the Masters of the Far East.* (6 Volumes) (Camarillo, CA: DeVorss Publishing, 1972), Vol. 2, p. 166.

2 What's BSMA? Downloaded on August 28, 2007, from http://www.bsma-int.com

3 For information, go to http://www.emdr-intl.com

4 For information, go to http://www.tftrx.com

5 For information, go to http://www.eftuniverse.com

6 For information, go to http://www.bmsa-int.com

7 Freeman, W. J. The Physiology of Perception. (*Scientific American*, Vol. 264, 1991), p. 84.

8 For information, go to http://www.tatlife.com

9 For information, go to http://www.seemorgmatrix.org/homepages/articles.html

10 Spalding, 1972.

11 Spalding, 1972, Vol. 3, p. 141.

12 Jung, C. G. *Dream Analysis: Notes from the seminar given in 1928 – 1930*. (McGuire, W. Ed.) Bollingen Series, XCIX. (Princeton, NJ: Princeton University Press. 1984), p. 675.

13 McAll, K. *Healing the Haunted*. (Goleta, CA: Queenship, 1996).

14 Hensley, D. *Hell's Gate: Terror at Bobby Mackey's Music World*. (Denver, CO: Outskirts Press, 2005).

15 Van Dusen, M. *The Presence of Other Worlds: The psychological/spiritual worlds of Emanuel Swedenborg*. (New York: HarperCollins, 1975).

16 Fleming, T. *You Can Heal Now: The Tapas Acupressure Technique (TAT)*. (TAT International, Redondo Beach, CA: Author, 2008).

17 Craig, G. *The EFT Manual*. (Fulton, CA: Energy Psychology Press, 2008); Flint, G.A. *Emotional freedom: Techniques for dealing with emotional and physical distress*. Rev. ed. (Vernon, BC: NeoSolTerric Enterprises, 2001).

18 Shapiro, F. *Eye Movement Desensitization and Reprocessing: Basic principles, protocols and procedures*, 2nd. Ed. (New York: Guilford Press. 2001).

19 Lipton, B. *The Biology of Belief: unleashing the power of consciousness, matter, & miracles*. (Santa Rosa, CA: Mountain of Love/Elite, 2005), p. 60.

Chapter 10

1 Adam. *DreamHealer: His name is Adam*. (Charlottesville, VA: Hampton Roads, 2003).

2 Read and permission granted.

3 Leahy, R. L. *Cognitive Therapy: Basic principles and applications*. (Northvale, NJ: Aronson. 1996).

4 Kraft, C. H. *Defeating Dark Angels: Breaking demonic oppression in the believer's life*. (Ann Arbor, MI: Servant Publications, 1992); Kraft, C. H. *Deep Wounds, Deep Healing: Discovering the vital link between spiritual warfare and inner healing*. (Ann Arbor, MI: Servant Publications, 1993).

5 Kraft, 1993, p. 229.

6 Kraft, 1992, pp. 123-124.

7 Sharaf, M. *Fury on Earth: A biography of Wilhelm Reich.* (New York:St. Martins/Marek, 1983), pp. 234-237.

8 Lipton B. (2005). *The Biology of Belief: Unleashing the power of consciousness, matter & miracles.* (Santa Rosa, CA: Mountain of Love/Elite Books, 2005), pp. 142-144.

9 Ortner, N. (2010). *Bruce Lipton: The tapping solution.* Retrieved on February 16, 2011, from http://www.thetappingsolution.com/blog/lipton

Glossary

This glossary gives definitions of the terms used in this book, which are either technical in nature or unique to Process Healing. Some of the usages are mine and idiosyncratic because I defined them based on my clinical experience. Understanding the definitions of words or phrases used in this book is the key to understanding the whole.

3D-Reality — the everyday experiences in our daily lives and everything that can be measured by scientific procedures.

Active Experience — a metaphor or construct for the brain activity involved in creating behavior. It contains all *active* memories and neural activity of the brain and body. It doesn't include dormant memories. The Active Experience construct simplifies thinking about the brain's activity and helps us make a distinction between dormant, unconscious, and conscious active memories in a meaningful way. The active memories are those triggered from a dormant state into the Active Experience. The triggers are stimuli, active content, or emotions in the Active Experience that are present in a dormant memory, which evokes the dormant memory into activity. Basic Neurostructure works on the Active Experience to create a collage from the Content and Emotion Memories, leading to a response and memory of the response.

Active Memories — memories that are active in the Active Experience. They are either unconscious or conscious active memories. Any active memory may be included in the creation of a collage of memories to run some brain or body activity.

Active Personality — a personality part with executive function that is active in the conscious or unconscious Active Experience in the present time. More than one personality part can be active at the same time.

Advanced Integrated Therapy — involves accessing unconscious material through ideomotor cueing (muscle testing) and moving energy through the material by "holding a touch" on a number of the body's major energy centers to eliminate symptoms, their causes, and after-effects. (See Clinton, 2000.)

Amassed Personal Field — consists of the Personal Fields (5th dimension) of all living beings and the Personal Field of all dead persons from the inception of humanity.

Amnesia — the lack of awareness between two memories, such as a trauma memory and an active personality part. The personality part does not know that the amnesic memory is active. In some cases, the amnesia is caused when few or no neural connections exist between memories with different memory structures. In other cases, the dissociative process causes the amnesia. Amnesic parts or memories of either type, can intrude into the Active Experience to cause some content or emotion in our experience.

Amnesic Part — a compartmentalized personality part of which other personalities are more or less unaware. During severe trauma for which 1) there is no previous memory to create a response to manage the situation and 2) when intense emotions independent of the Main Personality are present, the intense emotions rapidly activate memories to handle the crisis. The Main Personality is forced to go dormant by the rapid influx of memories. A new memory structure is formed that creates a compartmentalized amnesic part or memory. Amnesic parts with executive function can self-generate behavior and cause intrusions, such as unknown voices, images in a person's thoughts, or unexplained emotions. Amnesia between two parts can hide both parts from each other or operate in one direction only; namely, one part knows what the other is doing, but the other part is unaware of what the first part is doing.

Ancestral Field — a construct that refers to field phenomena carrying some positive or negative quality learned in a previous generation that is passed from generation to generation through the mother's or father's Personal Field to the fetus' Personal Field.

Associate *with* vs. *to* — all memories have a unique structure with which other memories associate. The memories associate *with* a structure to form a collage of memories (see Figure 1). When the structure is active, the collage of memories creates a unique response in our brain or body. Memories associated *with* a structure are easy to change. On the other hand, when a memory associates *to* a memory structure (see Figure 1), it is not possible to change the memories associated *with* the structure. The memory associated *to* the memory structure changes the neural plasticity. Until the memory associated *to* the structure is treated, the collage of memories associated *with* the structure cannot be

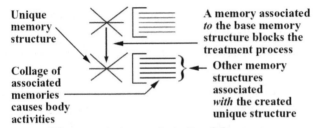

Unique memory structure

A memory associated *to* the base memory structure blocks the treatment process

Collage of associated memories causes body activities

Other memory structures associated *with* the created unique structure

Figure 1 Associated *with* vs. *to*

treated. A memory associated *to* a structure is a barrier to treating memories causing unwanted behavior.

Barrier — an active memory or activity in the Active Experience that stops treatment or communication with the subconscious or parts. A part, a belief, a memory structure problem, or a field can each cause a barrier in the Active Experience.

Basic Neurostructure — an assumed neurostructure that serves the specific function in our brain to create collages in memories that cause both the activity and memory for the behavior or activities of systems, organs, brain structures, and so forth. The Basic Neurostructure is believed to be the 10th dimension.

Behavior System — consists of the Basic Neurostructure, Memory I, Memory II, Memory III, the Active Experience, and other system-related structures. The Behavior System has a unique Basic Neurostructure that assembles collages of Content and Emotion Memories from all related active memories and neural activity in the Active Experience to create behavior. Collages of memories, created by the Basic Neurostructure, simultaneously create both responses and memories related to behaving.

Brief Multisensory Activation — a treatment method that involves doing two or three physical or mental activities at the same time while thinking about the issue to create change. This is called multisensory activation. This method is explained by a scientifically based neuropsychological theory that not only accounts for observed data but also allows for other therapeutic treatments to be derived.

Cellular Memories — located in the cellular structures of the wall of the cell.

Change History of the Personality — an intervention that treats the emotions of a trauma associated with similar memories created at any time following the initial trauma.

Circle of Friends — a community of volunteers who share the teachings of Bruno Gröning, who taught a way of living and an exercise that sometimes results in the healing of mental and physical problems.

Collage of Memories — a collection of memory structures that work together to run neural activity to make a response. There are always many active memories in the Active Experience. Some of these active memories are assembled into a collage to cause a response. The collage of memories associates *with* the neural activity present to form another unique memory structure.

Collective Subconscious — the entrained subconsciouses of all humans who have ever lived. The collective subconscious is believed to be a source of collective wisdom.

Compartmentalized Part — a memory with a unique structure that has executive function and is usually independent of the Main Personality and other parts. It is created by intense trauma, pain, or fear in a situation for which the person has no memory to manage the trauma situation. The pain or fear triggers relevant memories, forcing the Main Personality to go dormant, which leads to the creation of a compartmentalized part.

Complex Memory Structure — consists of a base memory structure with other memory structures associated *to* or *with* it.

Conception Virus — forms when a field virus entrains to the first cell at conception. This virus mildly distorts the DNA development throughout the brain and body (see Field Virus).

Conscious Active Experience — an awareness of emotions and behavior active in our conscious experience in contrast to the lack of awareness of emotions and behavior activity in the unconscious experience. Our Active Experience includes both conscious and unconscious active memories.

Content Memory — conscious memory includes all experiences, such as the visual, auditory, touch, taste, and smell, that are associated with the memory structure. Prior to treatment, the experience of content memory can include some ancillary experience, which is also associated with the memory structure but not to the content of the memory. This ancillary experience can include emotions, the need for air, food, and water, and other major brain and organ activity.

Dimension — the property of a matrix structure determined by the number of axes passing through a corner of the matrix. For example, a 3-dimensional matrix has three axes passing through each corner.

Dimensional Structure — a structure defined by the number of axes passing through the corners of the structure — for example, 5th dimension with 5 axes and the 7th dimension with 7 axes.

Dissociation — a process to move memories from conscious activity to unconscious activity. Active memories can be either conscious or unconscious. Memories that are not active are dormant memories. Dissociation is a normal process that causes the conscious and unconscious Active Experience. Dissociation is what we use voluntarily or spontaneously to hide memories that we don't want to remember or to hide skills that run automatically. Examples of dissociated skills or memories are the mechanics of driving a car or the composing and editing of speech or written prose. When one remembers the details of a trauma that are very upsetting and, later, cannot remember the details, then the details have been dissociated. We call these memories dissociated memories. A dissociative process works to dissociate some or all of a memory. Dissociated memories can be active in the unconscious. Repression or suppression is defined as involuntary or voluntary dissociation, respectively.

Dissociative Part — the memory of a repeated, painful experience moved to the unconscious by dissociation, where the memory causes little or no pain experience. Dissociative parts can cause intrusive behaviors that are memory-based and do not involve executive function. Content or emotions can trigger dissociative parts into your Active Experience. Dissociated memories can cause intrusions, such as hearing your name, or a comment in another voice, or seeing an image. However, some skills with apparent executive function can be dissociated and perform a task, such as composing and editing verbal behavior.

Dissociative Process — a part who associates with the content or emotions in a collage to cause the content or emotions of the memory to be active in the unconscious. The dissociative process can associate with all or some of the memories or emotions in a collage. The dissociative process is like a learned part. I call it the dissociative process to distinguish it from dissociative parts. Trauma can change the role of the dissociative process. The dissociative process can associate *to* memory structures to cause personality problems by creating memory structures difficult to change.

Distant Healing — occurs when an action of a person in the present location results in positive changes in the target person located some distance away. The intervention can be a prayer-like healing, an intention, or a direct treatment using an intervention such as EFT.

DNA Memories or Beliefs — hypothesized to be represented in a person's DNA structure in a way that these memories and beliefs can impact behavior. These memories can be treated.

Dormant Memories — memories that are not active in the Active Experience. The Active Experience consists of all active neural activity and memories that are used to create our behavior and experience. All dormant memories are available to be active. Most memories are not currently active. They remain dormant until they are triggered or cued into the Active Experience. The triggers are active content or emotions in the Active Experience that match those triggers present in the content or associated neural activity of a dormant memory.

Easy-entrainment — a brain process that allows fields to entrain easily. This process is caused by an unusual trauma situation that modifies a person's memory and the Basic Neurostructure to enable fields to easily entrain to that person.

Ego State — a system of memories dependent upon the cues of some specific situation. For example, a person may behave and feel differently in a church from the way he or she behaves and feels in a police department. These Ego States are state-dependent memories within the Main Personality.

Emotion Memory — a memory structure consisting of a collage of emotions that matches the present emotional experience. This Emotion Memory structure associates *with* the memory structure of the experience in the creation process. An Emotion Memory causes a positive or hurtful emotional experience. Emotions serve to motivate memory structures to be active and to cause a behavior, a thought, or an intrusion.

Emotion System — a system consisting of Basic Neurostructure, an Active Experience, and a memory of certain emotions. The Basic Neurostructure of the Emotion System creates a collage of Emotion Memories to match the emotion experience in the Active Experience during the creation of behavior or experience.

Emotional Freedom Techniques (EFT) — a treatment method that involves tapping on acupressure points to lower the pain associated with traumatic memories or unwanted beliefs. Emotional Freedom Techniques was developed by Gary Craig (2008). This is an offshoot of Thought Field Therapy (Callahan, 2001). EFT does not involve diagnosis, which simplifies its use by the public.

Entrainment — occurs when some characteristic, quality, or pattern of one waveform locks onto a matching characteristic, quality, or pattern in another waveform. When this happens, the waveforms are said to be entrained. A field can entrain to a living person — for example, when he or she has similar emotional experiences.

Executive Function — involves all aspects of the self-generation of behavior. This includes selecting information, planning, self-monitoring, self-correcting, problem-solving, decision-making, and controlling behavior. The 10th dimension manages the executive function.

Eye Movement Desensitization and Reprocessing (EMDR) — a treatment intervention that involves bilateral stimulation of the eyes, hearing, or touch to cause a reduction of painful emotions associated with a traumatic memory.

Family Constellations Therapy — a form of group therapy in which one member of the group, the patient, assigns group members as surrogates for each of his or her relatives. He or she then places them in a spatial relationship representing his or her family system. The group leader either gently guides the interaction between the patient and the surrogate family members or allows the process to evolve from the interaction between the surrogates and the patient (Hellinger, 2001a, b).

Field —

a) Field is used to represent activity in the 5th dimension to explain some aspect observed in our 3D-Reality.

b) Field is used as a metaphor for an intruding soul, the Personal Field of a dead person. When an alternative method is used to treat the field barrier, some patients feel a swoosh from their torso, chest, or some other part of their body.

Field Barrier — a barrier in our hidden reality entrained to field structures in our Personal Field that blocks communication or treatment. Field barriers can be treated by the subconscious to remove the barrier.

Field Virus — involves the entrainment of some content memory in the 5th dimension. Field viruses can entrain to content in our Personal Field and block complete treatment or cause disease (see Content Memory).

Flunots — basic structures that are assumed to be created and destroyed by zero points. Flunots have 10 axes crossing their core and are capable of joining with other flunots to form the 0th through 10th dimensional structures. Unused axes collapse to the core of the flunot.

Flux Theory — a geometrical string theory proposed by James C. Cranwell that explains all the particles of physics and the multi-dimensions of our hidden reality. It is a theory that unifies Quantum Mechanics and electromagnetism. (See String Theory.)

Generational Field — a field (soul) that has entrained to an intruding field (soul). The structures of multiple soul entrainments on an intruding soul can be complex. This is like a stack of poker chips, with each chip a field from a previous generation. Intruding fields, with generational fields (intruding souls), cannot be treated and released from the patient until the generational fields are treated.

Gravity — the force of electromagnetic attraction of all masses to each other in our universe. It is believed to be caused by flunots attracting each other.

Healing — the removal of pain. One can remove pain from an issue by treating the issue. This removal of pain is called healing the issue because an issue treated with this method, as with TFT and EFT, seldom returns. Healing, then, refers to the activity of treatment and the long-term positive outcome of the process of treatment.

Heart System — the Basic Neurostructure operating on the Active Experience and heart memory to run heart activity.

Hidden Reality — see Virtual Reality.

Hologram — a structure in which all information in the structure can be obtained from any point in the structure.

Ideomotor Responses — muscle responses, such as finger responses, that indicate, "Yes" or "No," and so forth. Ideomotor responses are used to communicate with the subconscious, parts, or aspects of the brain and body system

Integration — see Joining of Parts.

Intruding Soul or Field — a soul of a person, usually from a preceding lifetime, who is associated or entrained with a person. The entrainment is made possible because the soul has content or painful memory structures similar to the structures present in the living person. Intruding souls cause heightened motivation or atypical behavior that is problematic for the person.

Intrusion — a memory or part who becomes active and causes a behavior, a thought, an image, or an emotion in the conscious experience.

Issue — a mental or physical problem or concern, which requires a resolution. If the issue is not treated, then it will continue to be problematic for the patient.

Joining of Parts — an exchange of memories between two memory structures of the parts until they both associate with the same memories. More formally, the memory structures exchange associations until they have the same memory associations. After this sharing, the parts can create behavior without conflict. All memory structures remain unique and experience the same positive and negative experiences. This is not the usual definition of joining or integrating parts.

Kinesthetic System — the Basic Neurostructure operating on the Active Experience and the kinesthetic memory to run kinesthetic responses. The Kinesthetic System deals with feedback from our muscles, joints, and skin. Trauma to this system can give an "energy" experience in our brain or in different areas of our body. This energy experience validates thought intrusion or thought broadcasting in psychotic persons.

Layered Memory — a memory formed when another memory or part associates *to* a memory structure during its creation (see Associate *with* vs. *to*). A Layered Memory cannot be treated until the memory associated *to* the memory is treated. Trauma or unusual circumstances create Layered Memories. All people have some Layered Memories. Some beliefs or unwanted behaviors are Layered Memories.

Longitudinal Field — a construct that includes the 0th through 10th dimensions created by the zero points. Since all the dimensions are not measurable presently, the longitudinal field is a convenient construct to refer to all the dimensional fields created by the zero points that underlie our 3D-Reality.

Main Personality — the personality part with executive function who runs the body most of the time. The Main Personality starts forming at some point before or at birth. In people with extreme trauma history, a trauma part can become the most competent part and serve as the Main Personality. Sometimes, the damage to the original Main Personality is so severe that it never learns the skills to run the body. When this happens, other parts learn the necessary skills to run the body.

Manager — the name given the 10th dimension that maintains or manages the coherency between all objects and living matter in the universe. Since all living matter is assumed to have a history amassed in the virtual reality, the history is involved in maintaining coherency.

Manic-Depressive — a psychological condition where a person alternates between energized and depressed experiences, thereby experiencing highs and lows in mood.

Massive Change History — an intervention that involves the subconscious treating all memories in the brain and body distorted by a trauma memory from the date of the trauma to the present. A Massive Change History always follows a treatment intervention. (See Change History of the Personality.)

Matrix — a virtual or physical object consisting of multiple structures with a fixed number of edges to the structure. For example, a box is a 3-dimensional structure (length, width, height) with three edges connecting the corners. The unique assembly of more than one box, like a stack of boxes, forms a matrix of corners and edges.

Memory Elements — various kinds of memories with different structures. Memory elements with similar emotions can form a structure of memories because the emotions associated with the memory elements become associated in a structure.

Memory I — the type of memory that starts amassing shortly after conception. Memory I is state-dependent on neural activity. Shortly after conception, the Basic Neurostructure creates a response and memory from activity in the Active Experience. Activity in the Active Experience is the common feature of all memories in Memory I at this stage of development. Additional unique memory structures amass over time as state-dependent memories based on activity as the common property.

Memory II — the type of memory that starts amassing before birth and is state-dependent on both simple neural activity and primitive neural activity related to sensory stimulation, but not sensory experience. Memory II continues to amass until about age four. Predispositions are in Memory II.

Memory III — the type of memory that starts amassing shortly before birth and is state-dependent on simple neural activity, the five sensory experiences, reward and punishment, and basic needs. Memory III includes all memory structures that primarily run the brain and bodily activities required for day-to-day survival.

Memory Structure — the basic building block of all memories. All memories have a unique memory structure (see Figure 2). With the creation of each response, previously learned active memory structures

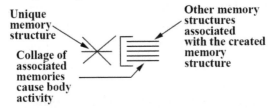

Unique memory structure

Collage of associated memories cause body activity

Other memory structures associated with the created memory structure

Figure 2 A Memory Structure

associate with a new memory structure that will cause the response. Because neural activity is always changing, all memory structures in a changing environment are unique. The memory structures that run neural activity and that merge to cause the response are collectively called a collage. The collage activates neural activity to run brain or body activity. It is as if each memory collage has its own memory structure based on the complexion of neural activity in the brain when the structure was created.

Metaphor — the application of a word or phrase to an object or concept, which it does not literally denote, in order to suggest a comparison with another object or concept, for example, using a rake to smooth out negative emotions just as you would use a rake to smooth out gopher mounds in your garden.

Motivation — positive or negative emotions associated with a memory that impel the memory into action or behavior. The more intense the emotions, the more motivated the memory — that is, the more likely it will become active. Intrusive thoughts, for example, are memories having emotions associated with them. When the emotions are replaced by neutral emotions in a treatment process, the memories are no longer motivated to intrude.

Neural — see Neurostructure.

Neurolinguistic Programming — a treatment method that uses brain processes to obtain change in behavior.

Neurostructure — a hypothetical cooperative network of neurons in our brain and body that are capable of creating behavior and memories. Reference in 3D-Reality is made to the neurostructure, neural activity, and neural pathways because, basically, all our behavior is caused by neural activity in our brain and body. There are interventions that operate directly on the neurostructure of a system. Being able to conceptualize some neural cause for the problem helps your understanding of the creation of behavior, memory that is more complex, and system structures. The Basic Neurostructure is a metaphor for the creation process of the 10th dimension — the Manager.

Nonlocal — refers to findings in physics that operations in one locality are observed to cause effects in another locality some distance away. Surrogate treatment is nonlocal.

Nonlocality — a property of the 11 dimensions (the virtual or hidden reality) that allows the dimensional structure of an object to appear to be available everywhere in the universe.

Out-of-phase — a condition where two waveforms start at a different position on the waveform, such as one starting at the bottom of the wave as opposed to the other starting at the top of the wave.

Part — a neural structure having associated memories that can give intrusions into the conscious experience or run the body when triggered. A part is either a compartmentalized or a dissociative part in Memory III that can independently run some of the activity of the brain. Dissociative parts are similar to skills or painful memories that are mostly active in the unconscious (see Dissociative Part). Severe trauma creates compartmentalized parts with executive function in a way that results in few or no neural associations between the trauma part and the Main Personality. The absence of neural associations causes the amnesia between the part and the Main Personality. Parts can be created in the memories of other systems, like the Heart System, Emotion System, and so forth.

Personal Field — a representation of our behavior from conception to now in the virtual reality (5th dimension).

Predisposition — the tendency to respond to a situation in a predefined way. Most Predispositions are memories in Memory II that are associated *to* or *with* parts or memories in Memory III. These memories in Memory III activate, when the predispositions are triggered, to affect our experience or behavior

Problem-Solving — consists of asking the subconscious leading questions to identify the memory structure of a barrier to determine the treatment or strategy for an intervention, such as whether an intervention is safe and the order for treating the structure.

Process Healing Method — a treatment approach that respectfully treats all aspects of a person's personality by coaxing them to join a Treatment Team. The Treatment Team members want to be treated, to have their positive qualities strengthened, and to join with the Main Personality. When all members of the Treatment Team grant permission, the subconscious is taught the treatment method. Then the memory structures of all the issues can be treated safely and painlessly by the subconscious.

Protector-Controller — see Subpersonality.

Reframe — a change in the experience of a negative situation or belief into a positive experience by giving an alternative explanation that has positive, self-empowering qualities. Reframes often cause positive therapeutic results in people. This is an intervention described in Neurolinguistic Programming.

Ritual Abuse — the name used to refer to any form of physical, sexual, psychological, electronic, or drug torture that involves some kind of repeated pattern of organization in its execution. The pattern of organization can be religious or idiosyncratic in nature.

Self-Healing — occurs what an individual uses the Process Healing Method to treat his or her problematic beliefs, emotions, or issues.

Self-Organization — when a system or process has an internal structure that increases in complexity over time without any external influence.

Soul — the name of our representation in the 5th through 9th dimensions that are amassed during our lifetime. After death, our soul continues to exist in the universe (see Intruding Soul).

Shadow Memories — memories induced or caused in the neural structures surrounding the primary neurological path of intense memory activity. After treating an intense traumatic symptom, it is often important to treat the Shadow Memory caused by the activity of the symptom for a complete healing to occur.

Stacked Fields — consists of a number of generational fields (old souls) entrained upon one another like a stack of poker chips, any of which can be the base for additional stacked fields.

Stacked Parts — two or more parts associated *to* each other. This is caused when the intense pain continues to increase to cause another mobilization of memories "pushing" the active personality part dormant. This can result in a number of new parts associating *to* preceding parts. With continuing and increasing pain, many parts can be stacked in a pyramid- or column-like structure that has to be treated by starting with the top part.

State-Dependency — a group of memories having some common triggers or cues that are necessary for inclusion in the state-dependent group. A memory with common cues with a group of memories would be a state-dependent memory. When most or all of the common cues are present, the memory becomes active.

State-Dependent Personality — a collection of memories in the Main Personality that are only active in particular situations. When the person is fully aware of these behaviors, they are called Ego States.

String Theory — describes our hidden reality as consisting of multidimensions, each of which consist of strings that amass information by vibrating in complex frequencies. Different dimensions have different geometrical structures. This is the string theory offered by James C. Cranwell (1998i-vii). There are at least five other string theories described by different mathematical assumptions.

Structure — There are two kinds of structures:

1. a unique neural state or structure *with which* or *to which* other memory structures associate (see Figure 1). The memory structures that associate *with* the unique memory structure form a collage that causes neural activity that can run brain or body activity.

2. a structure caused by the neural association of the common content and emotions of a collection of memories. The structure of memories is maintained by the emotions of the memories. The memories associated with the structure are called memory elements. When the emotions binding the memories together in the structure are treated, the structure falls apart and the memory elements can be treated individually.

Structure of Memories — see Structure.

Structured Torture Survivors — persons who were tortured to create an organized structure of compartmentalized parts, each with unique instructions, that serve specific purposes for the person or group that controls the victim. The structures are often imbedded in complex metaphorical structures like a theme from Disneyland.

Subconscious — a pervasive process that is created by the merging of the mother's and father's subconsciouses at conception. He or she is independent of memories of the 5th through 9th dimensions. The subconscious usually doesn't store memories and is not conscious or unconscious activity. The subconscious has your language, so one can communicate with him or her. The subconscious does not normally have sensory and emotional experiences but has access to the neural representation of all memory experiences in the body. The subconscious can access all active memories in the Active Experience and can work with brain processes to change the memory and behavior of all systems. In the current model of behavior, the subconscious is a part of us present, to varying degrees, in the 5th through 9th dimensions.

Sub-personality — consists of the Protector-Controller and other positive and negative tendencies called Predispositions. The subpersonality starts forming *in utero* and continues to develop through the first four years of life. A predisposition, like a part, provides a predetermined response to situations by creating behavior in the Active Experience that handles intrusions or specific circumstances. They are usually associated *to* or *with* structures in Memory III. (Adapted from Stone and Stone, 1989.)

Surrogate Treatment — involves a person in one location carrying out interventions intending to cause positive changes in the target person in another location. The intervention can be a prayer-like healing or direct treatment using an intervention such as EFT.

System — an Active Experience and memory working together to serve some function. A system runs every brain process, organ function, behavior, or body activity. The memory continues to amass as the Manager creates responses and memories from the activity in the Active Experience to run some brain or body activity — for example, the Behavior, Emotion, and Heart Systems.

Tandem Memory — a memory caused by activity overload in the Active Experience that operates in tandem with Memory III. Early in life, if the Active Experience is overloaded for any reason, another memory and Active Experience is sometimes created. This overload results in creating one or more additional and parallel forms of Memory III — Tandem Memories, each serving another Active Experience. Tandem Memories can have significant differences from the Memory III. Most people have multiple Active Experiences, each with a unique Tandem Memory.

Tapas Acupressure Technique (TAT) — a technique of applying gentle pressure to three acupressure points on your nose and forehead while putting your other hand behind your head. Tapas Fleming (2008) developed the Tapas Acupressure Technique. This is an effective technique to treat various mental health issues and allergies. I use it for treating obsessions.

Template — an example of beliefs or behavior in one person used to direct treatment when adding or removing beliefs or behavior in another person.

Thought Field Therapy (TFT) — a therapy using a technique of tapping on diagnosed acupressure points to resolve mental health or physical problems. Thought Field Therapy was discovered and developed by Roger Callahan (2001). Callahan developed algorithms to treat specific mental health issues like phobias, anxiety, depression, and so forth.

Torture — consists of constant, ongoing experience of physical, sexual, psychological, or drug abuse. It can include near-death experiences or can create a general feeling of helplessness and hopelessness that leads to voluntary compliance with the perpetrators to avoid anticipated death.

Trance — the loss or dimming of conscious experience as a person dissociates active memories and stimulation to quiet his or her conscious and unconscious experience.

Trauma — a hurtful experience that creates a unique trauma memory structure with associated pain.

Treatment by the Subconscious — a method of working internally to remove the emotions caused by trauma. The results are similar to treatment by external stimulation, such as tapping on acupressure points or eye movement. The tapping, stimulating neural activity, causes a learning process in which the present neutral-to-positive emotional experience replaces the trauma-Emotion Memories associated with the trauma memory. In this case, the subconscious engages in treatment by creating neural activity that is assumed to be similar to the treatment obtained by physical tapping.

Treatment Team — an imagined team formed by aspects or parts who want to have their negative emotions replaced with neutral to positive emotions, to have their positive beliefs and behaviors strengthened with positive emotions, to join with the Main Personality, and to run the body from morning to night. They create treatment plans for each other by consensus.

Unconscious Active Experience — made of active memories and behaviors created in the Active Experience that are not in conscious experience. The normal process of dissociation causes this unconscious condition. When the dissociative process associates with all or selective qualities of the collage of memories in a memory structure, the memory or those qualities become active in the unconscious activity of the memory. A memory can be active in both the conscious and unconscious Active Experience.

Virtual Reality — a real or imaginary multidimensional system that enables a person to imagine operations in the imaginary system to explain changes in our real-time reality or 3D-Reality (see Hidden Reality).

Well-formed Instructions — clear and precise details of what to change, the method of change, the intervention with which to cause the change (Wisdom, subconscious, sentence procedure, and so forth), and with what to replace the treated issue (self-empowering belief, love, peace, positive behavior).

Wisdom — the name for the positive knowledge that is assumed to be entrained on love in the 9th dimension. It is assumed to be a self-organized, intelligent field that can manipulate the 5th through 9th dimensions to create change in our 3D-Reality.

Zero Points — sources of energy in the vacuum of the universe that create photons and dimensional structures described as the longitudinal field. The photons are immediately destroyed, which suggests that the dimensional structures are immediately destroyed. This gives a movie-frame like unfolding of our universe. Groups of zero points create each structure in our universe.

References

Adam (2003). *DreamHealer: His name is Adam.* Charlottesville, VA: Hampton Roads.

Andrade, J. & Feinstein, D. *Preliminary Report of the First Large-Scale Study of Energy Psychology.* Retrieved on May 12, 2010, from http://www.eftuniverse.com/Research/andradepaper.htm

Bearden, T. E. (2002). *Excalibur Briefing: Explaining paranormal phenomenon.* Rev. ed. Bakersfield, CA: Cheniere Press.

Bearden, T. E. (2005). *Oblivion: America at the brink.* Bakersfield, CA: Cheniere Press.

Belanger, J. (2006). *Our Haunted Selves: True life ghost encounters.* Franklin Lakes, NJ: New Page Books.

Bartlett, F. (1967). *Remembering: A study in experimental and social psychology.* London, UK: Cambridge University Press.

Benor, D. J. (2000). *Distant Healing.* Retrieved on May 12, 2010, from http://www.noetic.org/research/dh/research/DistantHealing.pdf

Bradshaw, R. One-Eye Integration web site. Retrieved on May 12, 1010, from http://www.sightpsychology.com

Blizzard, R., Braude, S., Brown, R., Dell, P. & Nijenhaus, E. R. S. (2005, November). What is Dissociation? Panel presentation at the annual meeting of the International Society for Traumatic Stress Studies. Toronto, ON.

Boklage, C. E. (2007). Frequency and Survival: Probability of natural twin conceptions. In Hayton A. (Ed.) *Untwined: Perspectives on the death of a twin before birth.* St Albans, Herts, UK: Wren Publications.

Callahan, R. J. (2001). *Tapping the Healer Within: Using Thought Field Therapy to instantly conquer your fears, anxieties and emotional distress.* New York: McGraw-Hill.

Clinton, A. (2000). *Core Beliefs and Matrices & Protocol Book.* Self published by author. Accessed on May 12, 2010, from http://www.seemorg.com

Craig, G. (2008). *The EFT Manual.* Fulton, CA: Energy Psychology Press.

Craig, G. (2008). Vignettes retrieved on September 9, 2010, from http://www.eftuniverse.com

Cranwell, J. C. (1998i-vii). Flux Particle Theory – 101. Retrieved on May 12, 2010, from http://guitar.to/gravityboy

Cranwell, J. C. (1998i). Spatial Dimensionality. Retrieved on May 12, 2010, from http://www.gravityboy.gootar.com/docs/dimen.html

Cranwell, J. C. (1998ii). The Flux. Retrieved on May 12, 2010, from http://www.gravityboy.gootar.com/docs/fluxi.html

Cranwell, J. C. (1998iii). Gravity. Retrieved on May 12, 2010, from http://www.gravityboy.gootar.com/docs/gravity.html

Cranwell, J. C. (1998iv). Atomic Structures. Retrieved on May 12, 2010, from http://www.gravityboy.gootar.com/docs/atomic.html

Cranwell, J. C. (1998v). Relativity. Retrieved on May 12, 2010, from http://www.gravityboy.gootar.com/docs/relativity.html

Cranwell, J. C. (1998vi). The Big Bang Myth. Retrieved on May 12, 2010, from http://www.gravityboy.gootar.com/docs/fluxii.html

Cranwell, J. C. (1998vii). Miscellaneous. Retrieved on May 12, 2010, from http://www.gravityboy.gootar.com/doc./misc.html

Dell, P. (2005). Paper presented. See Blizzard (2005).

Dickason, C. F. (1987). *Demon Possession & the Christian*. Wheaton, IL: Crossway Books.

Edelstien, M. (1981). *Trauma, Trance, and Transformation: A clinical guide to hypnotherapy*. New York: Brunner/Mazel, pp. 53-54.

Esdaile, J. (1849). *Mesmerism in India and its Practical Application in Surgery and Medicine*. London, UK: Solis, Andrus & Sons.

Fleming, T. *How To Do TAT with a Stressful Event that You Experienced*. TAT International, Redondo Beach, CA: Author. Retrieved free on May 12, 2010, from http://www.tatlife.com

Fleming, T. (2007). *TAT Professional's Manual*. Redondo Beach, CA: TATLife.

Fleming, T. (2008). *You Can Heal Now: The Tapas Acupressure Technique (TAT)*. TAT International, Redondo Beach, CA: Author.

Flint, G. A. (1994, June). *Toward a chaos model of memory: A model based upon clinical methodology*. Paper presented at the 1994 Annual Conference of the Society for Chaos Theory in Psychology and the Life Sciences, Baltimore, MD.

Flint, G.A. (2001). *Emotional freedom: Techniques for dealing with emotional and physical distress*. Rev. Ed. Vernon, BC: NeoSolTerric Enterprises.

Flint, G. A. (2006). *A Theory and Treatment of Your Personality: A manual for change*. Vernon, BC: NeoSolTerric Enterprises.

Freeman, W. J. (1991). The Physiology of Perception. *Scientific American*, 264, pp. 78-85.

Freeman, W. J. (1994). Qualitative Overview of Population Neurodynamics. *Neural modeling and neural networks*, pp. 185-215. Retrieved on May 12, 2010, from http://soma.berkeley.edu/archives/ID9/94.html

Freeman, W. J. (1995). *Societies of Brains*. Hillsdale, NJ: Lawrence Erlbaum.

Gardner, M. (1957). *Fads and Fallacies in the Name of Science*. Rev. ed. Mineola, NY: Dover, Chapter 24.

Hammond, C. (1992). *Greenbaum Speech*. (Formerly called Hypnosis in MPD: Rituial Abuse), delivered at the Fourth Annual Eastern Regional Conference on Abuse and Multiple Personality, Thursday June 25, 1992, at the Radisson Plaza Hotel, Mark Center, Alexandria, VA. Retrieved on July 1, 2012, from http://cassiopaea.org/2010/09/17/the-greenbaum-speech/

Hayton, A. (2007). *Untwined: Perspectives on the death of a twin before birth.* (Ed.). St Albans, Herts, England: Wren Publications.

Hellinger, B. http://www.familyconstellations-usa.com/hellinger.htm

Hellinger, B. (1999). *Unraveling Family Secrets*. Interview by Humberto del Pozo in Santiago de Chile in September, 1999. Retrieved on May 12, 2010, from www.constellationsolutions.co.uk/familyinterview.htm

Hellinger, B. (2001). *Bert Hellinger Lectures and Articles* (see Taipei and Taiwan lectures). Retrieved on May 12, 2010, from http://hellinger-sciencia.com/index.php?id=119

Hellinger, B. (2001a). *Family constellation for teachers–Taipei University.* Lecture given at the Department of Education of Taipei University on October 10, 2001. Retrieved on May 12, 2010, from http://hellinger-sciencia.com/index.php?id=125

Hellinger, B. (2001b). *Introduction to Family Constellations*. Lecture given in Taipei on October 11, 2001. Retrieved on May 12, 2010, from http://hellinger-sciencia.com/index.php?id=126

Hensley, D. (2005). *Hell's Gate: Terror at Bobby Mackey's Music World.* Parker, CO: Outskirts Press.

Hersha, L., Hersha, C., Griffis, D. & Schwarz, T. (2001). *Secret Weapons: Two sisters terrifying true story of sex, spies, and sabotage.* Far Hills, NJ: New Horizon Press.

Ho, M. (1998). *The Rainbow and the Worm.* London, UK: Institute for Science in Society.

Ho, M. (2003). *Living with the Fluid Genome.* London, UK: Institute for Science in Society.

Jung, C. G. (1984). *Dream Analysis: Notes of the seminar given in 1928-1930.* (McGuire, W., Ed.). Bollingen Series XCIX. Princeton, NJ: Princeton University Press.

Kaku, M. (1994). *Hyperspace: A scientific odyssey through parallel universes,* time warps, and the 10th dimension. New York: Anchor.

Karriker, W. (2003). *Morning, Come Quickly.* Catawba, NC: Sandime Ltd.

Kraft, C. H. (1992). *Defeating Dark Angles: Breaking demonic oppression in the believer's life.* Ann Arbor, MI: Servant Publications.

Kraft, C. H. (1993). *Deep Wounds, Deep Healing: Discovering the vital link between spiritual warfare and inner healing.* Ann Arbor, MI: Servant Publications.

Lankton, S. R. & Lankton, C. H. (1983). *The Answer Within: A clinical framework of clinical hypnotherapy.* New York: Brunner/Mazel.

Leahy, R. L. (1996). *Cognitive Therapy: Basic principles and applications.* Northvale, NJ: Aronson.

Lipton, B. (2005). *The Biology of Belief: Unleashing the power of consciousness, matter, and miracles.* Santa Rosa, CA: Elite Books.

Retrieved on May 12, 2010, from http://arxiv.org/ftp/astro-ph/papers/0701/0701594.pdf

McCall, K. (1996). *Healing the Haunted.* Goleta, CA: Queenship Publishing.

McTaggart, L. (2001). *The Field: The quest for the secret force of the universe.* Hammersmith, London, UK: HarperCollins.

Medearis, L. personal communication, July 2, 2003.

MKULTRA, BLUEBIRD and STARGATE Projects. Download 20,000 pages of declassified CIA mind control documents from the US Government for $30. Instructions retrieved on May 12, 2010, from http://www.wanttoknow.info/mindcontrol10pg#ciadocs

Morehouse, D. (1996). *Psychic Warrior.* New York: St Martin's Press.

Miller, I. (2001). *The physics of conscious engineering, Part II.* Published by the Asklepia Foundation. Retrieved on May 12, 2010, from http://www.geocities.com/iona_m/Cosmology/conengineer2.html

Noblitt, J. R. & Perskin, P. (2000). *Cult and ritual Abuse: Its history, anthropology, and recent discovery in contemporary America,* Rev. ed. Westport, CT: Praeger Publishers.

Noblitt, J. R. & Perskin-Noblitt, P. (2008). *Ritual abuse in the twenty-first century: Psychological, forensic, social and political considerations,* (Eds.). Brandon, OR: Robert Reed Publishers.

Oglevie, S. & Oglevie, L. (1977, 1979). Working with Cult and Ritual Abuse. Workshops presented at the Elijah House, Mission, BC.

Ortner, N. (2010). *Bruce Lipton: The Tapping Solution*. Retrieved on February 16, 2011, from http://www.thetappingsolution.com/blog/lipton

Pearsall, P. (1998). *The Hearts Code*. New York: Broadway Books.

Pulos, L. (1980), Mesmerism Revisited: The Effectiveness of Esdaile's Techniques in the Production of Deep Hypnosis and Total Body Hypnoanaesthesia. *American Journal of Clinical Hypnosis*. Vol. 22, 206-211.

Pulos, L. (1994). Workshop on Ideomotor Questioning. Workshop presented at the General Meeting of the Canadian Society of Clinical Hypnosis (British Columbia Division), Vancouver, BC.

Rice, J. & Caldwell, L. Master Programmer training and certification at The Neurolinguistic Programming Center for Advanced Studies, Corte Madera, CA, 1986.

Roll, W. G. (2003). Poltergeists, Electromagnetism, and Consciousness. *Journal of Scientific Exploration*. Vol. 17, pp. 75-86. Retrieved on May 12, 2010, from http://www.scientificexploration.org/journal/jse_17_1_roll.pdf

Ross, C. A. (2000). *Bluebird: Deliberate creation of multiple personality by psychiatrists*. Richardson, TX: Manitou Communications.

Rossi, E. L. & Cheek, D. B. (1988). *Mind-Body Therapy: Methods of idiodynamic healing in hypnosis*. New York: W. W. Norton.

Rutz, C. (2001). *A Nation Betrayed: The chilling and true story of secret cold war experiments performed on our children and other innocent people*. Grass Lake, MI: Fidelity Publishing.

Sachs, A. & Galton, G. (2008). *Forensic Aspects of Dissociative Identity Disorder*. (Eds.). *London*, UK: Karnac Books.

Schlitz, M. & Braud, W. (2006). *Distant Intentionality and Healing: assessing the evidence*. Retrieved on August 28, 2007, from http://www. noetic.org/research/dh/studies.html

Shelfin, A. W. & Opton, E. M. Jr. (1978). *The Mind Manipulators*. New York: Grosset & Dunlap.

Sheldrake, R. (1999). *Dogs That Know When Their Owners Are Coming Home: And other unexplained powers of animals*. New York: Random House.

Shapiro, F. (2001). *Eye Movement Desensitization and Reprocessing: Basic principles, protocols and procedures*. (2nd Ed.). New York: Guilford Press, 2001.

Sharaf, M. (1983). *Fury on Earth: A biography of Wilhelm Reich*. New York: St. Martins/Marek.

Spalding, B. T. (1972). *The Lives and Teaching of the Master of the Far East,* (6 Vols.). Camarillo, CA: DeVorss Publishing.

Springmeier, F. & Wheeler, C. (1996). *The Illuminati Formula Used to Create an Undetectable Total Mind Controlled Slave*, Vol. 2. Clackamas, OR: Authors.

Stone, H. & Stone, S. L. (1989). *Embracing Ourselves: The voice dialogue manual*. Novato, CA: Nataraj Publishing.

Southerland, C. *About BMSA*. Retrieved on May 12, 2010, from http://www.bmsa-int.com/index.php?option=com_content&task=view&id=12&Itemid=30

Talbot, M. (1992). *The Holographic Universe*. New York: Harper Collins.

Targ, E. F. (2002). Research methodology for studies of prayer and distant healing. *Complementary Therapies in Nursing & Midwifery.* Vol. 8, pp. 29-41. Retrieved on May 12, 2010, from http://www.noetic.org/research/dh/research/ResearchMethodology.pdf

Targ, R. & Katra, J. (2007). *What we know about remote viewing*. Summarized from Miracles of the Mind. Retrieved on May 12, 2010, from http://www.espresearch.com/espgeneral/WhatWeKnow.shtml

Van Dusen, M. (1975). *The Presence of Other Worlds: The psychological/ spiritual worlds of Emanuel Swedenborg*. New York: HarperCollins.

Index

About the Author

Garry A. Flint was educated at Indiana University and received a doctoral degree in experimental psychology specializing in learning (1968). After treating abused teens for six years, he became a staff psychologist at the county mental outpatient clinic in Ukiah, California. It was at this time that he began to search for treatment techniques that worked faster than Behavior Modification. He obtained extensive training in hypnosis and Neurolinguistic Programming. Eventually, he became the  program manager of the psychiatric health facility, where he was able to work with severely disturbed persons. He has been in private practice since 1987 and has trained in Eye Movement Desensitization and Reprocessing (EMDR), Thought Field Therapy, and Tapas Acupressure Technique.

Flint developed an explanation of EMDR, which led to a memory-based theory of personality development and behavior — the basis for the Process Healing Method. This theory accounts for the formation of the personality and defined all symptoms as memory structures, which allows the therapist to simply treat the patient's symptoms.

It was while working with torture survivors that intruding souls became treatment targets. Flint found that Christian interventions worked, but he wanted to find a rationale and treatment approach more acceptable to practicing mental health professionals. Using a string theory to explain the spiritual world, a plausible theory and treatment for intruding souls developed that is an extension of his earlier theory of personality. This book is the culmination of 14 years of clinical experience working with intruding souls.

Flint currently resides in Vernon, British Columbia, where he is a practicing clinical psychologist. He has previously published two books: *Emotional Freedom: Techniques for dealing with emotional and physical distress*; *A Theory and Treatment of Your Personality: A manual for change*; and is coauthor of a third book with Jo C. Willems, *A Healing Legend: Wisdom from the four directions*.

Other Books by This Author

A Theory and Treatment of your Personality: A manual for change

A Theory and Treatment of Your Personality is a groundbreaking book that offers a new method of psychotherapy. The model of the personality and its development is based on learning theory. Flint redefines major constructs to bring clarity and consistency to treating personality issues. He develops the subconscious as a treater and treatment ally that proves to be very useful in treating and problem-solving difficult issues.

Emotional Freedom: Techniques for dealing with emotional and physical issues

Emotional Freedom is a manual for learning Emotional Freedom Techniques. Clear and concise, it has many interesting features, such as lists of issues you might not think to treat, shortcuts, and problem solving strategies for treating barriers. It includes a chapter that teaches you simply to ask your subconscious to treat an issue.

Over 10,00 copies sold in English Over 8,000 copies sold in Japanese

A Healing Legend: Wisdom from the Four Directions

In *A Healing Legend,* authors Garry A. Flint and Jo C. Willems use a Native American allegory and suggestions to teach readers of all ages a healing process to heal personal issues. The fictional story of Kidd is a way to explore the truth that the healing process can pass between family and friends.

All books are available in paperback or ebook formats.

Lightning Source UK Ltd.
Milton Keynes UK
UKHW020718110521
383528UK00004B/240